LET'S PLAY TWO

LET'S PLAY TWO

THE LIFE AND TIMES OF ERNIE BANKS

Doug Wilson

ROWMAN & LITTLEFIELD
Lanham • Boulder • New York • London

Published by Rowman & Littlefield
An imprint of The Rowman & Littlefield Publishing Group, Inc.
4501 Forbes Boulevard, Suite 200, Lanham, Maryland 20706
www.rowman.com

Unit A, Whitacre Mews, 26-34 Stannary Street, London SE11 4AB

Distributed by NATIONAL BOOK NETWORK

British Library Cataloguing in Publication Information Available

Library of Congress Cataloging-in-Publication Data

Names: Wilson, Doug, 1961– author.
Title: Let's play two : the life and times of Ernie Banks / Doug Wilson.
Other titles: Let us play two | Ernie Banks
Description: Lanham, Maryland : Rowman & Littlefield, [2019] | "Distributed by NATIONAL BOOK NETWORK"—T.p. verso. | Includes bibliographical references and index.
Identifiers: LCCN 2018025363 (print) | LCCN 2018032745 (ebook) | ISBN 9781538112304 (electronic) | ISBN 9781538112298 (hardback : alk. paper)
Subjects: LCSH: Banks, Ernie, 1931-2015. | Baseball players—United States—Biography.
Classification: LCC GV865.B24 (ebook) | LCC GV865.B24 W55 2019 (print) | DDC 796.357092 [B]—dc23
LC record available at https://lccn.loc.gov/2018025363

Printed in the United States of America

CONTENTS

CONTENTS

ACKNOWLEDGMENTS

In dealing with a subject such as this, certain traps and pitfalls to the truth must be navigated. The Ernie Banks story, as printed in newspapers and books, is littered with inaccuracies that have been printed hastily, cribbed, and reprinted throughout the years. Some stories handed down in the oral tradition have been embellished and contain more myth than fact. As much as possible, I sorted through the imprecisions and fact-checked with contemporary accounts, game records in baseball-reference.com, and personal interviews.

As usual, in any work of nonfiction, the author is indebted to the kindness of strangers who take their time to talk and share memories, and I was lucky to find a number of great storytellers. I cannot express enough gratitude for everyone who helped me.

A special note of gratitude is due to Robert Prince, Joe Kirven, and Robert Stinnett for sharing with me their experiences growing up in the North Dallas of Ernie Banks. These men lived through an important era of history, and they are national treasures. When they speak, we should all sit quietly and listen.

Similarly, men who played Negro League baseball are an important part of our history. Thank you to Ernie Johnson, Sam Taylor, and William Bell for speaking to me about their years with the Kansas City Monarchs.

Thanks to the following former Major League Baseball players for being so gracious to talk with me and share their memories: George Altman, Jim Bolger, Darrel Chaney, Doug Clemens, Dick Ellsworth, Ransom Jackson, Don Kaiser, Don Kessinger, Jerry Kindall, Hobie Landrith, Jim Marshall, Lindy McDaniel, Dick Nen, Rich Nye, Nate Oliver, Milt Pappas, Pete Richert, Bob Talbot, Lee Thomas, and Jim Willis.

ACKNOWLEDGMENTS

Due to the nature of talking to baseball players who played decades ago, sometimes they pass away before the book is published. I am appreciative of the opportunity and wish special thanks to the memories of Milt Pappas and Jerry Kindall. They were both very friendly and helpful in sharing their love for the game of baseball and will be missed.

I learned long ago that if you want to know how guys really behave off the field, talk to a batboy. I was lucky to be able to get in touch with George Incledon, Cubs batboy from 1956 and 1957. I enjoyed listening to his stories from what was probably the greatest job a 14-year-old kid could have in those days.

Thank you to Zach Sanzone, Shirley Marx, and Chuck Shriver for sharing their memories from their personal perspectives of the story. Also, thank you to Larry Davidson, Dennis Freres, Mike Filipiak, Kathy Hounihan, Steve Hullcranz, and Jerry Schuebel for sharing their personal stories of meeting Ernie Banks as fans at various ages.

It is always helpful to talk to journalists who worked during the period. They know the story from a personal point of view and also have the background information and knowledge of local lore that often is not printed. For this project, I was lucky to get help from three of Chicago's best: Fred Mitchell, Ed Sherman, and George Castle. Fred was gracious and helpful in explaining his relationship with Ernie Banks as both a journalist and friend for more than four decades. Ed was terrific and freely gave his time to talk to me and shared several articles. George has written more than 14 books on baseball, most of them about the Cubs; is a leader for the Chicago Baseball History Museum; and is probably the foremost Chicago Cubs historian. He provided clues to important aspects I otherwise might not have sniffed out and spent several days exchanging e-mails with me, playing the devil's advocate for several of my ideas. I cannot express my gratitude enough to these three men.

As a writer, Rich Cohen, a contributing editor at *Rolling Stone* and *Vanity Fair*, as well as a best-selling author, can sling words with the best of them. He also has a unique perspective as a lifelong Cubs fan and had the opportunity to meet Ernie Banks twice when he was young, then conducted what was probably the last significant interview Ernie ever gave. In that 2014 interview, perhaps because Ernie sensed his own impending mortality, Rich was able to access Ernie's true feelings on a number of subjects better than anyone ever had before. I appreciate the fact that he took his time to share his experience and opinions with me.

In addition to the books, articles, and online sources previously noted, an invaluable source for the understanding of what life was really like in North Dallas from 1930 to 1960 is found in the Marion Butts photo collection in the

Dallas Public Library Archives. Mr. Butts left hundreds of photos detailing virtually every aspect of life, from schools, entertainment, sports, landmarks, major events, and life in general. Examining these black-and-white images gives an unparalleled view into the past.

Special thanks to Mike and Mike, Harold, Brina, Lance, and the rest of the gang in the Goodreads Baseball Book Club for the stimulating baseball conversations, support, and laughing at my jokes (at least funny ones).

Thanks to Harold Kasselman for helping me to understand some legal situations in the story.

Thank you to the Negro Leagues Baseball Museum, the National Baseball Hall of Fame and Museum in Cooperstown, Jerry Schuebel, Steve Hullcranz, Larry Davidson, and James Brady for the use of pictures.

Thanks to Tyler Munn of the Bartholomew County Public Library for his great work obtaining hard-to-find stuff for interlibrary loan.

Thank you to the faculty of Kentucky Wesleyan College for teaching the value of a liberal arts education to this science major many years ago. Memories of red ink splattered all over my term papers from the vigilant grading pen of Dr. Marisue Coy in the Writing Workshop class inspire me to this day.

Thank you to my wife and family for their continued support.

PROLOGUE

This is the way it was supposed to happen.

After all those years toiling brilliantly for losing teams, remaining impossibly, improbably, inconceivably optimistic, Ernie Banks was finally in the postseason, playing a meaningful October game for the first time in his career. Late in the deciding game, the old man walked to the plate with men on base, carried by balky knees that had robbed him of the speed of his youth but not his enthusiasm. He stood blank-faced at the plate while his fingers incessantly milked the end of the bat. With one quick flick of his magnificent wrists, Ernie launched a dart that soared into the sunny sky and settled in the left-field bleachers of beautiful Wrigley Field. He bathed in the cheers as he toured the bases, happily doffed his cap to the adoring crowd, and disappeared into the dugout.

Later, after a futile effort to deflect praise toward his teammates, he sat in the clubhouse and patiently answered questions from the fawning press. "The pitch? Why it was a mediocre fastball," he said with a twinkle in his eye. After the clubhouse cleared, the old pro, alone with his thoughts, looked back and knew that the pain of the losing seasons had been finally purged.

Yes, this is the way it was supposed to happen for the most popular baseball player in Chicago history—the man who loved the game of baseball so much he was willing to play two games each day; a man unfailingly friendly to fans, media, and opponents. Everyone in baseball agreed: This is the way it should have happened.

But it didn't.

Ernie Banks never got to play that postseason game. For 19 years, he labored on some of the worst baseball teams of the era, hitting 512 home runs, becoming the first National Leaguer to win two consecutive Most Valuable Player Awards, and playing in 14 All-Star Games in a career as a first-ballot Hall of Famer and a member of the All-Century Team. His wonderful persona was so defining of his team that he acquired the moniker "Mr. Cub," which is still universally recognized. No other player on any other baseball club can lay claim to such a team-representing title.

But Ernie never played on a team that won anything more than the hearts of fans, sympathy, and sometimes ridicule. This burden, one of the cruel ironies in sports, often obscured his other accomplishments and followed him to the grave. For years, his was the first name conjured when anyone discussed athletic excellence without a postseason appearance.

But there is much more to the Ernie Banks story than smiles, unreasonable spring predictions of pennants, quick wrists, and bad teams. His career spanned an important epoch of social change, in and out of the game. He grew up indescribably poor in the segregated urban South, his life's course changed forever by the timely confluence of his own athletic ability and the admission of Jackie Robinson into the American game. He became the last player to go from the Negro Leagues to a Hall of Fame Major League Baseball career. He walked the tattered tightrope of a successful black man in a society that carefully watched such men. He knew the anxiety of trying to maintain his reputation and career, while feeling the sting of criticism from those who felt he did not do enough to promote the cause of his people.

And through it all, he retained his image—that of an amiable, optimistic man, unwilling to respond to slights with anything more than to ignore them; a man who preached tolerance and patience, on and off the baseball field; a man who appreciated what the game of baseball gave him and always reminded people of it.

It's an unfortunate product of our culture that a man can at once be universally known and also completely unknown due to an image that is so recognizable and so loved that no one bothers to seek anything further. We should resist the temptation to allow "Mr. Cub" and "Let's play two" to be the sole definition of Ernie Banks. But who was the real Ernie Banks, behind the happy clichés and optimistic veneer? How did an impoverished, shy kid from a segregated ghetto grow up to become not only the face of a franchise, but also the most celebrated athlete in one of the most segregated major cities in the country?

In attempting to write the true story of Ernie Banks, an obvious obstacle is Ernie himself. He freely gave interviews throughout his life but was so modest that he could not bring himself to make a self-promoting statement. His memories of early athletic endeavors invariably contained few feats of wonder, but rather his own wonder at why people thought he was good, as if they just always picked him for their teams, stuck him in the middle of the infield, and paid him money for no particular reason that he could fathom. His spoken memories of childhood were almost devoid of substance. The stories were unchanged throughout his life—the same precious few anecdotes, carefully packaged, told and retold: quaint generalities whitewashed with cheerful conclusions. His baseball stories were told with a relaxed, folksy style that, while entertaining, often does not stand up well to fact-checking—actual results and dates were less important than the intended moral or punch line. There was precious little concrete material of what it was really like or how he felt. He was never able to voice even a mildly negative thought about anyone or anything. Ernie certainly endured his share of disappointments, insults, and pain, but he tended to understate these or, more often, overlooked them altogether. To rely only on autobiographical accounts from Ernie would be to completely miss the most significant part of the tale.

The truly remarkable aspect of the Ernie Banks story lies not in his accomplishments on the baseball field, although they were considerable; rather, it lies in the impact he made on individuals and an entire city, the legacy of his persona, and the fact that he made it at all, given the time and place from which he came. Complete understanding of Ernie Banks is impossible without a clear knowledge of the forces at work during his developmental years. Critical examination is essential to fully appreciate the challenges he faced, how he responded, how he was viewed by the public, and his ultimate triumph. And so, some investigation is necessary.

1

DALLAS

A word of caution: It's not easy to find the childhood of Ernie Banks. He came from a time and place that no longer exists. It's been cast aside physically and mentally; perhaps because it's more comfortable to ignore that part of our past. But to fully understand the story, it is worth the effort—to do some searching, scrape off the societal paint and varnish, and see what lies beneath.

But where to start? How about Booker T. Washington High School in Dallas? Ernie graduated from there in 1950. The school stands in the same place it did back then, and kids still walk some of the same halls. Only everything is different now. When Ernie was a kid, the surrounding neighborhood was known as North Dallas. It was the black section of the city—the only place they were allowed to live. Today the school lies at the heart of the swanky Dallas Arts district. There is little trace of the houses and lives that once covered the area. And the name of the school is different. Today it is known officially as Booker T. Washington School for the Arts. It's a magnate school. Kids come from throughout Dallas County to attend—some from as far as 20 miles, kids of all colors. During Ernie's day, some of Washington's students traveled a distance also, but only because they had to—it was the only school in the city that would take blacks.

Look around the school. On the side of a hallway, near a stairwell, is a small area called Bulldog Corner. There is a plaque on the wall for Ernie Banks, the school's most famous alumnus. It was just put up a few years ago, after a campaign by some old friends. Nearby is a case that holds a bunch of tarnished-bronze trophies with football players on top—state championship trophies: 1941, 1946, 1950. . . . They don't even play football at Booker T. Washington anymore. Now the school produces world-class singers, dancers, and thespians. There is no other hint of the school Ernie knew.

Let's round up some old-timers from the area who knew Ernie back in the day, to find out what things were like. "There's only a few of us left," says Robert Prince. Dr. Prince, in his mid-80s now, has lived in the neighborhood all his life, except for a short time spent sitting on a hill in Korea holding a rifle in the early 1950s and his years of education. He is the unofficial historian of North Dallas. "I grew up a few blocks from Ernie. We were close. Where we grew up is practically downtown Dallas now, some of the most expensive real estate in the city. Of course, it wasn't like that back then."[1]

"It was very crowded in North Dallas," says Joe Kirven. Joe played on the Booker T. football team with Ernie. "There were a lot of people of color. And it was very segregated. People nowadays wouldn't even believe how things were back then. The history books will never tell how it really was."[2]

"Now, you have to know about Ernie's family," continues Kirven. "He didn't have much growing up."

"Ernie came from a rather large family who were relatively financially disadvantaged," says Robert Stinnett, an ex-military man who understates the obvious.[3]

"We were all poor," says Prince. "It was a poor, poor neighborhood. But Ernie's family? They were poor for black folks."

Knowing about Ernie's family starts with his father. Eddie Banks was born in 1894, near Marshall, Texas. Located on the eastern border of the state, Marshall had been the fourth-largest city in Texas during the Civil War, the seat of the richest county in the state—a county that held the highest per capita number of farms and plantations in the entire South just before the war. At the time, life in east Texas was the most identical representation of antebellum Old South in the state.

Cotton was the cash crop. The plantations provided enormous wealth and social standing for the owners. They didn't do much for the relatives of Eddie Banks, however. Eddie's people had the wrong color skin. They had worked the fields in and around Marshall for several generations, before and after the war. They were laborers, making enough to get by but little more.

Times had not been good for people who looked like Eddie Banks in Texas. The 1850 census counted 400 freed blacks in the entire state, a number that pales next to the estimated 58,000 slaves.[4] The emancipation of slaves in 1865 did little to improve the overall day-to-day lot for most. Some slaves were given small pieces of land by benevolent former owners, but most were simply turned out empty handed, unprepared to do anything other than what they had been doing—working the land to make money for someone else.

Although big farmers prospered after the war as the area once again became a leading cotton market, the majority of the county's citizens barely scraped by. Tensions between the races were high as everyone competed for jobs. The initial hope of reconstruction soon faded for African Americans as the White Citizens Party, Southern Democrats, and the Ku Klux Klan kept former slaves locked into poverty by intimidation and a series of laws that stripped the ability to vote and segregated every aspect of society—effectively restoring the old order. Historian Marvin Dulaney noted, "African Americans in Texas confronted a racial environment as rigid as that in other parts of the Deep South—a system of racial violence and segregation . . . a general pattern of apartheid that affected all aspects of African American life."[5]

Eddie's father, who had come to Texas sometime after he was born in Georgia in 1850, joined the scores of other poverty-stricken laborers in the area, trying to scrape out a meager living from the earth. Late nineteenth-century tenant farming in East Texas was called the "great open-air slum of the South."[6] The depth of poverty and dangers of raising a family in that era were illustrated starkly in the 1900 census, which recorded Eddie's mother, Francis, as having borne 19 children, but only seven were still living.

Across the state line, in Caddo County, Louisiana, lived the Durden family. Large numbers of Durdens worked the fields of Caddo County, going back to patriarch Moore Durden, who was born in Virginia in 1825, and brought to Caddo County in the 1840s. Like the Banks family, the Durdens toiled in the dirt and made money for other people. Essie Durden was born in Caddo County in 1912. "You never heard this in the papers, and I'm not sure Ernie even knew," says Prince, "but way back I remember some people around here saying something about Ernie and O. J. Simpson being related by their moms." Indeed. Essie's first cousin, Eunice, moved to San Francisco, married a man named Simpson, and had a son named Orenthal. He later went by O. J. and became a pretty good running back.

Eddie Banks served in the military near the end of World War I, most likely in one of the all-black service units. He returned to Marshall after the war and worked where he could. He met Essie Durden, and they were married in 1928, when she was 16 and he was 34. They would never tell their children stories of how they met or their courtship. The tales of romance would be lost to time, but the marriage would last until Eddie died 50 years later.

Shortly after marrying, Eddie and Essie boarded a Texas and Pacific Railway train and made the move west across the state, 150 miles to the growing city of Dallas. "A lot of black people took that train to Dallas from Marshall," says Prince. They were looking for a better life; maybe they would find it, maybe they wouldn't, but it had to be better than the no-prospect work of the east Texas farms.

Dallas had been a small town until the 1870s, when the population soared as it became the first railway crossroads in Texas—a strategic position for the transportation of goods north and east. In the 1930s, Dallas became the financial center for oil in Texas and experienced exponential growth. The population in 1930 was 260,000—up more than 100,000 from 10 years earlier—and it would swell to almost a half-million by 1950. Many of the newcomers were African Americans, drawn in by the increasing demand for labor in the growing city.

Eddie and Essie found a bustling, culturally rich African American community in North Dallas. It boasted the largest and most powerful Negro Chamber of Commerce in the country, a newspaper, and numerous black-owned theaters and businesses, providing almost all needed services. Deep Ellum, the named derived from a pronunciation of Elm Street, was the Dallas counterpart to Memphis' Beale Street, a place where jazz and legendary blues flowed like the nearby Trinity River.

Like the rest of the South, society in Dallas was totally segregated, by custom and law. Blacks and whites interacted as needed for work but little else. "Racism indelibly marked—and continues to mark—life in Dallas," wrote historian Harvey Graff in 2008. "Over the full span of the city's history, both implicitly and explicitly sanctioned violence sent clear messages about where power lay."[7]

Frequently, those messages came from the Ku Klux Klan. With 13,000 members in the 1920s, the Dallas chapter was the largest in Texas. At the time, the Klan dominated politics throughout the state—often running complete tickets. Candidates in many places had little chance for election without the Klan's overt support. At the state fair in Dallas in 1923, more than 75,000 citizens turned out to cheer a Klan parade and feted local dentist Hiram Wesley Evans, the national imperial grand wizard. The Klan actively maintained whipping posts near the black settlement of Joppa, just north of Dallas—trees whose lower limbs had been cleared away so a man could be bound to the trunk. Newspaper accounts included interviews with people who had been spirited away from their Dallas homes and taken out to Joppa in the middle of the night, either after a perceived indiscretion or simply as a warning to others.[8]

Signs throughout Dallas served as a constant reminder about the status of equality: "whites only" restrooms, "colored waiting room" at the bus station, hands pointing to the "white" entrance or "colored" entrance to theaters and other public establishments. One dunking booth at the state fair in 1946 advertised, "Hit the trigger and duck the nigger, 3 balls 10 cents."

Although the fairgrounds were only a short walk from North Dallas, African Americans were allowed to attend the Texas State Fair on one day only. For years the day was termed "Negro Day," but in the early 1950s the board of directors, in an effort to make it more palatable, renamed it "Negro Achievement Day." Several years later, protesters derided it as "Negro Appeasement Day."[9] In 1953, facing pressure, the board decided to allow African Americans to attend any day but only with the stipulation that they were not allowed on certain midway rides that carried the risk of physical contact among riders, lest the inexcusable act of touching between the races were to occur. This was the Dallas of Eddie and Essie Banks.

The young couple moved into a flimsy wooden-frame house on the edge of an unpaved lane called Katy Street in the middle of North Dallas. They lived amid a stretch of unpainted houses that had crooked poles holding up sagging roofs and crumbling porches. The only heat was from a round-bellied woodstove, and during the winter they had to put paper around the windows to keep out the cold. There was no running water; the bathroom was out back. Electricity was a luxury that would be added amid great fanfare a decade later. Rent was $20 a month.

Eddie and Essie soon began to build a large family. They welcomed a daughter, Edna Mae, in 1929. The couple's first son, Ernest, was born in 1931. He was born at home, delivered by a midwife, as were all children in the area because the only Dallas hospital that would admit blacks was a 14-bed North Dallas structure not equipped for deliveries. "It was almost 1960 before a black baby could be born in a hospital in Dallas, if you can believe that," says Prince. Children continued to arrive in the Banks house, one every year or two, until the last child, Donald, was born in 1956, making an even dozen.

Ernie frequently said in later interviews that the overriding memory of his childhood was how hard his father worked. Many days he watched Eddie leave the house in the early morning darkness and return in the evening when it was dark once more. Eddie loaded trucks, washed cars, and shined shoes. He picked cotton when it was in season. He worked wherever he could. During the hard years of the Depression, he landed a coveted job with the Works Progress Administration. "The WPA was mighty good for us poor people," he told a reporter later.[10]

In 1940, Eddie was hired as a janitor and porter at the Texas Wholesale Grocery Corporation and kept that job for more than 20 years. There was some trouble at the grocery between blacks and whites, but Eddie never talked about it—he only warned his oldest son to look elsewhere for employment. That was

Eddie's way: Work hard, don't complain, just deal with things and take care of your own—but learn.

Thin and wiry with large, strong hands, Eddie was neat and always wore a hat. A sober man, Eddie's wife and kids never were at a loss when it came to his whereabouts. When not working, his idea of a big time was to hold out a couple of bucks before turning over his pay to Essie, buy a half-pint at the corner grocery, and share it with his brother while playing checkers or dominoes on the porch. "Ernie's dad acted like he didn't have a care in the world," says Kirven. Eddie seemed content with his life; he never expressed a desire to buy a house or even a car. If he ever had any ambition more than simply making ends meet—and have everyone leave him alone and allow him to exist—he never showed it.

But Eddie Banks didn't show a lot of things. He was not a man given to frivolous emotional expression. Smiles were rare. He was uncomfortable, guarded even, around strangers, and anyone not family was a stranger. Eddie would later be described by his son as a thinking man who kept his thoughts to himself. He would answer direct questions, but anyone waiting for Eddie to volunteer anything had best find a comfortable chair. Attracting attention and speaking about himself was not Eddie's style. As a young man, he had learned to keep his head down; he had seen what could happen to a man in North Dallas who stood out.

While Eddie worked, Essie ran the house. An attractive woman in her day, Essie was strong-willed and provided the emotional glue of the family. The opposite of her husband, she was very outgoing; she enjoyed being around people, talking, and laughing. She was a true matriarch, and Ernie, who would remain close to her throughout her life, would long quote her words of wisdom, tolerance, and hope. Her lessons were liberally sprinkled with words from the Good Book. Even when Ernie was older, Essie would remind him of a specific scripture, something to live by for the day.

Times were hard everywhere—and worse in North Dallas. Work was a way of life for the Banks family. Everyone worked—not to get ahead, but just to survive. Ernie sold newspapers, mopped floors in a hotel, shined shoes, and picked cotton to help out. "I can clearly remember a large truck would pull up early every morning in the summer in front of the YMCA," says Prince. "Those who wanted to go pick cotton out in the county would get on, and they would bring them home in the evening." He added, "Ernie's entire family, when they were old enough, would go. Sometimes they'd have to miss school for working and picking cotton. Some of them didn't even make it through high school because they had to work. It was tough."

They rode out to the cotton fields, eating dust as they stood crowded together in the back of the truck. It was hot, sweaty work—Texas hot, at 105 degrees or more. Bent over, crawling on their knees on the hard clay, battling stickers and fire ants, they got paid $2 for each 100-pound bag. Five dollars was a good day's work.

Amid the struggle to survive, education was considered a luxury in the Banks household, a luxury most members of the family couldn't afford. Eddie had finished the third grade, Essie the sixth. Ernie would be one of the few lucky ones among the Banks kids who got to finish high school.

Essie had to use her imagination to feed her ever-growing family. "It's amazing to see how they made it with nothing," Ernie said in 2004. "She could make a dollar talk."[11] A big can of lard and a sack each of beans, flour, and meal might provide dinners for a month. Sometimes there were food rations from the welfare truck. Sometimes, especially during the war, when things were tight all over, Ernie and Essie would walk to a nearby supermarket and go through the trash to pick out pig feet, pig tails, ox tails, and other things she would fix in a stew.

Ernie never spoke of any bitterness or self-pity. "I just thought that was the way things were," he said in 1970. He continued,

> We never had anything, and being brought up the way we were I never had a burning desire to have more than we had. Actually, when I look back, they were happy times. My father never showed signs that we were down and out. He had a happy attitude and assured us that somehow we would always have what we needed. As a result, I never had the feeling that we were really poor.[12]

While Ernie frequently offered similar comments—an old man's euphemistic view of an idyllic childhood—and no one would ever question his membership in the glass-is-half-full club, there comes a moment in every impoverished child's life when he undeniably *knows* that he is really poor; and watching his mother go through trash to find the family's dinner is that moment.

At the time, Jim Crow hung over North Dallas like a nor'easter cloud—dark and foreboding, with the threat of a deadly tornado kicking up at any time. Kids learned the rules early. "You didn't go downtown by yourself if you were black," says Kirven. "If you had business there, you went there and got the heck back to our neighborhood as fast as you could."

"Everything was segregated back then," says Prince, continuing,

> Separate but certainly not equal. Our school always got the worn-out desks and books from the white schools. For us kids there weren't many parks in our part of town; really just the one and it didn't have anything. It was basically just an empty lot. Sometimes we would slip off and go to the parks in the white section. Reverchon Park was really nice; it had a baseball diamond, swings, everything a

park is supposed to have. We looked at that place like it was Heaven. We would go and play there, but somebody would always call the police. We would play until the police would show up and run us off.

The neighborhood houses were too small for anything other than living. Ernie spent most of his time outside, like the other kids. "We made our own fun," says Prince. "Touch football in the streets, stickball in the street until a window got broke—then we'd scatter." Homemade scooters—made by attaching wheels to the bottom of scrap wood—to race in the streets, kites built out of pieces of fruit crates covered with newspapers, the kids used their imaginations when it was time to play. Sometimes play included shooting rats with BB guns.

Their entire world, including the elementary, junior high, and high schools, was contained within a few blocks. The heart of North Dallas life centered on the triad of three historical institutions: St. Paul Methodist Church, the Moorland YMCA, and Booker T. Washington High School. All three were a great source of pride and accomplishment for the community—institutions built by blacks for their own advancement. Within easy walking distance of the Banks home, they played a major role in the foundation of the childhood of Ernie Banks.

Established as a congregation in 1873, St. Paul was the first place ex-slaves in Dallas were able to learn to read and write. The building was started in 1901, based on a design by architect William Sydney Pittman, Booker T. Washington's son-in-law. Black workers brought home whatever extra bricks they found each day from various parts of the city, contributing to the different colored bricks throughout the building that persist to this day. Each Sunday, Essie Banks dressed her kids in their nicest clothes and marched them down the street to St. Paul.

A YMCA in North Dallas, the first YMCA for African Americans in the entire Southwest, was formed in 1928. It was a three-story brick building with cast stone ornamentation and an impressive arched entrance. It had a gym, an indoor pool, and a dorm with 37 rooms for use by visitors during a time when there were only two other hotels in the city that accommodated African Americans. In addition to sports, it offered the African American community a place to congregate and became a meeting place for professionals and clubs. The Moorland YMCA was such a vital part of North Dallas life that when money was needed for a large addition in 1947, the community responded by raising $65,949, the "largest amount ever raised by Negro citizens from Negroes in any campaign in North America," proclaimed the *Dallas Morning News*.[13] Ernie, like all the kids in the area, spent many hours at the Y. He frequently worked there in the office. "I don't know what we'd have done without the Moorland YMCA," says Prince. "It was the biggest thing for us kids." It had the only pool in the city black kids could jump into when the Texas summers boiled over.

A high school had been established for blacks in Dallas in 1892. Booker T. Washington High School replaced the generically named Dallas Colored High School in 1922 and remained the only high school in Dallas County for black students until 1939, when Lincoln High School was opened about five miles away in North Dallas to alleviate the overcrowding, which had swelled to 1,400 students in a school built to hold 600.

The name of the school was significant. Booker T. Washington was the dominant leader in the U.S. African American community at the turn of the century. While he worked tirelessly to advance his people's interests, he promoted the long-term goal of building the community's economic strength and pride by focus on self-help and education, and encouraged compromise, working with the white community, and patience rather than the militant opposition of Jim Crow—a philosophy similar to the one Ernie Banks would one day advocate.

Booker T. Washington High School's principal, John Patton Jr., was also a North Dallas institution. An alumnus of the old Colored High School, he had attended Prairie View College, then returned and taught history until taking over as principal in 1939. While teaching, Patton developed a course on Negro history to give the kids a better understanding of the struggles and problems their people faced and a proper social consciousness and pride in their achievements. This course continued as required class work when he became principal. Patton dressed impeccably in a suit and tie every day and tolerated no nonsense. In addition to Patton, Washington had a number of excellent, dedicated teachers who considered teaching a mission. "All of our teachers were inspirational," says Prince. "They knew what we faced, they had been through it. They tried to prepare us. My father was a math teacher there, and he emphasized getting a good education."

The kids took great pride in their school and the crimson and gray Bulldogs of Booker T. Washington. Graffiti on their building was unheard of, and the stands were always packed for football games, everybody cheering wildly when the sharply dressed band strutted onto the field at P. C. Cobb Stadium, led by baton-twirling majorettes and a high-stepping drum major. The football team regularly played for state championships. "We had the best track program in the state," says Kirven. "The white schools couldn't touch our times."

"The pride in our school didn't just go for sports," says Prince. He elaborated,

A lot of passion was put into athletics, but many of us were just as enthusiastic as academic rivals. I couldn't play any sports. The coach said I ran like a white boy. Academics were my thing. It was a big deal to get into the National Honor Society. I never thought of not going to college.

In 1956, Essie Banks told a reporter Ernie had been almost a model boy. She said he never prowled at night and was a regular at Sunday school and church. He liked to stretch out on top of his bed and read for hours but to the best of her memory was an average student in school.[14]

By all accounts, Ernie was as advertised by his mother. "Ernie was one of the nicest and quietest guys in the neighborhood," says Stinnett.

"I never met anyone like him," says Kirven. "Ernie was different. Very quiet. On the football field he just did his job. You know how athletes will get together and shoot the bull; some guys talk a much better game than they play. Ernie wasn't like that. He never bragged."

"Everybody liked Ernie." says Prince. "Everybody knew he was mild-mannered. That's just the way he was. I never knew him to get in an argument. As a kid you always had arguments and fights on the playground over games and stuff, if someone got bumped too hard or the games were close. But I never knew Ernie to."

"I never even saw him get mad," says Kirven. "Never heard him use foul language. He got along with everybody. He was unusual that way."

"He didn't talk tough and didn't fight, but Ernie never had any trouble because everybody respected him for his athletic ability," says Prince.

Aw yes, athletic ability. It didn't take long for everyone in North Dallas to figure it out: That Banks kid could play some ball. "It was quite obvious that Banks (what I called him) was head and shoulders better than most of the kids, to include the next best players," says Stinnett.

"Sports came easy to Ernie," Washington's football and basketball coach, Raymond Hollie, said in 1977. "He was good in everything. Not particularly fast, but very talented."[15]

Ernie had the kind of athletic ability that made a shy kid stand out, whether he wanted to or not. "No one was more pure of an athlete than Ernie," says Kirven. "I went to college on an athletic scholarship, and I played with and against a lot of guys. But I never saw anyone who was as good of an overall athlete as Ernie. He could play anything. He might have been the best all-around athlete to ever come out of Dallas."

"Ernie played the wrong sport," said one longtime North Dallas sports follower in 2005. "He was a better basketball player than he was a baseball player.

I never saw anyone who could shoot a basketball like Ernie."[16] But basketball was not quite a glory sport at the time. Booker T. Washington didn't even have a gym; the boys practiced and played their home games at the Moorland YMCA. The tiny gym wasn't built for spectators—fans had to stand lining the court or perched above on the catwalk track. And there wasn't much space between the basket and the wall, a fact worth remembering while charging down the court on a fast break.

Long and lean with silky movements and great hands, Ernie stood out on the basketball court. "Ernie had a good shot," says Kirven. "He was a good rebounder too. We had a good basketball team, a lot of talented players, but Ernie was the best." Reliable records are hard to come by from the era, but by one account he averaged more than 20 points a game; another said 15. The exact number is not as important as the fact that in most games, Ernie Banks was the best player in the gym.

Ernie was also a good track man. More of a middle-distance runner than a sprinter, he was good enough to do a 51-second quarter mile. He also high-jumped 5 feet, 11 inches.[17]

While Ernie was a standout in basketball and track, he made his most lasting North Dallas impression on the football field. And here he benefitted from his association with another area landmark, Coach Raymond Hollie. By the time Ernie got to Washington, Hollie, who had been there since 1939, had already established a powerhouse program. He was one of those coaches who could take some guys with a little talent and mold them into a strong team; he could take guys with real talent and turn them into champions. "Raymond Hollie was a great coach," says Kirven. "Very smart. No nonsense. Very disciplined. He would have been a good coach anywhere if the times had been different."

"He was a very stern coach who had a great influence on my life," Banks said in 1999. "He was like Green Bay's Vince Lombardi. Coach Hollie pushed us along."[18] One year, Ernie broke his collarbone early in the last game of the season. Afraid to tell the coach and risk disapproval, he finished the game in pain.

"There wasn't any fooling around if you were going to play for Coach Hollie," says Kirven. "You had to be in shape and you had to follow orders. Ernie seemed to easily conform to and reflect Coach Hollie's high standards of behavior. No smoking, no drinking, or any other habits that might be considered bad."

Hollie placed an emphasis on physical conditioning. "Treat your bodies like they are temples," he would tell his players. "He challenged his athletes to give everything they had, on and off the field, to lay everything on the line and give 100 percent each and every play," said a former player. "He [Hollie] was one of the best coaches ever in this country—black, white, green, or purple. The football atmosphere was one of discipline. Mr. Hollie made sure you did the things you were supposed to do."[19]

And Ernie Banks rarely needed encouragement to do what he was supposed to do. "He [Ernie] was one of those kids who are a delight to coach," Hollie said later.[20]

The long, tough practices were not infrequently concluded with the aid of headlights from coaches' cars clearing the darkness. This was rough, hard-hitting, no-face-mask football. Texas style. The meek didn't make it through practice. "He always told us that we had to fight for things," said Ernie. "That we couldn't expect from life any more than we were willing to put in it ourselves."[21]

The Bulldogs competed in the Prairie View Interscholastic League, commonly referred to as the Negro League. Set up and operated out of Prairie View A&M near Houston, the PVIL set the schedules and ran the state tournaments for black schools until Texas sports integrated in 1967. The league had many great players, for instance, future NFL stars Dick "Night Train" Lane of Austin Anderson and Ollie Matson of Houston Yates. Powerhouses in the state were Houston Wheatley, Houston Yates, Fort Worth I. M. Terrell, Galveston Central, Corpus Christi Coles, and Booker T. Washington of Dallas. From 1941 to 1958, Washington appeared in eight PVIL state championship games, winning three and tying one. The tie came in Ernie's freshman year, 1946, and they lost, 6–0, in the championship game in 1948, when he was a junior.

Games in the PVIL were played on Wednesday nights, often with long bus rides, getting the kids back home in the early morning—in time for an hour or two of sleep before getting ready for school, and going to school the next day was required by Coach Hollie. Football was the high school dream game in Texas, regardless of color. "We usually had big crowds for football," says Kirven. "We played the Lincoln Tigers in the Cotton Bowl every year."

Everyone wanted to be on the football team. Jimmy "Iron Claw" Hill, a Washington graduate who went on to an 11-year pro football career with the Cardinals and Chiefs, told a reporter in 1956, "I was a senior at Washington High when Ernie was a freshman. His father used to bring him to football practice, and Ernie was mad because he couldn't get in the scrimmages. . . . Later on, Ernie played football at Washington, and we all figured he could have played in college."[22]

Ernie was captain on the football team and one of the stars. Again, records were kept sporadically, but he reportedly caught eight touchdown passes in one season. According to another account, he scored 22 touchdowns in his junior and senior seasons combined. The numbers vary, but there is no mistaking his impact. "Ernie played right end," says Joe Kirven. He added,

I was the other end. I was much faster than Ernie. I was a track man, but he had the surest hands on the team. He had pro hands. He could have played pro football. Our offense was geared for passing and running, and Ernie was a great third-down player. When our football team had a tight game, Coach Hollie would tell the quarterback to get the ball to Ernie. On third down, Ernie often got double coverage by the opposition, but he usually made the play anyway. When things got tough, the quarterback knew where to go.

The Washington–Lincoln game was a focal point of the North Dallas community each year, timed with Negro Day at the Fair, frequently drawing crowds in excess of 20,000. Residents talked about the game for months; close games were talked about for years. One of those was the game in which Ernie might have stepped out of bounds while making a late, crucial catch in 1949. Or he might not have. The play still triggered spirited debates among Dallas old-timers a half-century later. Robert Thomas, the Lincoln defender and later Dallas Independent School District athletic director, always maintained Banks had a foot outside the line. Washington fans would forever believe he was in. But the call went to Lincoln, and they won the game and eventually the state that year.[23]

North Dallas held dangers that derailed the future of many teens. More than a few kids dropped out of school and headed for the dead end of Deep Ellum, hanging out with the pool sharks, numbers men, and street toughs. Ernie watched several friends and siblings get into trouble with the law. He later recalled that when he was 17, a friend "got involved with marijuana." Banks continued,

> I could have smoked pot, too, but I didn't. . . . He got nabbed and spent a couple of years in the state penitentiary. I've thought about that a lot. We played ball together . . . and I went to the [professional] clubs while he went to jail. All because he got involved with the wrong people and I was lucky enough not to.[24]

Only it wasn't really luck. "There was no risk of Ernie getting in trouble," says Kirven. "He always knew how to avoid it."

Ernie seemed to have an innate sense of timing—of when to dodge impending trouble. He perfected the fade-out. He might be walking down a street with a group of guys, joking and laughing, looking for something to do. When talk among the group drifted to something that sounded like trouble, or girls, they would turn around and Ernie was gone. Disappeared. Quietly faded away. Ernie had an internal barometer—acutely attuned to changes in the atmosphere that warned of approaching squalls and gales—that helped him avoid hazards that sidetracked other kids.

While Ernie was quiet around the guys, he was nearly paralytic around girls. He rarely dated and later said he only went to one dance and that was because his mother made him. It did not turn out well. He long remembered the kidding he received from buddies when his date went home with someone else.[25]

In none of the accounts of his high school years do we find the continually talking, upbeat Ernie Banks. There is no record of him predicting championships each year for Booker T. Washington. Joe Kirven does not remember him ever exhorting his teammates to play two football games. He was never referred to in the yearbook as "Mr. Bulldog." That character did not exist yet. What did exist was a quiet, cautious kid with an unusually acute moral compass that would always keep him out of trouble, a kid eager to please and be liked, who found speaking in front of others painful, who preferred not to attract attention, but who possessed a unique form of athletic ability that always made him stand out.

This was Ernie's world. With time, he always said good things about his childhood and hometown, as was the case in an interview in 1999, when he said, "I enjoyed growing up in Dallas. Everything was within walking distance: the school I went to, the YMCA, my friends in the neighborhood, the park I played baseball on. Everybody knew everybody."[26] He never discussed the racism of his childhood or the harsh conditions.

But a wound remained from those years that would never mend. "There was a lot of hatred here growing up," says Prince. He added,

> Ernie had bad memories of how things were. He may not have talked about it, but I know it had an effect. I think that's why he never came back here; only for funerals or to visit his mother. Dallas ignored him too. When he was doing great, there might be a small blurb in the back of the paper and that was it. It was like guys from our part of town didn't exist.

"Things were pretty tough," says Kirven. "You had to be careful. You couldn't go in certain stores, had to sit in the back of the bus. But we didn't know anything different. We just accepted it and tried to make the best of it. And looked forward to a time when it would be better. We survived."

The segregation of Ernie's Dallas was generally accepted without outward complaint. That was the way things had always been as far as they knew. While hoping that someday things would improve, surviving in the present was the main thing, and that was often a full-time proposition. There were certainly no protests when Ernie was growing up—everyone knew about those hitching posts in Joppa. The weight of history crushed many dreams.

"All of us kids knew how things were," says Prince, continuing,

> I don't really think any of us kids ever thought we would see the day when segregation would end; not in our lifetime. Many tried to run from it—go to California, out west where it wasn't as overt. But it was still just going from one ghetto to another. Many of us were bitter. A lot of guys just gave up and became thugs. But Ernie was not like a lot of us who grew up with a chip on our shoulder for some reason. Ernie kept it inside.

Changes were coming to Dallas and the rest of the country, but they would be slow and hard fought. Dallas schools would not integrate until a federal mandate forced them to in the mid-1960s. Housing integration would come much later. By then, Ernie Banks would be long gone. The vibrant community of North Dallas that Ernie knew would eventually disappear—when changing laws made it no longer necessary. First, a freeway sliced through the heart of the neighborhood like a scythe. Urban renewal took care of the rest, leaving little trace—only a few landmark buildings, a historical plaque or two, and memories of old-timers.

It is a mistake to assume, as some do, that the kids of North Dallas had little chance of improving their lot in life due to their circumstances and the times. There were opportunities, although not as many as kids had in other places—and it often took unusual foresight, determination, and luck for the opportunities to materialize—but the kids did have a chance.

"As a boy, I grew up three blocks from Baylor Medical School," says Prince. He further explained,

> I would stand on the corner and admire the students as they went in. When I told my dad I wanted to go to Baylor and be a doctor, he said, "Son, sit down. I don't know if you noticed, but the only kids going in there are as white as their coats. You can't even use the library." He explained how things were, but he also encouraged me. He said, "Right now you can't go there. But study hard. Maybe by the time you're ready, things will change. Prepare yourself for when the time comes."

Prince used the GI Bill to go through college and medical school, became the first black obstetrician in Dallas, and served the community for 60 years.

"Everything eventually changed for the better," says Kirven. "Of course, we weren't allowed in any state colleges at the time, but I was fortunate. I had some breaks. I went to Wiley College [a traditionally black college in Marshall] on an athletic scholarship." Kirven eventually formed a service company in Dallas that grew to 192 employees and made him a wealthy man. He was chosen as one of five outstanding young Texans in 1968—the first black ever selected—and later served on the board of directors of two universities.

After attending Prairie View, Stinnett joined the army and became one of the first black helicopter pilots. He distinguished himself in the Battle of Ia Drang (which was later made into a Mel Gibson movie called *We Were Soldiers and Young*), in which he repeatedly flew through a hail of gunfire at a nearly over-run landing site to extract wounded soldiers, collecting more than 100 enemy bullet holes in his Huey and winning the Silver Star in the process. He retired as a colonel.

There were opportunities—for the smart, the lucky, and the brave. For Ernie Banks, the opportunity came in the form of a small, round white ball. "Ernie was usually gone in the summers," says Kirven. "We didn't see him around. He would be back in the fall for school in time for football. But he spent his summers off playing baseball."

Yes, baseball. We can't leave Dallas without discussing baseball, because without it, no one outside Dallas would have ever heard of Ernie Banks.

2

BASEBALL

He loved baseball—always had, always would.

He never dreamed the game could provide a means of escape from a life of hard labor and poverty; he just loved to play. He loved the give-and-take with other players, the chance a man had to show he was as good as or better than another man based solely on what he did on the field, not what he looked like. He loved the Saturday and Sunday doubleheaders—two games were hardly enough. He loved the game of baseball so much he would continue to play into his 40s, still enjoying himself even though age had taken its toll on his body. Yes, Eddie Banks loved baseball.

Ernie, on the other hand, was another matter.

Young Ernie was not interested in going out in the yard and playing catch; his father sometimes resorted to bribing him with nickels or dimes. The man who later famously loved baseball so much he wanted to play two games every day had to be bribed just to have a catch with his father? That was Ernie's story, and he stuck to it. He first related this in a newspaper profile in 1955,[1] and repeated it often throughout the years, prominently telling it to reporters the weekend of his Hall of Fame induction in 1977, and he was still repeating it in 2006. He would tell about the spring day in 1937, or was it 1939, could have been 1941 (the year changed but the story never did), when his father came home from work with a five-and-ten-cent store glove he had purchased for $2.95 and took him into the backyard. Ernie claimed he didn't really care for it but only participated "because dad used to throw in an occasional nickel to keep up my enthusiasm."[2]

In the later version, Ernie claimed that while playing catch with his father, "I was always thinking, 'Why is he doing this?' Because no blacks could play in the major league. But somehow in his mind he had a vision that things would change and be better."[3]

Was Eddie really hoping for a miracle, that someday his son would be allowed to play in the major leagues? Or was he just like thousands of other stoic fathers of the era—unable to verbalize his love for his son but using baseball to engage him in something they could share together? He never said. But the fact remains that Eddie loved both baseball and Ernie enough to offer the kid nickels, during a time when nickels, not unlike smiles, were rarely thrown around frivolously.

In those years, baseball was perhaps a more prominent part of black society than it was among whites. The annual Juneteenth celebration of emancipation often featured all-day baseball marathons. Eddie had played on both organized and sandlot teams throughout his youth in eastern Texas and kept it up long into his adult years in Dallas. It was reported that Eddie had played several years as a pitcher and catcher for the Dallas Black Giants in the 1920s, traveling throughout the Midwest. He had a half-dozen crooked fingers testifying to his years toiling behind the plate.

When Ernie was growing up, with hungry mouths to feed, Eddie's traveling baseball days were long over, but he still played on weekends, mostly for the Dallas Green Monarchs, a team sponsored by Joe Maniscano's supermarket in the fast Dallas semipro league. Ernie enjoyed being the batboy, walking home with his father and talking about the game (Eddie was much more expansive on baseball than any other subject). "He was still so small his mother had to cut the store uniform they bought for him to about half its original size," Eddie said in 1960. "He'd be playing catch with some of the players when he should have been doing his regular chores. Ernie was such a happy-go-lucky kid nobody minded too much that he was spending more time playing than working."[4]

Eddie reportedly was a good hitter. Did he have the wrists his son would later make famous? It was never recorded. Eddie did tell inquiring reporters in the mid-1950s that he could always hit, just not with the power his son showed. But he usually added the caveat that the balls used when he was young and strong were mostly mush-balls, and there is no way of telling how far he might have hit one of these shiny modern balls. Throughout the years, printed retrospective accounts of Eddie's baseball career varied wildly regarding the teams and cities in which he supposedly played, and since no record was kept of the various semipro black teams from the era, the true nature of his baseball exploits are lost to history. What is fact is that Eddie played a lot of baseball, and he was good enough that people wanted him on their teams long after his 40th birthday—and that he shared his passion for the game with his oldest son.

"We used to play catch every afternoon after I came home from work," Eddie said, continuing,

> The bat came later, and that almost wrecked everything. Drives off Ernie's bat broke so many windows in the neighborhood that we were always in trouble. In fact, his mother used to yell at me: "Why don't you quit that silly baseball and help Ernie get a job? He'd be better off delivering newspapers or cutting grass." He smashed so many windows that I was almost broke trying to pay for them. That is when I learned something new. I'd roll out tin cans, cut them to the size of the window, and use them as replacements for the broken glass. . . . You'll never know the number of tin windows we had in our home.[5]

Maybe when Eddie was younger, he had possessed enough skill to have moved on up given the chance; maybe not, but he never complained of missed opportunities. He played the game and passed it on to his kids, teaching them to enjoy baseball for itself and not getting caught up in other worries. Eddie tutored his boys in baseball. Ben became an accomplished player and was signed by the Cubs three years after his brother. In 1956, Eddie was managing a youth team that featured a battery of 13-year-old Sammy Banks pitching and 15-year-old Eddie Banks Jr. catching. "You can't start too early," Eddie told a reporter. "I taught Ernie how to catch the ball right, how to trap it and get rid of it. But those home runs was more than I expected. I guess he knows how to use his wrists."[6]

In Ernie's younger years, Dallas had a team in the Texas League, the Dallas Eagles, but the first black would not play for them until 1952. African Americans had their own team, the Dallas Black Eagles, a minor-league team for the Negro Leagues. Throughout the 1930s and 1940s, there were numerous amateur and semipro teams, sponsored by North Dallas businesses.

Everyone knew there were opportunities for those who could play. African American kids who dreamed of baseball, dreamed of a spot in the Negro Leagues, like their heroes, Satchel Paige and Josh Gibson. Quite a few guys from North Dallas made it. Then, in 1947, Jackie Robinson took the field for the Brooklyn Dodgers and everything changed.

Booker T. Washington High School did not field a baseball team until the early 1950s, after Ernie had left. In fact, there were no organized baseball teams for black kids in Dallas at the time, only adult baseball teams. Fast-pitch softball was the thing for kids. And it was big. While Ernie played for several different teams in the area, the St. Paul Methodist Church team was the best. It was run by J. W. Whirl, a good guy with an eye for talent who regularly fielded the strongest teams in North Dallas. Whirl made Ernie his shortstop. Pretty soon people started taking notice of the St. Paul shortstop. "We took that softball very serious," said Raymond Hollie years later. "There were some red hot rivalries going on. . . . Word got around pretty fast about how good Ernie was."[7]

One of those who heard the word was Bill Blair. The 5-foot-9 Blair was a feisty little dude, fond of cigars and fedora hats, and rarely seen without both. Blair was a fixture in North Dallas; he knew everyone and everyone knew him. He had been a quick, tough halfback for Washington in football[8] and a pitcher with good velocity and a drop-dead curveball—good enough to play in the Negro Leagues for the Indianapolis Clowns, where his roommate was famed Harlem Globetrotter Goose Tatum. During the fall, he was a high school football official in the PVIL. A natural leader, Blair had reportedly been the youngest black first sergeant to serve in the U.S. Army during World War II, and in 1948, he founded the *Southwest Sports News*, a newspaper that specialized in publishing scores from African American college games. The paper would be renamed the *Elite News* in 1960, and became an important voice for Dallas-area African Americans in the next five decades. In 1947, Blair was 27 years old and running a semipro baseball team based in Amarillo, Texas, called the Detroit Colts.

Although for years Blair would enjoy telling people about the day he discovered Ernie Banks, he had known Ernie and his family for a long time. On the day often quoted, when the Colts had a break in the schedule, Blair was back in his hometown and decided to check out the local talent. Blair's trained eye noticed the way Ernie moved about the infield and swung the bat. Early in the game, Banks slugged a long home run. It was just the start. The opposing pitcher was a kid named Brannon who had a reputation. "Brannon was the fastest pitcher I had ever seen," Blair said. "I never saw anyone who could throw like him. I never saw anyone get the licks off him. And here was this willowy kid walloping ball after ball off him. Ernest, I could tell right away, was going to be something special."[9]

After the game, Blair talked to Ernie and invited himself to the Banks house. "They lived about four doors down from me," he said. "I knew his daddy, Eddie. I told Eddie I was taking his boy with me."[10]

Ernie later said he and Eddie were all for it, but, "We had to talk fast to convince Mom I should leave home."[11]

Blair promised Essie, "We'll take good care of him."

"Make sure you get him back so he can go to school [in the fall]," she replied.[12]

The next day Ernie and another North Dallas teenager were driven 360 miles west to Amarillo. It was a learning experience, a grand adventure. Other than the short rides outside Dallas on the cotton-picking truck and high school football trips, Ernie had never set foot out of his neighborhood.

Blair later reflected that Ernie didn't have a suitable glove so he bought him one. Once Ernie was equipped with a good glove, Blair had no hesitancy about putting the 17-year-old in the middle of his infield of adults. "I put him at shortstop," he said. "I knew he had all kinds of agility and natural athletic ability because I had seen him play basketball in high school. He could move. He looked like a natural-born shortstop to me."[13]

Ernie also impressed Blair as a quick learner. "You had to show Ernest everything one time and he learned it," Blair recalled in 1977. "The talent was all natural."[14]

The Colts were called a semipro team, but usually it was more semi than pro. The players divided up the gate receipts from each game, and a good day's take was maybe five or six bucks each.

The overhand pitching was much different than what Ernie had been accustomed to in fast-pitch softball, but the quick swing required in softball paid off. In Ernie's first game with the Colts, in front of the Amarillo crowd, he hit a home run to break a scoreless tie in his third at-bat. Blair greeted him at the dugout, "Get up in the stands and pass your cap," he told the confused youngster. Blair explained that it was customary for a player to pass his cap for donations after a home run. Ernie obliged and was rewarded with about $6 in pennies, nickels, dimes, and a few quarters.

After two home games, they left on a road trip. They traveled on an old bus throughout Texas, Kansas, Oklahoma, Nebraska, and New Mexico, stopping in small towns along the way. They played against American Legion teams, semipros, teams of college stars, and minor-league teams—anyone who had a field and a gate, and the gate was often optional.

Occasionally, the team stayed in hotels, but usually they split up and stayed with local black families. Blair seemed to know everyone in every town. Frequently, he had called ahead, and the players were greeted with their names on placards, urging citizens to come out and see them play. The older players accepted the two youngsters, but "let the kid do it" was a frequent comment when an errand or odd job needed to be done.

Ernie enjoyed his first season on the road. The total financial haul for the summer was almost $200, and when he returned home, he dutifully turned over most of it to Essie. Then he started his sophomore year of high school.

Ernie played for the Colts the next two summers. Statistics are unreliable, but in 1953, it was reported that Ernie's averages with the Colts were .355, .330, and .350.[15] Whatever his average, Ernie showed he had talent.

"He was younger than most of us," Frank Adams, a Dallas man who played for Amarillo, said in 1977. "But there wasn't any doubt about him being able to play with the big boys. When you see a guy who's got it, you know he's got it. . . . Ernie was going places, no doubt about it."[16]

Ernie was going places all right, but in 1947, the question was where? That summer Jackie Robinson had integrated the major leagues, but the thought and dream had not yet taken hold in every level of baseball; the future was still uncertain. "The major leagues for Ernest?" Blair responded to a question years later. "That was the furthest thing from my mind. It wasn't the way you thought back then."[17] But Blair thought Ernie had enough talent to make it to the Negro Leagues.

So did Negro League scouts. During Ernie's second summer with the Colts, the team played the Kansas City Monarchs' second team, the Stars, in a tiny Texas town an hour southeast of Amarillo called Memphis. The Stars, used by Monarchs owner Tom Baird to train players until they were ready for the big team, and also to scout the country looking for black talent, were managed by "Cool Papa" Bell. Universally called "Cool," Bell had been a legend as a player, one of the greatest in the Negro Leagues. Everyone who played with him had a "Cool-Papa-was-so-fast" story. The classic belonged to Satchel Paige: "Cool Papa was so fast he could turn out the light and be under the covers before the room got dark." After giving up the game as a player, Bell became famous for his ability to spot a ballplayer.

That day in Memphis, the Colts shortstop got three or four hits and showed defensive sparkle. "Son, you can play this game!" Bell told the teenager after the game.[18] Bell inquired about Ernie's plans for the future but made no commitment.

At this point it is uncertain whether Ernie truly believed in the opportunity that lay at his feet. Blair later said, "Ernie was an exceptional ballplayer, but he was not fond of the game and did not think of a life in professional baseball until the many talks we had about my experiences and the experiences of people like Goose Tatum, Josh Gibson, and Satchel Paige."[19] Ernie began to understand that baseball might take him somewhere.

The next spring, Ernie was at the Moorland YMCA when William "Dizzy" Dismukes arrived in Dallas looking for him. Dismukes was the head scout, traveling secretary, part-time pitching coach, and anything-else-that-needed-to-be-done man for the Monarchs. College educated at Birmingham's Miles College, Dismukes also doubled as a journalist, covering events for the *Chicago Defender* and *Pittsburgh Courier*. He was an astute baseball man who recognized talent and potential. A right-handed submarine pitcher, he was regarded as one of the best pitchers in black baseball in the 1910s and 1920s, mostly with the Indianapolis ABCs. He had been instrumental in acquiring Jackie Robinson for the Monarchs in 1945 and, recognizing Robinson's deficiency at shortstop, had helped convince him that short was not his best long-term position.

At Dismukes's suggestion, Ernie took him home to meet his parents. Dizzy offered Ernie $300 a month to play for the Monarchs. This was big money to Ernie's parents, who had never come close to making that amount. With little discussion, Ernie agreed to join the team. For his part in the story, Blair later claimed that Dismukes gave him a finder's fee. "Gave me three 10-dollar bills," he said in 2012.[20] A better bargain for a future baseball player would be hard to find.

Before leaving for professional baseball, Ernie had a big day coming. When he walked across the commencement platform to graduate from Booker T. Washington High School in May 1950, he was both proud and uncomfortable. The unmistakable sense of pride came from being the first member of his family to finish high school. The discomfort came from the first store-bought suit he had ever owned—well, store-bought of sorts. Essie had found it at the local Goodwill store for 20 cents. Ernie later told an author that the ill-fitted dark graduation suit still hung in his closet, next to the fancier clothes he had been able to buy, as late as 1970—an appropriate symbol of the transition from the poverty of his youth to his future success. As Ernie walked across the stage, he knew he had the opportunity for success—he was going places. The day after graduation, he was on a bus to Kansas City to join the Monarchs.

3

KANSAS CITY
MONARCHS

*We were like the New York Yankees. We had that winning tra-
dition and we were proud. . . . Waste no tears for me. I didn't
come along too early. I was right on time.*

—Buck O'Neil[1]

Although he may not have fully appreciated it at the time, Ernie Banks could not have picked a better situation for his start in professional baseball. The Kansas City Monarchs were the flagship team of the Negro Leagues. Charter members of the Negro National League in 1920, they boasted such alumni as Satchel Paige and Jackie Robinson and had won more championships (10) and would send more players to the major leagues than any other team. The Monarchs had an aura and a national following. Tweed Webb, who wrote for the African American weekly the *St. Louis Argus,* summed up, "To play for the Monarchs, you had to be the best."[2]

More important for Ernie's personal development was the team's manager, Buck O'Neil. When he appeared in Ken Burns's 1994 series *Baseball,* O'Neil introduced himself to a new generation of baseball fans as the sweet-talking oracle of the Negro Leagues, but in 1950, he was simply one of the most respected men in black America. As a player, starting with the Monarchs in 1938, he had been a slick-fielding, better-than-average-hitting, three-time All-Star first baseman. He became player-manager in 1948. In 1950, at the age of 39, he confined himself to the dugout most of the time but could still swing a bat well enough that when he looked around the dugout for a pinch-hitter, he would often say, "Wait a minute. Hand me my wood."[3]

O'Neil possessed a singular personality with a positive outlook on life that was as contagious as the common cold. The universally respected O'Neil was the type who would later be referred to as a player's manager. "The only thing I can say about Buck is that he was one of the finest men I ever knew," says Sam Taylor, who played for the Monarchs in 1953 and 1954. He added,

> If you couldn't get along with Buck there was something wrong with you. He never pulled punches; he would tell you exactly how it was. But he knew how to handle people, that was the key. He made everybody on the team want to play hard. Guys wanted to play for Buck. He could keep everybody happy. It's one thing to know baseball; it's another to know how to manage men. Buck knew both.[4]

"Buck O'Neil was the kind of manager that left it up to you as far as what you needed to do and what kind of career you wanted to have," says Bill Bell, who played for the Monarchs from 1948 to 1953.[5] Buck expected everyone to be ready to play every day. He always had his players' backs and knew when to use the carrot on a stick and when to crack the whip.

"Buck O'Neil was a wonderful person," says Ernest Johnson, a Monarch from 1949 to 1953. "If you played the game the way he taught, he was okay with you."[6] The way O'Neil taught was to play smart, fundamentally sound, aggressive baseball—and always hustle.

Although players feared his disapproving looks, O'Neil seldom raised his baritone voice when a player committed an on-field sin. "When a fellow makes a mistake, you don't ride him," he explained in 1962. "You show him what he's supposed to do and make him believe he can do it. You have to make him believe in himself."[7]

More than anything else, Buck O'Neil was a leader. The men on the team looked to him, whether for a sign with one out and a man on first or for which restaurant to go to after the game. It was difficult to spend much time around him without his philosophy and personality rubbing off. O'Neil would play a major role in shaping young Ernie Banks as a person and a baseball player, and Ernie was always quick to give him credit: "A teacher and a leader, he was all that and more," Ernie said in 2006. "He was the most positive person that I have ever been around. I transferred that into my life. He helped build up my confidence so I would know what to do and what to say and where to go."[8]

The team didn't spend a lot time in Kansas City, but when there, they were celebrities in the African American community. They played in the stadium of the New York Yankee AAA farm team, the Kansas City Blues, and would frequently outdraw their white counterparts—more than 20,000 on Opening Day.

The Monarchs drew fans from throughout the Midwest, even whites. Black churches would end services early when the Monarchs were in town; preachers knew better than to keep the crowd of fidgeting kids—and adults—late. Fans would parade into the park in their Sunday best. A Monarchs game was a downright social event.

Kansas City was segregated at 27th Street—north was white, south was black. Monarch players quickly learned the rules. "It was a nice city, but we never went downtown," says Johnson. "There was still a lot of discrimination there in theaters and restaurants. We stayed in the black area. But we enjoyed ourselves there." At the time, there were those who would say Kansas City had the best blues, the best barbeque, and the best baseball, and it would be hard to argue with them on any of the three. For Monarchs players, Kansas City life centered around 18th and Vine Streets, on the east side of town. Count Basie, Charlie Parker, and Pearl Bailey routinely torched joints like the Blue Room and the Reno Club. Basie came to Kansas City so often he named his band the KC Seven.

Like the other players, Ernie took a room at the Streets Hotel in Kansas City and was treated like royalty. The Streets was in a three-story, red-brick building with a barber shop and a big restaurant called the Rose Room on the first floor. It was steeped in tradition, located in the heart of the black commercial district, not far from the building in which Rube Foster had founded the Negro Leagues in 1920.

The rookie shortstop was assigned to room with 21-year-old Elston Howard. A Monarch since 1948, Howard was considered to have a bright future in the Negro Leagues. Big and powerful, he was a tough, smart competitor. Away from the ballpark, he was good-natured and reserved. He loved pinball and shooting pool but was a model citizen who didn't smoke, stay out at night, get drunk, or chase women. "Shoot, I never had to worry about Elston off the field," O'Neil said later. "He was a fine young man. With Elston it was always baseball, baseball, baseball."[9] Well educated, from a middle-class family in a segregated neighborhood in St. Louis, Howard appeared to young Ernie Banks to be the picture of worldly sophistication, and Ernie had an immediate role model and friend.

"I can still see his smile," Banks said years later, continuing,

He smiled a lot. We talked a lot. We did everything together. We went to the movies, the park, shared the same seats on trips, ate together in restaurants. He had more experience than I did. I would follow his lead. Wherever he would go, I would go. We talked about almost everything. We became brothers.[10]

With Howard at his side, Ernie was introduced to high living. A big steak dinner at the Rose Room was a dollar and two cents tax. Players called it a "dollar-two." A plate of eggs, bacon, and grits for breakfast was 35 cents. Not far from their room was a legendary barbecue joint at the corner of 18th and Brooklyn—ribs so good, as they would say, they'd make your tongue reach back and slap the back of your head. The owner, Arthur Bryant, was a baseball fan and would often let players eat all they wanted for free. Howard, who liked fine clothes, introduced Ernie to the tailor at Myers Tailor Shop, where the impeccably dressed Buck O'Neil got his suits and argyle socks.[11] Most players dressed sharp. Some had a different suit for each day of the week—color coordinated, with socks matching their shirt and handkerchief.

By 1950, the glory days of Negro League baseball, which at one time had been the third-largest African American–run enterprise in the country, were rapidly receding in the bus rearview mirror; killed off by the very thing they had long sought—integration. Negro fans flocked to watch the Jackie Robinsons, Roy Campanellas, Larry Dobys, and Monte Irvins compete in the major leagues, leaving the Negro Leagues to die a rather rapid and inglorious death. The Negro National League had folded in 1948. The Negro American League consisted of 10 teams in 1950: the Baltimore Elite Giants, Cleveland Buckeyes, New York Cubans, Philadelphia Stars, Houston Eagles, Chicago American Giants, Indianapolis Clowns, Memphis Red Sox, and Birmingham Black Barons, along with the Monarchs. Only the Clowns and Monarchs still consistently drew crowds. Tom Baird, the white owner of the Monarchs, had taken to selling off his best players to help meet expenses and keep afloat. Each spring the team reloaded with fresh faces. Major-league scouts frequently lurked in the stands of Monarchs games, like buzzards waiting for the choice parts of a carcass. "The older guys were always talking that it wasn't the way it used to be," says Taylor. "We had some pretty small crowds sometimes."

Ernie was one of the younger players on the Monarchs and, since he had missed the one-week spring training, was forced to learn on the fly. He had been signed solely on the word of Bell; neither O'Neil nor Dismukes had seen him play. The day after Ernie arrived in Kansas City, he found himself getting ready for a doubleheader against the Indianapolis Clowns in Blues Stadium. Ernie, who had never seen so large a park or one in which a grounds crew drug and raked the infield, was put right into the lineup as the shortstop. The skinny 19-year-old had big shoes to fill—the two previous Monarchs shortstops, Jackie Robinson and Gene Baker, now plied their trade in white baseball.

O'Neil worked with Ernie at shortstop when he could, but with games every day and the travel, there wasn't much time, especially since O'Neil had no other coach with him except for occasionally Dismukes, who helped with pitchers. Ernie was raw initially and, like the other newcomers, had to rely on the experience of the older players to learn the finer points of the game. He had the benefit of a smooth-fielding double play partner in 21-year-old second baseman Curtis Roberts. Already a veteran of three seasons with the Monarchs, Roberts was from Oakland and had attended the same high school that, in a few years, would produce Frank Robinson, Vada Pinson, Curt Flood, and basketball player Bill Russell.

Players knew it was an honor to be playing in the Negro League, and they played hard, knowing someone always wanted their place. The young players heard stories about a practice called Dutch: If a guy hadn't been putting out as expected, he might be sent into a grocery store with enough money to get home, told to go buy food for lunch for the team, and when he came out, the bus would be gone. The 18 men on the roster had to be ready each day; there was no injured reserve list. "There was not much sympathy for an injured player in our league," said Bill Blair, talking about his Negro League days. "There were no trainers. If you were injured, you were carried to the side and left there. No one cared for you or cried for you. That is just the way it was. Each of us knew if we got hurt we would lose our jobs. So we just played through the pain."[12]

Once, Ernie got hurt in Muskegon, Michigan, and hobbled to the dugout. Buck approached him with, "You got to play. We sympathize with you, but we need somebody to play shortstop."[13] That was the end of Ernie's injury.

Among teammates that first year, Banks was a shy kid who sat in the front of the bus and hardly spoke other than to Howard and Roberts. "He was a nice guy," says Johnson. "Very easygoing, rarely raised his voice, got along well with everyone."

"Got along, but never had a lot to say," says Bell.

"Shy beyond words," said Buck O'Neil of Ernie's first year. Sometimes Ernie appeared to be brooding. O'Neil lectured him, "Be alive, man! You gotta love this game to play it."

Decades later, when he was told Banks had said he learned how to play the game from him, Buck disagreed. "No, Ernie Banks knew how to play, but what he did learn was how to play the game with love."[14]

The one constant about playing baseball in the Negro Leagues was the travel; the vast majority of games were on the road. The organized Negro League schedule ran from April to September, about 125 games. In between, they played a lot of nonleague games in small towns to help cover expenses. Frequently, they would hook up with a team like the Clowns and tour with them for several weeks, playing games each day in a different place. Other times, they would play town teams or local semipros.

"We would be in the Catskill Mountains, and the next day we'd be in Columbus, Ohio," says Bell. "We would sleep on the bus while it drove to the next town. We did a lot of sleeping on the bus. We'd go to Memphis, then head down to Florida, then back up to Birmingham, then work our way up to Indianapolis."

"We would start out at 6 o'clock after a doubleheader in one town, bounce along for ten or twelve hours and arrive in the next town in time for two more games," said Howard in 1965. "We would eat cold hamburgers in the bus." Food and sleeping arrangements weren't the only concern. "Sometimes we would drive an awful long distance to find a garage which would allow Negroes in the bathroom."[15] Not infrequently, they pulled over and headed for the woods to answer nature's call.

When in heavily populated African American areas, for example, Chicago, Detroit, and Harlem, they stayed at the best black hotels, ate in good restaurants, and enjoyed the best music in the world. But in small towns, they sometimes had less hospitable arrangements. Dismukes and O'Neil frequently had the inside track on local African Americans who would allow players to sleep at their houses, but oftentimes there were no accommodations. "Once we were down in Tampa and we slept on the bus three nights in a row because there was no place to stay," says Bell. "We went to the bus station [to go in the colored waiting area] when we had to go to the bathroom."

They soon developed a routine—play, pack, ride, play again—performed with meticulous precision that would make an army logistics officer smile. It was not unusual to play the next day in a damp uniform.

In the South, they searched for restaurants that would serve blacks, marked by a sign that read, "Colored." Since they were not allowed in restaurants in many areas, players would chip in their three- or four-dollar-a-day meal money and go to a supermarket for baloney, sardines, bread, peanut butter, and drinks to be consumed on the bus—and they learned not to be goofing off when the food was passed around, because it didn't last long.

Playing in the South presented more challenges than just finding a place to eat. "Oh man, it was rough," says Bell, who grew up in Iowa, adding,

I'll never forget the first time we were in San Antonio. I was about 18 or 19. I saw a sign that said, "Nigger chicken served here." I asked Willard Brown what that meant. He just shrugged, "Oh, that's just what they call dark meat chicken down here." It was a different mindset down there.

Growing up in Dallas had prepared Ernie for the trips through the South. There was little he hadn't seen. But he still listened intently as Buck and the older players talked about the hazards before each stop, often adding a legend of bad things that had happened to a black man who hadn't obeyed the rules in that part of the country.

"Buck and the other guys would always tell us when we went to a new place, to keep us out of trouble, to make sure we didn't step out of line," says Bell. And they would warn them particularly to avoid the deadly sin of reckless eyeballs. Said Bell,

> Once in Memphis my first year [1948], I needed to get a pair of socks and Willard [Brown] told me, "You get down to the store and then get your black ass straight back here." Memphis was really bad. You had to be careful. They said you might pass some white women waiting for a bus or something and sometimes, they liked to show everything they got. They said, "Don't even look. It might be the last thing you ever look at."
>
> I remember once in Little Rock, the older guys told me, "See that white man coming down the street? He's not going to get out of your way. You're going to have to get on the damn grass. And he doesn't want you to look him in the eye. You have to look down." They wanted to belittle you; take your dignity. Birmingham was the worst. Let me tell you, when we played there, we didn't go nowhere. We just stayed together, played ball, then got the hell out of town.

Players realized that there was nothing they could do about the racism. "To me, that's just the way life was," says Johnson. "We didn't know any better. It never occurred to me that things could be different. I never really had any anger about things, that's just the way it had always been."

"We had become conditioned to racism," said O'Neil later. "You accept what's around you . . . we thought it would change some day. We just waited for it to change."[16]

O'Neil refused to give in to hatred. Hate only weakens the hater, he reasoned. He focused on the positives. "We've always had more good people than bad, but we just let the bad people do things that we shouldn't let them do. We are living in the greatest country in the world. And it's going to be greater."[17] Spending so much time together, playing, riding on the bus, Ernie bathed in O'Neil's philosophy.

Most of the players were making between $300 and $400 a month. "A kid had to really love the game to do all that," says Bell. "And he couldn't have any obligations to worry about. It was pretty rough at times." But they all knew deep in their hearts that it beat the heck out of work. And most of them came from poor families where the conditions had been much worse.

"We had a lot of fun. Everybody got along good on the team and had fun together," says Bell. "We never had guys who caused any trouble. Buck wouldn't have stood for that; he would have gotten rid of them." Riding, joking, listening to stories, they were like a family by the end of the long season. The atmosphere of the team formed a protective cocoon against the outside world and its prejudice.

"I didn't mind the conditions or travel," says Johnson. He continued,

> I enjoyed the guys we were traveling with. But then, we all got along great. You couldn't spend that much time together on the road and have someone who didn't get along. And I loved to play baseball. I was just happy I was getting to play every day. And I was able to see a lot of the country—parts I would never have seen, parts most people never get to see. So we learned a lot about this country.
>
> That was the best part of my life. I loved playing with the Monarchs. I played baseball, I got a chance to travel this whole country, and I got paid to do it. We lived a pretty good life as ballplayers, better than the average black person.

The shared hardships and fun forged a bond among the teammates. It was a bond that would last throughout the years—future meetings would quickly dissolve into smiles and laughs, stories and lies, as they relived the good and the bad. "[Negro League] players were more like family than teammates," Ernie said in 1998. "You really cared about the other people you were playing with."[18]

The 1950 Monarchs went 52–21, and finished in first place in the Negro American League western division. Ernie hit .305 with 15 home runs, well enough that he attracted attention as one of the up-and-comers of the league. After a game with Indianapolis during the last month of the season, the manager of the Clowns sought out Ernie and asked him to call him at the end of the season. Ernie was invited to meet him in Jacksonville to join a barnstorming tour with the Jackie Robinson All-Stars.

The Negro League squad was made up of the core of the Clowns plus a few other players to round out a quality roster. Each player got $400—big money. Large crowds—black and white—turned out. The All-Stars included Campanella, Newcombe, Doby, and Irvin, but Robinson was the obvious main attraction. In addition, crowds came to watch the Clowns do their famous pregame routine and watch their headliner, King Tut. Performing a routine similar to that made famous by Meadowlark Lemon with the Globetrotters, Tut went into the stands, threw popcorn and water on fans, snatched wigs from women and put them on his head, and sat in the laps of fat people. His favorite crowd-pleaser involved putting a little dog in a box and turning the handle, making frankfurters come out.

Ernie was living the dream, playing on the same field with the biggest names in the business. Some games, he competed on the major leaguer's team and received pointers around second base from Jackie. When the tour reached Dallas, Ernie got the thrill of playing in front of his parents and then introducing them to the famous stars after the game.

Paid off with a wad of cash at the end of the tour, Ernie bought a new suit and returned to Dallas feeling like a big shot. Even though he turned over most of the money to Essie, word got out quickly and some of the neighborhood regulars soon showed up. One former friend, a questionable character who later spent much time in prison, wanted Ernie to go to a show with him. On the way, oh yeah, he suddenly remembered something—just need a quick stop. They turned into a pawnshop and after some fast talking, Ernie found himself handing the clerk $15 to get the guy's watch out of hock. It was a scene that would be repeated throughout the years, as Ernie was unable to turn down a friend with a good story and an empty hand.

Before he could consider the next season, Ernie received a letter containing greetings from the president of the United States. He had been drafted. In the army, which had been officially desegregated by an executive order by President Truman in 1948, Ernie worked and played with whites for the first time. He was assigned to the 242nd Antiaircraft Unit and spent most of the next two years at a base in Mannheim, Germany. An officer soon showed up and asked the men if any played professional sports. And that's how Ernie came to lob more baseballs than shells during his time in the military. He played both baseball and basketball on service teams. "I went in a private and I came out a private," Ernie would frequently tell reporters seeking tales of military heroism.[19] In reality, Ernie was promoted to NCO and became base athletic director, reportedly one of the first African Americans to hold the office.

While in the army, Ernie had the opportunity to play a basketball game with the Harlem Globetrotters—leading to the legend that he had narrowly failed to make their team. "My basketball coach at Fort Bliss, Texas, was a lieutenant who knew Abe Saperstein," he later explained. Banks elaborated,

> So when the Trotters came into El Paso one weekend, he arranged for me to work out. They gave me a suit and let me sit on the bench. Late in the game, Saperstein turned to me and asked me if I wanted to play. I told him, "Okay, but I'm playing straight." He let me play for two or three minutes. I scored a basket.[20]

This made Ernie one of the few men, along with Fergie Jenkins and Bob Gibson, to both score with the Globetrotters and become a member of baseball's Hall of Fame.

The 1950 season and the postseason barnstorming trip had given Ernie a reputation. Fresco Thompson, the Dodgers' farm director, heard reports and corresponded with Ernie while he was in the army. The Indians' Bill Veeck and the owner of the Dallas Eagles of the Texas League also expressed interest in Ernie, but nothing solid came from any of them.

Someone else was waiting for Ernie when he got back from the army: He got married. His bride, Mollye Ector, had been a high school sweetheart, according to reports. "I was playing softball one afternoon when I noticed this girl on the sideline," Ernie explained to a reporter in 1955. "I went over and talked to her. She gave me her phone number. I guess you'd call it love at first sight, but we went together eight years before we were married."[21] The "eight years" was most likely a typographical error or an exaggeration, as Ernie was 22 and Mollye 18 when they got married. It also contradicts Ernie's later claims he was so shy he never talked to any girls or was interested in dating while in high school.

Mollye's version, told in 1956, was: "Ernie and I both played on softball teams. One summer a park recreation director introduced us at a social. Ernie walked me home. Early that winter we met at high school and Ernie asked me to a movie. We went out regularly from the time he was a senior." After high school Mollye attended Wiley College in Marshall, Texas. While Ernie was in Germany, she came home from college and found a letter that had arrived containing Ernie's proposal. "It took me five minutes to write back that I'd marry him when he got out of the service."[22]

The couple was married on April 6, 1953, in North Dallas. "Mollye was a beautiful girl," says Robert Prince. "Very outgoing, just a wonderful personality. She came from a good family. Her grandfather was a well-known evangelist minister. I forget what the denomination was but we called them holy-rollers. She and her sisters were very smart; good students."[23] Mollye was a member of the choir at St. Paul. Soon after the wedding, Ernie left for spring training with the Monarchs. Ernie had called Buck O'Neil when he got back to the United States, and O'Neil had enthusiastically said he had a uniform waiting for him. Later that summer, Ernie and Mollye found an apartment in Kansas City.

It was a vastly different league that Ernie Banks rejoined in 1953. The hemorrhaging of the best players had accelerated, and the league was on life support. While Baird and the other owners had met operating costs by selling their best players to the major leagues during the first years of integration, major-league teams were now scouting and signing their own young black players, eliminating the need for the Negro Leagues altogether. Both Howard and Roberts were long gone—Howard signed by the Yankees in late 1950 and Roberts by the Braves in 1951.

In 1953, the Negro League consisted of only four teams: Kansas City, Indianapolis, Birmingham, and Memphis. Ernie's reputation preceded him for the 1953 season. "The return of Ernie Banks, 22-year-old shortstop, brought a smile to the face of manager John (Buck) O'Neil," reported the *Sporting News*.[24] O'Neil later said that when Ernie returned from the army, he was a new man. He played hard, ran the bases with abandon, drove the ball with authority, dove for grounders, and hustled nonstop. His personality was now coming out also. He smiled constantly and talked it up on the field.[25] He was now a force.

"Ernie started out with a bang in 1953," says Bell. "He was a different ballplayer. All baseball. Smooth in the field. Had great wrists. You could start to see it now—he was better than the other guys."

"Ernie Banks Plugs Hole for Kaycees," touted the *Chicago Defender* in May, noting that the "gangling six-footer" dazzled Monarch fans with "spectacular play" at shortstop and power at the plate.[26] Ernie was leading the league in hitting, with an even .400, when he was selected for the East–West All-Star Game in August.

The Negro League East–West All-Star Game had long been the highlight of every season. "Except for a radio broadcast of a Joe Louis fight, this game was the biggest sporting event in black America," wrote Negro League historian Larry Lester.[27]

Held annually in Chicago's Comiskey Park since 1933, the game brought thousands to Chicago. Special train coaches were added to carry fans from throughout the country. Black businesses in Chicago advertised All-Star Game tickets to pull in customers, and scalpers did a brisk business in the Grand Hotel lobby, the epicenter of black America for the weekend. It was a 48-hour holiday, a who's who in black entertainment and society—they were all in Chicago. Game attendance reached 50,000 in the early 1940s, often outdrawing the major-league All-Star Game.

While the major-league All-Stars were selected by sportswriters, the East–West All-Stars were selected by fans throughout the country who voted through the nation's two largest black newspapers, the *Chicago Defender* and the *Pittsburgh Courier*. The significance of the method of selection was not lost on the astute. "That was a pretty important thing for black people to do in those days, to be able to vote," Buck O'Neil later wrote. "Even if it was just for ballplayers . . . they sent in thousands and thousands of ballots."[28]

The games were hotly contested because the players played for not only pride, but also positions on other teams the next year, for a chance to show the entire black world who they were, and, increasingly, to show white major-league scouts what they could do. "It was clear that our game meant a lot more than a big-league game," wrote O'Neil. "Theirs was, and is, more or less an exhibition. But for black folks, the East–West Game was a matter of racial pride."[29]

By 1953, the East–West Game had followed the fate of the league. Interest and attendance had waned for several years. The 1953 game, played on August 16, drew only 10,000 spectators.

The decreased interest from fans did little to dampen the pride and enthusiasm of the players, however. "It was still a big deal to play in the East–West Game," says Ernie Johnson, who also was selected. "I had grown up in Chicago following it, so it was great to finally get to play in one."

The West, managed by Buck O'Neil, won the game, 5–1. The game was otherwise forgettable, except for the West shortstop. Reported the *Chicago Tribune*,

> Ernie Banks . . . who played the full game at shortstop for the West, went hitless in four times at bat but lived up to advance notices in the field as he accepted seven chances without error and made one of the game's fielding gems with a spectacular stop of Verdes Drake's smash in the third inning, taking the ball on a short hop and throwing Drake out from deep short.[30]

"All-Star Tilt Fails to Impress Scouts from Big Leagues," read the Wendell Smith headline in the *Pittsburgh Courier*. While there appeared to be few major league-ready stars left in the Negro Leagues, Smith judged, "The best prospect in the contest was a 22-year-old shortstop owned by the Kansas City Monarchs, Ernie Banks."[31]

The 1953 Monarchs were the class of the Negro League. They had winning streaks of 14 and 16 games, and although the Barons challenged them as late as mid-June, they finished with a record of 56 and 21, a full 20 games ahead of the second-place team.

While some players thought about making the jump to the major leagues, Ernie later said the Negro leagues were his comfort area. He didn't want to leave. If true, he was the only one. "By 1953, everybody was trying to get to the next level," says Bell.

"We didn't call it the major leagues," says Taylor. "We called it 'going to Heaven.' Guys would be talking and they'd say, 'You hear about so-and-so?

He's going to Heaven.' That meant he got signed. That's all we thought about—getting seen and then getting signed."

Ernie later claimed he had no idea he was even being considered as a prospect for the major leagues. But he had definitely caused interest among scouts. In July, before the All-Star Game, he had badly twisted his ankle sliding into a base and was sent home to Dallas to recuperate. He was home for nine days and, during this time, was offered a chance to work out with the Dallas Eagles. "It was odd the way it happened," Ernie said in 1958, adding,

> I was sitting on the doorstep one day when Buzz Clarkson came up to me and asked if I wanted to work out. Clarkson had been in the big leagues briefly and was then playing with Dallas. I was glad for the chance, and so the next night I took batting practice with Dallas. I remember it very well because I took four or five swings, and I must have hit two or three balls out of the park. Then I took infield practice.
>
> At the time Jerry Doggett [radio announcer] was working the Dallas games. Jerry came up to me and said, "We could use you here." He intimated that the Dallas owners were interested in buying me from the Monarchs. That was the first time I realized I had a chance to get into Organized Ball. But nothing much happened, and I rejoined the Monarchs. I didn't particularly like the life. I was lonesome, and one day I went up to Tom Baird (the Monarchs owner) and mentioned that I was thinking about quitting. Mr. Baird sat me down and said, "Now listen, I don't think you know this, but you're going to wind up in the big leagues. The Chicago White Sox are interested in you." That news almost floored me.[32]

The White Sox were indeed interested and had a shot at picking up Ernie, as did a number of other teams, all of whom let him slip through their fingers. Former Monarchs pitcher Connie Johnson came up to the White Sox in 1953, from their Colorado Springs minor-league team, and badgered manager Paul Richards about Banks. "He's a major leaguer right now," Johnson said. "He can't miss."[33] Richards sent a scout to see Banks, and the report was that he showed good possibility as a hitter but had a weak arm. White Sox general manager Frank Lane later said, "Our scouts had seen Banks and were not impressed. Cincinnati didn't think much of him. The Yankees had turned thumbs down."[34] At the time, some major-league scouts seemed to look for reasons for Negro Leaguers to fail rather than see the true potential.

The lowly Pirates also had a shot at Banks. Dom Caniglia, longtime scout for the Pirates, later said he was on Ernie's trail. "After following Ernie for 12 games, I told Mr. Rickey, he [Banks] couldn't miss as a major leaguer. What

impressed me was the way he hustled. . . . He had a strong arm, he was fast."
Rickey gave Caniglia another assignment and sent his son, Branch Jr., to look
at Banks. Junior's report said, "Tremendous glove, fast, but won't hit major-
league pitching." And the Pirates, doormats of the National League, moved on
in search of other talent.[35]

Bill Veeck, owner of the St. Louis Browns, was alerted by his top scout about
Banks early in 1953 season and wanted him badly. Baird reportedly asked for
$35,000. Veeck, cash strapped to make his own payroll, pleaded with Baird
to take $3,500 down and the rest later, but Baird wanted the entire amount on
delivery and Veeck had to pass.

Other teams also had a chance to see and sign Banks. The Monarchs and
Clowns played a series of games against one another in major-league parks
Briggs Stadium (Detroit), County Stadium (Milwaukee), and Crosley Field
(Cincinnati), as well as Comiskey. None of the teams recognized the talent play-
ing in their own stadiums.

Meanwhile, the Chicago Cubs were nibbling at the hook. And, as so often
happens in baseball, a bit of serendipity changed history. "When Ernie Banks
was first spotted, the scout came to see me," says Ernie Johnson.

Tom Gordon, the general manager at Macon in 1953, needed an outfielder
and, since his fellow South Atlantic League team, Jacksonville, had recently
seen a spike in attendance due to their African American star Hank Aaron,
decided his gate could be increased with the addition of a Negro League
player. "Vedie Himsl [Cubs scout] told me the Monarchs, who were playing
in our territory, had a boy I might be interested in," he said in 1956. That
outfielder was Ernie Johnson. Gordon drove to Columbus, Georgia, to see
the Monarchs play, but it was the team's shortstop, not any outfielders, that
caught his eye. Gordon related,

> He was batting, and I remember I had this stopwatch in my hand . . . out of idle
> curiosity I clocked the boy going down to first. It was just over four seconds. Not
> bad when you consider he was running out a pop fly to short. That got me inter-
> ested in him . . . that night this shortstop did it all. He came in on slow rollers,
> had to go in the hole, cover the left field foul line, and made the double play. He
> made it all look so easy. Then, late in the game, he hit a curveball over a 60-foot
> fence that was 360 feet from home plate. That was enough for me.

Gordon wrote the Cubs' director of player personnel, Wid Matthews, with
a glowing report about Banks: "I'm no baseball expert, but this kid looks like
a natural."[36]

"That scout saw Ernie Banks play shortstop, and he forgot all about Ernie Johnson playing outfield," says Johnson, who was eventually signed by the Browns in 1954, and played in the minor leagues until 1959.

Not trusting one man's opinion, Matthews called scout Ray Hayworth in North Carolina and instructed him to meet up with the Monarchs and follow them several games but didn't tell him which player he was interested in. Five days later, Hayworth told Matthews the Monarchs had a shortstop who could play in the majors right now. He also reported that manager Buck O'Neil had stated that Banks "has good habits and is an aggressive type that likes to play the game."[37] The "good habits" part was important because white owners were wary of signing an African American player with "bad habits."

Matthews checked his file on the Monarchs and was surprised to learn that there was nothing on a shortstop named Banks. "Ray learned Banks was just out of the army, which explained why we'd had no scout reports on him," Matthews later said. Matthews called Tom Baird to check on the availability of Banks and was told that all Monarchs stars would go to the highest bidders.

Still not convinced (one wonders how many separate checkers Matthews sent to scout some of the other players he signed to bonuses who never made it), Matthews ordered three more scouts to see Banks. The report was the same each time: He was a can't-miss prospect. One of the scouts, Ray Blades, reported back, "Wid, you've got to see him to believe it." Matthews finally took a look himself when the Monarchs were in Des Moines and agreed. He was further convinced while watching the All-Star Game in Chicago. He talked to Baird, who wasn't ready to make a deal yet.

The day after a Monarchs game at Comiskey Park in early September, Wendell Smith picked up Banks and 19-year-old pitcher Bill Dickey, along with Buck O'Neil, at the Persian Hotel on the South Side of Chicago. Ernie later said that he didn't know, and didn't bother to ask, where they were going. As they were talking, they stopped in front of Wrigley Field. They were escorted to the office of Wid Matthews, who announced he wanted both players in a package deal. Baird had agreed on a price of $20,000 for the two. "You guys look pretty good," Matthews told the stunned players, "and we're going to sign you with the Cubs. Dickey, we're going to sign you to a contract at Cedar Rapids, Iowa." Then he turned to the shortstop. "Ernie, we think you can play here right now."[38] Ernie was offered a major-league contract to play for the Cubs for $800 a month, almost triple the amount he was making with the Monarchs.

The 57-year-old Matthews, from Jackson, Mississippi, had been a career minor leaguer who hit exactly one big-league home run. He had worked for

Branch Rickey in St. Louis and Brooklyn before coming to the Cubs in 1950. While with Brooklyn, Matthews had shown his baseball instincts by sending in a negative scouting report on a 17-year-old whiz who played for the Birmingham Black Barons—the kid couldn't hit a curveball, according to Matthews. The kid, named Mays, later signed with the Giants and proved Matthews wrong. By 1953, Matthews was in the process of presiding over seven of the most dismal seasons in Cubs history. "I do not infallibly state that Wid had a knack for doing the wrong thing," wrote *Chicago Tribune* columnist Dave Condon in 1975. "Let me say that had owner Wrigley sent him for a package of gum, tho [*sic*], Wid probably would have returned with Beechnut."[39] As Banks, O'Neil, and everyone else left his office that day, Matthews had no idea he had just completed the best deal he would ever make in his baseball career.

Conventional thinking among baseball people at the time was that the Negro Leagues were not of a high enough caliber to prep a player for the majors. Even the best Negro League players needed a year or two in the minor leagues, in "Organized Ball," to be ready. Jackie Robinson, Monte Irvin, Roy Campanella, Willie Mays, Hank Aaron had put in some time in the minors. The fact that the Cubs offered Ernie Banks an immediate shot at the majors was significant, and rare. "I was sort of surprised," Banks said in 1958. "I knew a few other teams had turned me down, and I never expected to get signed. I had just got an apartment for my wife and me in Kansas City, and then I had to call her up and tell her we were moving to Chicago."[40]

"I was surprised by a long-distance telephone call," Mollye told a reporter in 1956. "It was Ernie asking if I'd mind living in Chicago. He said I'd better not mind, because he had just signed with the Cubs."[41]

Ernie also called Dallas and told his parents. "I thought he was going to cry," Ernie said of his father's reaction. "He said to me, 'I hope you can make it, and I know you can.'"[42]

As part of the agreement with Baird, the two signees finished out the last few weeks of the Monarchs season before joining the Cubs organization. Ernie played his final Negro League game on September 13, 1954, against the Indianapolis Clowns in Pittsburgh's Forbes Field, and hit a couple of balls over the left-field wall. After the game, Ernie left for Chicago. Hank Rigney, veteran press agent and promoter for the Negro American League, later explained,

I put Banks on a plane at Pittsburgh when he was joining the Cubs. Baird called me and said, "Give him 20 bucks?" I said, "Only 20 bucks?" Baird asked, "What would you give him?" I said, "Oh, a thousand anyway." Baird laughed and told me, "You'd spoil him. Right now he thinks I've done him a favor. If I give him a thousand dollars he'll begin to think he did me a favor. Give him 20 bucks and see how it works out." So I gave him 20 bucks, and Baird was right.[43]

Ernie signing with the Cubs was historic—the team had yet to field an African American player. "Dallas Negro Set to Become First in Cubs' Lineup," the *Dallas Morning News* informed his hometown readers.[44]

"Cubs First Negro Player in Game Here Yesterday," the *Pittsburgh Post-Gazette* announced on September 14, 1953, with the subheadline, "Shortstop Eddie [*sic*] Banks Leaves Monarchs for Chicago Trial Today." The article quoted Banks as saying, "I just hope I can do them some good next season. I don't even know whether I'll get to play the rest of this season with them, but I want to tell you it will be great just to put on that Chicago uniform." The article noted that Ernie hit .380 in 180 total games in 1953, with 22 home runs in 125 league games. He concluded saying, "I think I can hit major-league pitching. I only want to be an asset to the Cubs. I'm grateful for the opportunity to find out if I can."[45]

Opportunity. That's all any of them had ever asked for. Ernie Banks was going to Heaven.

4

CHICAGO

A lot had changed in the six years since Jackie Robinson took the field for the Brooklyn Dodgers, but the United States was still not ready for the full participation of African Americans in baseball—or society—at the time the Cubs acquired Ernie Banks. Two stories that appeared in the same *Sporting News* issue that announced the Cubs' signing of Ernie Banks illustrate the climate. A U.S. district judge in Hot Springs, Arkansas, dismissed a civil rights suit taken out by Jim Tugerson, a former Indianapolis Clowns pitcher, against the Cotton States League. Tugerson had signed with Hot Springs; however, the league refused to allow him to play because of his color (he wound up signing with Knoxville and won 29 games, with 289 strikeouts, that year).

The other story reported that Jackie Robinson's life had been threatened by mail in St. Louis and that FBI agents had been assigned to protect him. These were mere signs of the times for African American baseball players.

Ernie Banks arrived in Chicago just before the Civil Rights Movement began in earnest. Change was coming, but it was still moving at a glacial pace. Thurgood Marshall, legal counsel for the National Association for the Advancement of Colored People, was working on taking down the 1896 separate-but-equal decision of *Plessy v. Ferguson* and was pleased with progress on trains. "We have nearly ended discrimination in dining cars," he told the *Chicago Defender* in 1952. "We are now working on coach cars."[1] Bigger events were just around the corner: *Brown v. Board of Education* would be decided in 1954, and Rosa Parks would refuse to take a back seat on a bus in Montgomery, Alabama, in 1955.

In 1950, Chicago was the second most populous city in the United States, with more than 3.5 million people. The *Chicago Defender*, the nation's largest black newspaper, with a circulation of more than 250,000, had promoted the city to a generation of blacks in the South, encouraging them to participate in the Great Migration. As Southern blacks answered the call and poured into the city, the black middle class boomed, and a South Side area known as Bronzeville became a cultural epicenter for jazz and African American literature, rivaling Harlem as the capital of black America.

But Chicago was a divided city—housing was segregated by not only race, but also ethnicity—and embers of trouble needed only a small breeze to erupt. During the 1950s, many Chicago restaurants still did not seat blacks, and most hotels would not accommodate them. Hotels in the Loop didn't start accepting African Americans until 1953. African Americans had been "redlined" into housing in a strict area of South Chicago; this was enhanced by the construction of a freeway that served as a concrete barrier, widely felt to be government's effort to contain the movement of blacks. Chicago slums were considered to be some of the nation's worst. Edwin Berry, executive director of the Chicago Urban League, called Chicago the "most residentially segregated city in the United States."[2]

According to Mike Royko, the city's preeminent political and cultural columnist of the last half of the twentieth century, "Most Chicago whites hated blacks. The only genuine difference between a Southern white and a Chicago white was in their accent."[3] It is disturbing to note that incidents of violent negative persuasion occurred often enough that the term "housing assaults" was added to the language to describe what happened when blacks tried to move into white neighborhoods. In 1951, a riot involving an estimated 4,000 whites had occurred after a black family rented an apartment in the previously all-white suburb of Cicero, an area that had once provided comfortable sanctuary for Al Capone to run his empire. Hooligans destroyed property and fought with the U.S. National Guard, yet the Cook County grand jury failed to bring charges against a single member of the mob; instead it indicted the owner of the apartment and the family's lawyer for inciting the conflict. This was the Chicago in which the plane from Pittsburgh carrying 22-year-old Ernie Banks landed.

The Chicago Cubs were a miserable team—on their way to a 65–89 record and a seventh-place finish—and had been drawing poorly in 1953. They were struggling to make 750,000 fans, a drop of more than 200,000 from the previous year. The Cubs had once possessed a proud history of championships, but that was long ago. Since 1947, they had finished either last or second to last every season except one.

There was just something about the Cubs, an attitude pervasive in the dugout and throughout the entire organization. The exact source of the attitude was, like a man's uvula, hard to put your finger on, and the more you tried, the more likely you were to gag and throw up, but undoubtedly it emanated from the top with owner Phillip K. Wrigley. According to who you talked to, P. K., as he was known, was either a benevolent soul who managed the old family team with heart-wrenching care, eager to try innovative steps to provide a winner for the citizens of Chicago, or a bumbling fool whose ego prevented him from allowing more knowledgeable people to run the team and under whose mismanagement the team went decades without a winner. The truth, most likely, lies somewhere in between.

P. K.'s father, the flamboyant William Wrigley Jr., had made a fortune in the chewing gum business and been equally successful with the baseball team he had purchased in 1916. Legend has it that the elder Wrigley extracted a deathbed vow from his son Phillip to keep the baseball team in the family, and the team in Chicago. Phillip was much more interested in cars than baseball, but he stayed true to the pledge—he would keep the team until turning it over to his own son upon his death in 1977.

P. K. Wrigley was unquestionably a brilliant chewing gum man. His genius lay in marketing: product recognition and convincing people that chewing gum was good for them. A handshake man whose word was as good as a contract, he was intensely loyal to those loyal to him. In fact, at least when it came to baseball, it could be said that he valued allegiance over competence—men who kept their mouths shut and followed the party line were ensured a spot, some spot, in the organization for life, regardless of aptitude or performance. Because of this, he built much goodwill during his career and maintained a legion of supporters on the baseball field and among the media. But his record as a baseball owner speaks for itself, and that inspired many critics.

There were those who thought Wrigley loved his namesake ballpark more than the inhabitant Cubs. He spent freely on the upkeep of Wrigley Field, and perpetual renovations allowed it to outlast others built in the same era. Once, when asked about the needs of the team, which had finished last the preceding year, he mentioned only that Wrigley Field restrooms needed updating. Frustrated fans pointed to the fact that Wrigley's personal fortune placed him among the top five wealthiest baseball owners of the time; the Wrigley family stash was worth $100 million and would grow to $2.7 billion by the end of the century. Had he wanted, he could have dipped into his deep pockets and bought a pennant-contending team. Instead, he insisted that the baseball team stand on its own, with no financial help from the chewing gum company. This was unfortunate, for both fans and the team, because a series of Wrigley fumbles ensured that the team did not make the money needed to be competitive.

In the early days of television, Wrigley virtually gave away the broadcast rights. Similarly, he failed to bargain when the Braves moved to nearby Milwaukee and later gave away the franchise rights to Los Angeles (which he held for his AAA Angels team) when Walter O'Malley wanted to move his Dodgers there in 1958. And his refusal to play night baseball cost the team immeasurably at the box office (every other major-league team had lights by 1948). Wrigley eschewed the time-honored methods of acquiring and developing solid players used by virtually every successful team. Instead, he reveled in trying a never-ending variety of hokey schemes in the guise of being a pioneer. That, along with a reliance on inept cronies, doomed the team to perennial bottom-feeder status.

Phillip K. Wrigley was a living paradox. He was an astute, innovative, successful businessman, yet his baseball team stood as a model of old-time inefficiency. He claimed to be private and publicity-shy, but his picture and words filled more sports page space than those of any of his managers or players. He claimed to be open-minded, accessible to his employees, and a proponent of free speech, yet he ruthlessly dispatched anyone who offered anything other than an optimistic appraisal of the organization or dared to publicly disagree with him. He claimed to love baseball; however, he never went to his own ballpark to see a game himself. He claimed to have only the fans' interests at heart and wanted to make a trip to Wrigley Field as pleasant a family experience as possible, but he staunchly refused to allow night baseball, making it difficult for a working man or school-aged children to attend games. He claimed to be progressive in race relations, yet . . .

There was a story that Wrigley's supporters like to throw around concerning an incident that occurred when he was developing Catalina Island in California, one of his family holdings. A real estate agent called and informed him, "A Negro wants to settle on Catalina? What should we do?" Wrigley replied, "See if you can find a history book and read the Constitution of the United States."[4]

The story, possibly apocryphal, is meant to illustrate Wrigley's true feelings on integration. But apparently Wrigley felt that the U.S. Constitution, while well and good for such items as equal-opportunity housing, did not cover the important institution of baseball. Wrigley's name appeared, along with the other major-league owners, except Branch Rickey and Bill Veeck, on a petition calling for the commissioner of baseball to nullify the Dodgers' contract with Jackie Robinson in 1945. And as his team floundered throughout the late 1940s and early 1950s, Wrigley ignored the abundance of black baseball talent that paraded through Chicago to compete against the Chicago Elite Giants and play in the East–West All-Star Game—undeniable talent that was available for the picking, cheap.

As with everything else in his life, Wrigley's stance on race was open to interpretation, and the most charitable explanation is that he was a man of his times, no more, no less. Obviously, the final decision to integrate the Cubs lay in the hands of the autocratic ruler—whatever he decided, everyone else would have capitulated. Had he truly favored equal opportunity, he could have fielded a team with black stars in the late 1940s that would have ruled the league along with the Dodgers. But while Wrigley was amiable and always said the right things amid several newspaper campaigns and meetings with civil rights leaders beginning in the mid-1940s, when it came time to act, he did absolutely nothing.

By 1950, Branch Rickey's Brooklyn Dodgers had won four consecutive Rookie of the Year Awards with African American players (Robinson, Newcombe, Black, and Gilliam), illustrating the type of talent that could be found in the Negro Leagues. No longer was there any rational debate about African American players' ability to play at the highest level. After watching the Dodgers, Giants, and Indians not only integrate, but also win pennants after doing so, African American journalists and activists began calling for the integration of baseball in Chicago. The White Sox brought in Minnie Minoso, a dark-skinned Cuban, in 1951. While he had to endure some name-calling by opponents, Minoso quickly won over Chicago fans and the press with his hustling style of play and warm, agreeable personality.

Comiskey Park, situated on Chicago's South Side, became a drawing point for the city's African American fans. Comiskey's owners had long-held relations with the Negro League, providing use for league games, as well as the annual All-Star event. Wrigley Field, located in the midst of Chicago's totally white North Side, rarely saw an African American, except for those who traveled up from the South Side to cheer for opponents like Robinson, Monte Irvin, Willie Mays, and Sam Jethroe.

The Cubs, meanwhile, remained exclusively white. They signed Negro League pitcher Booker McDaniels to their AAA Los Angeles Angels in June 1949. While McDaniels had once been a hard thrower, he had never been considered an elite player in the Negro Leagues—he was the veteran of only one East–West All-Star Game—and in 1949, he was 36 years old and had control problems. Cynical observers felt that the move was solely for publicity and that the team had no intention of ever bringing him to Chicago, and they were right. McDaniels went 11–13 for the Angels in two seasons before being released.

Next, the Cubs signed Kansas City Monarchs shortstop Gene Baker in March 1950 (opening the Monarchs shortstop position for a young Ernie Banks) and assigned him to their minor-league system. Baker played well at Davenport,

Iowa, and was promoted to Los Angeles, where he impressed observers—everyone, apparently, except those who made the decisions regarding who to promote to the Cubs. Despite being acknowledged as the best shortstop in the Pacific Coast League, Baker remained in Los Angeles for four years, at one point accumulating a record of 420 consecutive games played, a streak that speaks as much to the myopia of the Cubs as to the reliability of Baker. In March 1951, the Cubs signed another African American, a fleet 20-year-old center fielder from Little Rock, Solly Drake, and assigned him to Class C Topeka. Drake showed promise, hitting .324, but then was lost for two years to the U.S. Army.

Calls in the press for Baker's promotion were ignored. In 1952, an announcement was passed around by the Cubs, obviously aimed at proponents of Baker, stating that the team would not call up anyone from Los Angeles during the season to avoid affecting the Angels' minor-league pennant hopes. In other words, the Cubs cared more about their minor-league team's success than their own.

While the integrated White Sox had vaulted into the first division and were averaging more than 1 million fans per year, the Cubs stood pat and continued losing both games and potential fans. Baker attended spring training with the Cubs in Mesa, Arizona, in 1953, but he was deemed not ready and sent back to Los Angeles. The move stunned observers. Bobby Bragan, a former Pirates and Dodgers player who was managing Hollywood in the PCL at the time, called Baker the "best shortstop I ever saw, and that includes Pee Wee Reese."[5]

As Baker once again turned in a fine season in L.A., hitting .284 with 20 home runs, the Chicago press, especially the *Chicago Defender*, became increasingly vocal about the travesty of not bringing him up to Chicago. Wendell Smith wrote in August,

> The most controversial player in the Chicago Cubs organization is a 28-year-old shortstop who plays 2,000 miles from here. He is Gene Baker of Los Angeles, the Cubs' number-one minor-league affiliate. Are the Cubs purposely overlooking this smooth-fielding shortstop, for whom they paid $6,500 to the Kansas City Monarchs of the Negro American League in 1950?[6]

James Enright of the *Chicago American* took the time to poll PCL managers about Baker. He reported that they were unanimous in their opinion about where he belonged. "If I were a major-league manager, I would consider him ready for an immediate opportunity to play in the major leagues," he quoted one as saying. "Purely on playing ability, [Baker] is a big-league player," said another.[7]

The situation would have been defensible if the Cubs had a stellar shortstop, but they did not. Roy Smalley, who had held the job for the previous five years, was one of the worst regular shortstops in the National League. Smalley,

27 years old in 1953, had hit 21 home runs in his third season, in 1950, but otherwise he was an annual disappointment. He was never able to hit better than .250, he struck out a lot, and his fielding was much below average. His arm was so erratic that the refrain from Cubs fans at Wrigley Field on a ground ball to second baseman Eddie Miskis (sadly reminiscent of the famous Tinkers-to-Evers-to-Chance) was "Miskis to Smalley to Addison Street." Smalley also committed the sin of loafing a few times to first base on popups and ground balls, a fact that angered fans.

After so much wrangling and perhaps due to the fact that the White Sox had integrated two years earlier, the September 1953 announcement that the Cubs had signed Ernie Banks and were calling up Gene Baker was met with surprising indifference in the Chicago African American community; Cubs integration was viewed as overdue—old news. Wrigley had missed a grand opportunity by waiting too long. An article in the *Defender*, with the title, "Cubs to Bring Gene Baker Up," noted, "Under extreme pressure from both the fans and newspapers . . . the Chicago Cubs have finally signed Negro ballplayers."[8]

The arrival of Baker was the real news to the press and fans; Banks was an unknown. There is a story that originally appeared—unsourced—in a 1990s book on Cubs history and has been retold numerous times since, in which Wrigley is surprised when informed that the Cubs were adding Ernie Banks. "We're already bringing up a Negro player this year!" he exclaims. "Why did you go out and get another one?"

"We had to have a roommate for the one we've got," he is told.

The story, while possibly amusing, is almost assuredly false—the product of a writer's imagination. Although decidedly inept at baseball, Wrigley was not a buffoon, as the story implies. It is common knowledge that African Americans were often brought up two at a time, for rooming purposes, but this was not done exclusively. The Cubs were bringing in Ernie Banks because he could play—he would be no man's caddy. Banks had been scouted, overscouted even, as much as anyone they ever signed. They knew he would help and soon. In addition to the previously mentioned checks and cross-checks, a scouting report exists, dated July 28, 1953, by Hugh Wise, which notes he observed Ernie in a total of 13 games. Above the question "Years before major league?" Wise typed, "Can play now." And, once Banks arrived, he was inserted into the starting lineup within a few days by the manager.

That manager, 36-year-old Phil Cavarretta, was a native Chicagoan who had been in the organization since he was signed at age 17. A fan favorite for years, he had been the National League Most Valuable Player on the pennant-winning 1945 team after hitting .355. A natural leader, he had reluctantly taken the reins as manager in June 1951, upon the exodus of Frankie Frisch, believing he still had time left as a first baseman. The no-nonsense Cavarretta said little, but his words brought immediate reaction from players. Respected for his previous talent, along with his knowledge of baseball, he possessed a hot temper that flared just enough to keep everyone in line.

As team captain in 1947, Cavarretta had called a meeting of Cubs players and informed them that every club in the league had voted to refuse to play the Dodgers if Jackie Robinson took the field. The team agreed to go along with the boycott[9] (commissioner Happy Chandler squashed the revolt by threatening players with permanent banishment). But attitudes had changed in six years. By 1953, Cavarretta was just looking for anyone, of any color, who could help his lousy team win a ball game.

By and large, the 1953 Cubs Banks and Baker joined were an easygoing, friendly bunch. The leaders were outfielders Hank Sauer and Ralph Kiner, two aging behemoths who had been on the short list of baseball's top sluggers in the not-too-distant past. Sauer, 36 years old in 1953, was a man of enormous natural strength. The only thing larger than his hands was his nose, a proboscis of truly ponderous proportions, so much so that his nickname was "Honker." A Cub since 1949, Sauer was the team's resident All-Star. At heart a good ole country boy from Pennsylvania, he was called the "Mayor of Wrigley Field" by his adoring fans, who bathed him with packs of his favorite chewing tobacco from the outfield bleachers.

Kiner, who was in the latter days of a Hall of Fame career, had joined the Cubs in mid-1953, in a 10-player trade with the Pirates. He had won seven straight home run titles and was on his way to a 35-homer season, but a bad back was rapidly eroding his effectiveness. Kiner had the type of personality to go along with his accomplished major-league résumé, which allowed him to quickly become a leader in the clubhouse. Friendly and well liked by everyone, as the highest-paid player on the team he didn't hesitate to reach for the check when dining with teammates.

In between the Jurassic right and left fielders, termed the "Quicksand kids," was speedy center fielder Frank Baumholtz. A consistent .300 hitter, the 5-foot-11 Baumholtz had been an All-American basketball player at Ohio University and was a good enough all-around athlete to play two seasons of professional basketball.

Third baseman Ransom Jackson was a quiet, likeable guy with a dry sense of humor. A graduate of Little Rock Senior High School (later to be called Little Rock Central), Jackson was a great athlete who had started in the backfield of two-consecutive Cotton Bowl football teams while in college. He was so laid back and unexcitable in his mannerisms that writers and managers often questioned his desire, even as he made All-Star teams with his performance.

The incumbent shortstop, 27-year-old Smalley, was in the process of hitting .249 (the highest batting average of his six-year career to that point), with six home runs and 25 RBI. The catcher was a mediocre-talented motormouth with a gift for making people laugh named Joe Garagiola. First baseman Dee Fondy, a .280 to .300 hitter with little power, and second baseman Eddie Miksis, a serviceable fielder and .250-hitter whose major contribution was that he showed up every day and provided fiery rhetoric to keep the rest of the infield awake, rounded out the lineup.

While the Cubs fielded a fair everyday starting eight, the pitching staff was abysmal. Seven different men started 10 or more games in 1953, and none had an ERA of less than 4.00. Only one, 29-year old Turk Lown, had a winning record—he was 8–7, with a 5.16 ERA.

Since players came and went with regularity, the team was not cliquish. It was a relaxed, if not exceedingly fun, clubhouse that Baker and Banks joined. With little tradition other than losing, Cubs players were unburdened by the stress of the expectation of anything more than playing out the schedule and trying not to embarrass themselves. A loss was no call for screaming or gnashing of teeth—Cubs players, and their fans, had become accustomed to finishing the day on the wrong side of the score. The fans at Wrigley Field, while not numerous, were friendly and treated the players well, with the exception of Smalley.

There were certainly still rednecks in baseball who resented players based solely on their skin color, but few of those were on the Cubs. There was no resistance in the clubhouse to Banks and Baker. Ransom Jackson says his only thought when they walked in was, "They must be good or they wouldn't be here. I hope they can help us win."[10]

"I'm from the South," says Jim Willis, a Louisiana native who was a 26-year-old Cubs pitcher in 1953, "but I didn't have any problem with them coming in." He continues,

> And I didn't hear anyone else say anything either. As a pitcher, if they bring somebody up who can help you win, that's great. They looked like they could play. That's all I cared about. And also what helped was that you could immediately tell that they were both not only good players but good guys.[11]

Ernie Banks arrived at Wrigley Field on Monday, September 14, 1953, as the Cubs were hosting the Brooklyn Dodgers. Two other rookies were called up from the Los Angeles Angels along with Baker: pitcher Bill Moison and outfielder Bob Talbot. Ernie was greeted in the clubhouse by Ralph Kiner, who showed him around and told him which group to hit with during batting practice. Clubhouse man Yosh Kawano handed Ernie a uniform with the number 14 on it and assigned him a locker next to Hank Sauer. Manager Cavarretta said little to any of the new players.

Ernie felt as if he were in a fog as he was shuttled from the clubhouse to the field, met numerous strangers, and shook bunches of hands. One of those hands belonged to Jack Brickhouse, the Cubs' broadcaster. "You'll do fine," Brickhouse told the rookie. "Just go out and play."

Ernie didn't realize it, but he had just made a lifelong friend. "It was not his broadcasting," Ernie said years later. "It was his feel for people. He was like a brother, like a lawyer, like a judge. He was always there for you."[12]

During batting practice, Jackie Robinson spotted Ernie and walked over to talk to him. Jackie, who remembered Ernie from the 1950 barnstorming trip, welcomed him to the big leagues and gave him some paternal advice: "I'm happy you're here. Play hard and listen and you'll learn."

The words from Robinson meant a lot to Ernie. "It kind of wiped out the fear I had. . . . When he said a few words to me, that relieved me."[13] But Ernie didn't need the advice to keep his mouth shut—he was already doing a good job of that. Other than the military, he had spent little time among white people in his 22 years and almost none as supposed equals. Although Ernie had met Dodgers Robinson, Campanella, and Newcombe on the barnstorming tour, he knew no one else. Being alone in a strange land, he relied on his father's example of keeping quiet and being as inconspicuous as possible.

Gene Baker was having a much easier time of it, exchanging greetings and insults with former teammates from the minors. "I had played with Baker since 1950," says Bob Talbot, who continued,

A lot of guys who came up through the system knew him. He was a good guy. Most everybody liked him. So they just welcomed him to the team along with us other guys from Los Angeles. But Ernie was different. He was an unknown to all of us. We knew he came straight from the Negro League and was supposed to have been good there, but that was it. Ernie looked like a young kid when he walked in. He was nice but didn't say much.[14]

Once in the batting cage, the social awkwardness disappeared. It was just Ernie and the ball. He launched the first batting practice pitch he saw over the left-field wall, turning some heads. In the next few days, teammates sized up the new arrival. In the clubhouse, he was unimpressive—even more so when he removed his shirt. Although there did not appear to be an ounce of fat anywhere on his body, neither did there appear to be any muscle. He was decidedly skinny, with narrow shoulders and almost no upper body mass—his chest was as flat as his stomach. But on the field, and especially in the batting cage, Ernie was fascinating to watch. He had a smooth, almost effortless swing. There was no neck-vein popping, red-faced straining; he looked as though he was half asleep in the box. But the swing, the swing was the thing; it was at once beautiful and savage, like he was cracking a whip.

"You could see the talent immediately," says Talbot. "His hands were so quick—he could wait and hit the ball out of the catcher's mitt."

"He was an average fielder," says Jackson. "Good enough to play in the major leagues, which is pretty darn good, but average. He had a great arm and could cover a lot of ground, but he wasn't polished. Hitting, though, you could tell right away that he had it. It was surprising how far he could hit a ball being so skinny." Teammates noticed how the ball jumped off his bat—that one coveted trait, immediately recognizable by baseball men, inexplicable, impossible to teach. Everybody wants it. Ernie had it in spades.

And Ernie's initial impression of the Cubs and Wrigley Field? In the version he would tell in countless smiling interviews for the next five decades, incorporated smoothly and naturally into his myth, he immediately fell in love with the friendly confines of beautiful Wrigley Field—so much so that he actually wanted to live there in an apartment at the facility. It was the most beautiful sight he had ever seen, and he swore he never wanted to leave. In 2014, however, Ernie told Rich Cohen for *Sports Illustrated* that wasn't exactly so. "I was shocked when I first walked onto that field," the 83-year-old Banks finally admitted. "I was expecting the big-time major leagues, a gleaming castle, seats up to the sky, but the place was falling apart, half empty, shoddy, and I thought . . . is this all there is?" The product on the field did not impress him either. The team he had just left in the Negro League had been running away with first place. The Cubs? Well. Said Banks, "I went from playing with the best to playing with some of the worst."[15] Ernie carefully guarded these thoughts—it would be six decades before anyone ever heard Ernie Banks say a discouraging word about the field or the team.

When Baker and Banks had reported, Cubs management had been met with an immediate problem: They had two very good shortstops on their hands, neither of whom had played much at any other position. But Baker arrived with an injury sustained in Los Angeles, a pulled muscle in his side that would keep him out for several days, which perhaps made the decision easier. After watching Ernie in batting and infield practice for three days, Cavarretta felt it was time to see his new player in action. He didn't say much more than, "You're playing today," offering no advice.[16] Ernie took the field at home against the Philadelphia Phillies on September 17, and played without distinction in a 16–4 drubbing, going 0-for-3 at the plate and committing an error at shortstop.

Ernie started again the next game and this time responded with two hits and a walk, and took part in three double plays in a 5–2 Cubs victory. A day later, in Sportsman's Park in St. Louis, Ernie hit his first major-league home run, off Gerry Staley, and added a triple and a single. Gene Baker, his leg feeling better, debuted as a pinch-hitter. The next day, in a curious intersection of future Chicago icons, Ernie was approached around the batting cage by 39-year-old Harry Caray, who was in his eighth year of doing Cardinal radio broadcasts, his first on powerful radio KMOX. "Ernie Banks!" Caray enthused in his famous voice, no doubt dripping with beer and spittle. "You hit a tremendous pitch out of the ballpark last night! You are going to be a great hitter." After getting little more than a smile and a one-word grunt in reply, Caray wished him well and walked off to talk to other players. Ernie later said he didn't think it was anything special—he didn't know about the celebrity-making potential of radio men since the Monarchs had never had any—until Baker started laughing and told him that KMOX had a range of 500 miles and that Ernie was going to be famous now.

By the time Baker was healthy, Banks was hitting .417 and certainly not leaving the lineup. Baker had originally been working out at both short and second. After the first few games Ernie played, Cavarretta, apparently having seen enough to be certain about the future of the team's shortstop position, asked Baker to come out mornings for extra work at second with the coaches.

September 22, Banks and Baker were in the lineup together both games as the Cubs split a doubleheader in Cincinnati, forming the first African American keystone combination in major-league history. They played the last six games of the season together, and the Cubs won three and lost three. Ernie started the last 10 games of the 1953 season and hit .314, with two home runs and six RBI. Everyone in the Cubs organization was impressed. Most scouts had underestimated him, thinking no one could be that good with no minor-league service and only two years of Negro League play.

After the last game, Ernie returned with his wife to Dallas, where he worked as a bellman at a local hotel and a counselor at the Moorland YMCA, still uncertain about his place in Major League Baseball. In a move that perhaps signified the Cubs' thinking about Ernie's place, Gene Baker was sent to the Puerto Rican winter league to learn the nuances of playing second base.

5

BINGO BANGO

If there were any doubts during the winter as to the future of the shortstop position for the Chicago Cubs, they were quickly put to rest during spring training in Mesa, Arizona. Ernie Banks was simply brilliant. "It's been a long time since the Cubs have had a rookie who seems certain of stardom in his first year and who stirs the imagination with the possibility of his greatness," Edgar Munzel of the *Chicago Sun-Times*, who had been covering the Cubs since 1929, wrote in early spring. He continued,

> But no longer. They have such a kid in camp this spring in Ernie Banks . . . manager Phil Cavarretta and personnel director Wid Matthews say he can't miss, and wherever the Cubs play this spring, rival managers and players line the dugout in fascination when the young man is hitting.[1]

The Cubs remained content with their decision to go with Gene Baker at second and Ernie at short. The most frequent explanation was that Ernie's stronger arm was better suited for short. Also, it was felt that the smooth-fielding veteran Baker would be able to make a position switch easier. More and more the plan looked good. Ernie showed great hands at short and was better than average at turning double plays, but it was his bat that had everyone talking. The fact that the bat was carried by a middle infielder was an added bonus. Management had been encouraged by Ernie's potential in the short trial the previous September, but now, seeing him every day, they were amazed. "He's the best batter against breaking stuff of any rookie I've ever seen come to the big leagues, and I'm not barring anybody," said Wid Matthews.

And they were already noticing those glorious wrists. "The answer is in his wrists," said 37-year-old veteran catcher Clyde McCullough. The backstop further stated,

> I've never seen any better wrists on a hitter than Banks has. That kid throws his bat at the ball like Jack Dempsey used to throw a punch. It travels only a few inches, and when the bat connects the ball just seems to jump to the outfield. It's his powerful wrists that give the bat that snap before it meets the ball.[2]

Cavarretta, overall disheartened at the lack of talent available from the Cubs farm system, was immediately impressed with his young shortstop. "The only one [prospect] I could see who had great potential was Ernie Banks," he said years later. "I said, 'This guy has to play . . . because this kid is going to be great. You don't have to be Einstein to see it.'"[3]

The secret got out quickly. Midway through the preseason, Fred Lindstrom told his radio audience, "The Cubs have themselves a great shortstop and one who'll hit . . . he gets that club around like Eddie Mathews. He's born to be a star."[4]

All-but-forgotten veteran shortstop Roy Smalley, hitting .071 to Banks's .500 in the spring, was traded on March 20. Wrigley benevolently announced that the trade was made for Smalley's own good. "We have decided to trade Roy simply to help him," P. K. told reporters. "He's an intelligent young man . . . Cub fans . . . were brutal in their treatment of him."[5] While new surroundings might have been nice for Smalley, everyone recognized he no longer fit into the club's plans.

Still, there were skeptics. Tired of hearing the raving reports, Orioles manager Jimmie Dykes made a bet with Munzel that Banks wouldn't stick. Dykes, who in his previous job as manager of the A's had been known as one of the most leather-lunged racial-baiting bench jockeys in the league, declared, "I still say that he won't hit .240, and he'll be out of the National League by June."[6] Dykes would prove to be more than just a little wrong in his assessment, and Munzel would win a dozen golf balls on the wager.

It was big news when the Cubs announced that Baker and Banks would be their regular keystone combination for the 1954 season. The fact that made headlines was not just that they were both rookies, but also what *kind* of rookies they were: "Two Negro Rookies May Solve Cavarretta's Problem," read one headline[7]; "Cubs' Boss Thinks Pair of Colored Rookies Will Be Hot," read another.[8]

Any ambition for the team's season was shaken when manager Phil Cavarretta was suddenly let go as they broke camp—the first manager ever to be axed during spring training. His crime had been giving the owner an honest appraisal of the team—that he couldn't win with the talent assembled. Rather than accept the view of the seasoned veteran baseball man and attempt to obtain more talent, Wrigley did the next best thing—he canned him. The stunned Cavarretta told reporters (in words that foreshadowed the coming despair for Ernie's career), "I believe the biggest headache a Cub manager faces is the future outlook of the club . . . the material just isn't there . . . there just isn't any good new talent coming up . . . the Cubs have to get some big-league ballplayers or they're sunk."[9]

Wrigley, promoting from within, as was his custom, summoned Los Angeles Angels manager Stan Hack to run the Cubs. "Smiling" Stan had been a solid third baseman for the Cubs for 16 years, retiring in 1947, with a .301 career average. He had remained in the organization and worked his way up the managerial ladder. The easygoing Hack was universally viewed as a nice guy. He didn't get too upset when the team lost, which was fortunate, because they were destined to lose a lot. "We lost 10 or 11 in a row and his attitude was, 'Boys, let's have another beer and get 'em tomorrow,'" pitcher Johnny Klippstein later said.[10]

After leaving Arizona, the Cubs played a series of exhibitions with the Orioles, working their way east and north. In Dallas on March 30, Ernie hit a solo home run in front of his friends and family. When the Cubs stopped in Hattiesburg, Mississippi, the hometown of Wid Matthews, Banks and Baker achieved another historic first. "White, Negroes in Game First Time in Hattiesburg," was the headline. There had never been a mixed-race baseball game in the town. Munzel wrote, "The event brought no noticeable reaction from the crowd of 2,352,"[11] a fact that seemed to amaze some.

But times were definitely changing. Whereas only six of the 16 major-league teams had integrated by the time Ernie Banks stepped onto the Wrigley Field turf for the first time, five other teams would do so during the 1954 season, leaving only four, the Yankees, Red Sox, Tigers, and Phillies, yet to make the move. In January 1954, a *Chicago Defender* article had touted "Large Crop of Negroes in Majors."[12] A total of 27 black players were on major-league rosters at the start of the 1954 season. The season would become a watershed year for the integration of baseball. African Americans were stars, and young players like Ernie, Willie Mays, and Hank Aaron served notice of a spectacular future.

Although the racial makeup of the major leagues was shifting, individual attitudes changed slower. It was a feeling-out period for Cubs players. Some from the South had never before played on an integrated team. Just as awkward, many white players from the North had never experienced segregation and so had no idea of the challenges Ernie and Gene faced on a daily basis.

On the field, they were all teammates who supported and cheered one another. In the clubhouse they laughed and joked together, particularly the outgoing Sauer, Kiner, and Garagiola. Away from the park, however, they went separate ways. Like Baker, Ernie and his wife, by necessity, took an apartment on the South Side of Chicago, a long way from Wrigley Field and the rest of Ernie's teammates, most of whom lived near the ballpark. Ernie and Gene stuck together almost all the time and rarely went out with other players. They were not welcome in the North Side establishments near Wrigley frequented by teammates, and few Cubs dared to visit the South Side. Interaction during the winters would be rare.

The two rookies met little open resentment, in the city or among their new teammates. Both were genuinely liked; everyone could easily appreciate their talent and attitudes. "Baker and Banks were both great guys," says Ransom Jackson. He added,

> They were the first two black players I had ever played with. I don't remember any trouble. By that point, guys had pretty much accepted it. Remember that was about seven years after Jackie Robinson broke in. My view was whoever could help us win was good to have on our team, and it was obvious both of them were good players and were going to make us a stronger team. The black thing never entered my mind. I don't remember anybody making a big deal about it. Some guys may have said something, but if they did, it was quietly and among themselves.[13]

"A lot of clubs had black players by then," Baker said in 1997. "The fans in Chicago were great to us. There was no prejudice against us."[14] Despite the statement four decades removed and Ernie's lifelong proclamations of mutual love, the two were forced to ignore some negative things. Ernie heard scattered boos when he first took the field. Soft-spoken Billy Williams would receive letters that started, "Dear N*****," when he broke in with the Cubs in 1960,[15] so it's safe to assume Ernie and Gene were sent similar greetings.

Says Jim Willis,

> Some guys called them niggers. Not to their face, but just when talking about them. It wasn't right, but that's just the way some people talked back then. And guys would yell things at the blacks on other teams. I remember Hank Aaron was always killing us, and one of the coaches down in the bullpen would yell every time he got a big hit and call him a nigger. I'm sure Ernie and Gene heard that. At Wrigley Field everybody in the place heard that. Looking back, that had to hurt.[16]

Once, as the team train, heading south toward St. Louis, picked up Banks and Baker at the 63rd Street Station, a part of town unfamiliar to the other players, Ernie heard one of his teammates remark, "Where are we stopping, at South Africa?"[17]

The worst came in the spring, particularly when the team broke camp and worked their way through the South, to Texas, Louisiana, and Mississippi. Ernie and Gene were exposed to the full treatment accorded African Americans in the mid-twentieth-century American South—that is, separate lodging, rest-rooms, drinking fountains, and eating arrangements, and don't let the sun go down on your ass in town.

During the regular season, Ernie and Gene stayed with teammates at hotels in every National League city except St. Louis, where the Chase Hotel would be the last holdout to integration. While teammates unloaded their gear from the bus in front of the Chase, Ernie and Gene carried their bags to the curb and tried to get a cab—often a difficult task, sometimes waiting 30 or 45 minutes, as white cabdrivers would drive by upon seeing their faces—and then ride across town to the black Adams Hotel. The Adams had no air conditioning and was unbearable during steaming St. Louis summer nights. They kept the window open, even with trolleys running on the street below, and soaked sheets in ice water and put them on the bed to make it tolerable.

They accepted the conditions and silently bore the burden without com-plaint. "And that was a new thing to Gene because he had always stayed with us in the PCL," says Bob Talbot. "A lot of guys didn't notice or think about it. But I think most of us felt that was wrong. We felt they should have been able to stay with us, but we were just ballplayers, we didn't make the rules. Nobody said anything about it. But I know it was hard on Ernie and Gene."[18]

"That's just the way it was," Baker said later. "You couldn't speak out. If you did, no one would listen anyway."[19]

Although they stayed in the team hotel in cities other than St. Louis, Ernie and Gene rarely went out with teammates. In places like Cincinnati, where many players crossed the bridge to Covington, Kentucky, which had lively nighttime entertainment, they knew they were unwelcome. It became a lonely year.

"A lot of guys would just go different directions after games," says Willis. He continued,

Because so many guys were coming and going on the team, it was hard to make real friends anyways. You didn't have time to get close. It was a new roster every spring, so you didn't have guys who played together three or four years and became friends like on the Dodgers. And then, with conditions being the way they were, we just didn't see Baker and Banks much after games. I don't really know what they did after games.

"We didn't socialize with them away from the park," says Talbot. "If we were in Chicago, we all went home to our wives. On the road, they went back to their hotel I guess."

Like all teams at the time, the Cubs traveled by train, and the trips to New York, Boston, Philadelphia, and Cincinnati were long, giving the players a lot of time together. Groups gathered for card games, to drink or just talk. Some sought solitude to sleep or read. Ernie usually sat alone or with Baker.

An iron curtain of misunderstanding descended. "In Chicago, white and black players could have socialized together without there being any questions at all," said Jim Brosnan, the pitcher and author who played for the Cubs from 1954 to 1957, who may or may not have correctly gauged the atmosphere, "but Banks and Baker didn't mix with the white players. As far as I knew, they didn't ask to."[20]

Ernie's personality certainly didn't help. While to Ernie the white players were an unknown possible hazard, to them he was a riddle, wrapped in a mystery, inside horsehide. Not that he was a wide-eyed yokel—he had more experience and exposure to the world than most of his teammates had at a similar age. He had traveled the Southwest with the Colts and traveled the country with the Monarchs. He had been to Europe with the U.S. Army. But while he had done these things, he had always had a protected layer of comfort—the older players on the Monarchs and Colts, the military. Now he was out on his own. He kept to himself and rarely spoke unless addressed first, and then, more often than not, his eyes roamed, looking for a chance to escape. Polite formalities seemed to exhaust his vocabulary. "Ernie was so quiet that he wouldn't talk to anyone," Sauer said.

"He was shy, but Hank Sauer and I would talk to him every day after the game," said Frank Baumholtz.[21]

"It was so different for me," Ernie said in 2006. "When I first joined the Cubs, I didn't talk very much. Just watched everybody. It was a learning experience. . . . It was a major challenge in my life."[22] There was also a silent fear: "Would I be accepted? What's it like to compete here? Can I stay? All these things were in my mind."[23]

In Ernie's perpetually sunny personal myth, he always maintained that he was welcomed by his new teammates with open arms. In his later years, however, he admitted that it hurt that few of them talked to him. "I felt like I was there but not there," he said in 2004. "Like Casper the Ghost. There was not a lot of camaraderie [the first year]. Sometimes I felt invisible."[24] Ernie knew absolutely no one other than Baker, whom he had only known for the few weeks the previous September. Normally reserved and slow to warm up anyway, Ernie felt like the only uninvited guest at a noisy party.

The discomfort increased as he watched his parents in his new surroundings. Eddie and Essie Banks took a train (neither would ever fly) to Chicago to watch their son play. Eddie experienced a cultural shock. "He had never been around whites," Ernie said later. "He had worked for whites but had never been around whites. He would walk around the stands, he was so nervous every time somebody would come over to ask for an autograph."[25]

Things were much easier for Gene Baker. He had been playing with white players since 1950, attended spring training with the Cubs several years, and played in the minors with at least half of the men on the roster. In addition, he was 29 years old (six years older than Ernie) and was naturally outgoing. A former college student who was raised in the relatively integrated community of Des Moines, Iowa, he mixed easily with reporters and other players.

Banks and Baker were not entirely on their own. African American journalist Wendell Smith acted as advisor to them, much as he had to Jackie Robinson in 1947. Smith would later be viewed as a giant, an undeniable force in the integration of baseball and, consequently, society. And he managed to pull it off without appearing militant—he worked calmly and logically within white society to further the cause. He was an invaluable mentor to the players. Early in the year, Smith emphasized to the two rookies that they were representing their race and that their behavior off the field, as well as on it, was constantly being judged.

Other National League black players also welcomed them and gave advice. Once, as they were walking to their hotel from Ebbets Field in Brooklyn, easygoing Dodgers catcher Roy Campanella pulled up in a big Cadillac and gave them a ride, along with tips on how to handle themselves in the big leagues. A common bond existed among black major-league players, from shared experience, familiarity on barnstorming trips, and the knowledge they were all in it together to a certain extent. They would frequently talk around the batting cage before games and exchange tidbits on cities and opponents, warnings, and intelligence. This camaraderie did not prevent guys like Don Newcombe and later Sam Jones from throwing at Ernie and Gene more frequently than white pitchers, however. No quarter was given on the field.

The two new Cubs were immediately welcomed on the South Side of Chicago. Their neighbors, who previously had little cause for interest in the Cubs, let them know they had support at home. "In my own community, people were really proud of me," Ernie said in 1997. "They assisted me, made sure I got to bed on time, congratulated me. . . . It wasn't like I was a star or a hero. It was like I was taken in, like a family."[26]

Ernie and Gene clearly understood the significance of their awesome responsibility. "I felt the spotlight was on me and Gene . . . to be a good example," Ernie later said. "We had to play well, have good character, all those kinds of things. . . . You felt like you were always being watched."[27] But how does one deal with potentially crushing expectations by your entire race while swimming in murky waters, with unknown dangers beneath the surface, with no familiar hand to grasp for help? And all while still not quite sure of being good enough to stick in the majors.

Ernie did what he did best—play baseball. He betrayed no emotion, good or bad, but just went about his business playing the game. And he played hard. He sprinted through first base like a man running from a fire even on routine infield popouts. He never threw a bat or cursed after a strike out. At the plate, he took his position and stared at the pitcher with an absolute blank face, waiting on the pitch before unleashing his explosive swing. His play in the field appeared effortless. The grace and emotionless demeanor initially gave the impression of almost indifference, yet, there was the hustle, the refusal to ever leave the lineup, the hard-nosed approach after being knocked down at the plate and while dodging spikes-high slides at second base. He left little doubt that he was a player, and a good one.

The rookie combo at shortstop and second (the first in the majors since Rizzuto and Priddy with the Yankees in 1941) was quickly acknowledged as one of the best in the league. In early April, they brought the crowd to its feet when Baker ranged far to his right to snag a grounder backhanded and made a glove-hand flip to Banks, who turned it into a quick double play. The two were soon going by the nicknames Bingo and Bango. Cubs catcher Joe Garagiola explained to a reporter, "The nickname just seemed to pop up, and now everybody calls them that. It just seems to fit them, the way they've been playing for us. They've got rhythm."[28] The nicknames, generally credited to announcer Bert Wilson, would prove beneficial when first baseman Steve Bilko played briefly with the Cubs that year, setting Wilson up with the wonderfully alliterative call "Bingo to Bango to Bilko" on double plays.

Ernie was solid from the start—not spectacular, but solid. Then he went 4-for-4 against Cincinnati on April 25, and had three more three-hit games in the next seven. Like a baseball met flush on the sweet part of a bat, his career took off, headed on a majestic arc. "Inside the first few months, he really developed and turned into a great hitter," says Jackson. "Through the season, watching the balls he hit, how far they went, the timely hits that helped us win ballgames, you began to realize he wasn't just good, he was special."

Gene Baker was not too far behind initially. Baker was a slick fielder and a solid hitter. More importantly, he knew the game of baseball and was fundamentally sound. He could bunt, hit-and-run, hit to the right side to move runners, and steal a base, and he was very consistent. In short, he was a professional. He had earned the respect of everyone who played with him. Baker became a big brother to Ernie. They were not only roommates, but also good friends, almost inseparable during the season.

Baker took the move to second base easily and taught Ernie the nuances of the game he had picked up in his years at shortstop. They discussed opposing hitters and pitchers, often replaying the day's game. And Baker worked to get Ernie to loosen up. He was not above tying Ernie's clothes in knots on the road or dumping ice down his shirt; he would do anything for a laugh and to help Ernie relax. They went to a lot of movies and ate almost every meal together. They were regular bowling companions in the offseason. Baker's influence was immeasurable. "He was one of the greatest people I've ever known," said Banks in 2012. "I wouldn't be here if it wasn't for him."[29]

The 1954 Cubs team got off to a fast start with Kiner, Baumholtz, Garagiola, Sauer, Jackson, and Banks all hitting better than .300 by the end of May. But the June swoon, that hated malady of every Cubs team that would haunt Ernie's career, hit especially hard in 1954. Kiner's knees and back went bad, and he limped to 22 home runs—the worst season of his career. Garagiola hurt an ankle, Jackson got an infected hand from a spider bite, and Baker missed three weeks in June with a broken wrist after being hit by a pitch. The Cubs were only four games out of first on Memorial Day; by the end of June they were 21 out, and the season was essentially over. A late August stretch of 17 losses in 21 games finished them off. Despite Sauer's 41 home runs, they crawled to the third-worst season in team history—perhaps vindicating Phil Cavarretta's preseason assessment.

No one could blame the rookie keystone combo for the poor finish, however. Joe Garagiola quipped, "The kids around second base kept them [Cubs fans] from dropping to double A—Alcoholics Anonymous."[30] And he was probably right. Banks and Baker were involved in more than 100 double plays together in 1954, more than the combined eight other men produced the year before for the Cubs. They hit an identical .275; Ernie had 19 home runs and drove in 80, Baker had 13 and 61. Ernie played every game of the 1954 season—every inning except one. Both were named to the rookie All-Star Team by the *Sporting News*.

In the Rookie of the Year voting, Wally Moon of the Cardinals, who hit .304, with 12 home runs and 76 RBI, won with 17 votes; Ernie finished second with four. Braves outfielder Hank Aaron, who had signed in 1952 and spent two years in the minors, was fourth with one vote.

While baseball formally frowned upon fraternization between opponents, baseball's black players maintained a collegial relationship. One day in the spring of 1955, a seemingly innocent pregame conversation with a foe proved to have a momentous impact on the career of Ernie Banks. Before an exhibition game, while talking to the Giants' Monte Irvin around the batting cage, Ernie picked up Irvin's 31-ounce bat. He immediately liked how it felt compared to the 34-ounce model he had used in 1954. Irvin encouraged him to try it out. In the cage, Ernie noticed that the ball flew off his bat. He was even able to pull outside pitches over the wall in left field. He decided to stick with the lighter bat. Few sluggers at the time used light bats; many swung lumber weighing as much as 38 ounces. Ernie didn't know it at the time, but with the switch to a 31-ounce bat, he was about to became a pioneer.

"He loved that bat," said Irvin years later. "That's when he became a really good pull hitter. . . . He could whip it."[31]

Ernie hit three home runs in the first four games of the 1955 season. After a short dry spell in early May, he ripped one with the bases loaded against the Dodgers at Wrigley Field on May 11, to help the Cubs to a 10–8 victory. Suddenly, everything coming off his bat was a rocket. He added another grand slam on May 29, against Lew Burdette and the Braves. The hits, and home runs, kept coming. When Hank Sauer slumped in late May, Ernie was written into the cleanup spot (he had started the season in the six slot) for the first time—a rare move for a shortstop. He exploded for 17 home runs in a little more than a month, hitting .381 (43–113) during that span.

Home run number 19, equaling his total for 1954, came on July 1. People were beginning to call Ernie Banks the best shortstop of the decade; some were looking even further back. The National League record for home runs by a shortstop was 23, by Glenn Wright of the Dodgers in 1930, and it was in danger before midseason. Baker and Banks were acknowledged as the best double play combination in baseball, no longer with any color qualifiers.

And the Cubs were playing great. As they invaded the East to open a June road trip, they had won 15 of 18 and were in the rarified air near the top of the standings for the first time this late in years. Cubs fans started talking like the team was for real. Big crowds were showing up at Wrigley Field, and not just for the sunshine. "The era of the contented Cubs, which covered many dull years following the club's last National League pennant in 1945, seems at last to have ended," wrote Edward Prell in the *Chicago Tribune*. "The Cubs started taking on a new character last year when Ernie Banks and Gene Baker became a dazzling double play combination . . . the revitalization continued this season. . . . Long-suffering Cub fans are hoping all these signs aren't too good to be true."[32]

Alas, they were. The normal order of the universe was soon restored as the Cubs hit quicksand in June, then lost 14 of 15 on a brutal July road trip. But Ernie continued his dazzle. As he came to the plate in the third inning of the second game of a doubleheader at Wrigley on July 3, PA man Pat Piper was naming the All-Star squad and announced that Ernie Banks would be the starting shortstop. The crowd of 35,176 burst into applause and gave Ernie a standing ovation. He rewarded them by lining a home run into the left-field bleachers.

In a close vote, Ernie had beaten out incumbent Johnny Logan of the Braves for the All-Star team 2,097,466 to 1,964,528. Baker was named to the squad as a backup by manager Leo Durocher. They took the short train trip with fellow All-Star Jackson to Milwaukee for the game. In the All-Star Game, which Stan Musial won with a home run in the bottom of the 12th, Ernie went 0-for-2. It was the first of what would become an annual midseason trip for Ernie.

After the break, Ernie picked up where he left off. On July 8, in Busch Stadium, he hit two home runs, giving him 23 for the year, tying the National League record for home runs by a shortstop. He hit his third grand slam nine days later.

As Ernie gained confidence due to his performance on the field, his clubhouse personality changed. "Once he got used to the other players and came out of his shell, he lightened things up a bit," said Sauer.[33]

In a June game, Ernie was hit on the top of his nose near his left eye by a pitch from Pittsburgh's Ron Kline. He sprawled in the dirt, momentarily stunned, but got up on his own and headed to first, refusing aid. In the clubhouse after the game, Sauer suggested that Ernie should make a better effort to keep his nose out of the way of fastballs. "True enough," Ernie replied to the man with the enormous schnoz, "but if you had been hit on the nose it would have been a single."[34]

"He had been really quiet at first," says Jackson. "I think he was trying to find his place on the team. As he finally realized that he belonged, that he was there for good, he settled down and his personality came out. He was the nicest guy you'd ever want to meet. He had a good sense of humor."

Teammates also noticed the unusually sunny aspect of his personality. "Ernie was pretty quiet, but he was very confident," said Johnny Klippstein. "One day a knuckleballer came in to pitch against us. Nobody liked to hit against a knuckleball. Nobody. Someone told Ernie, 'Watch this guy because he throws a good knuckleball.' He said, 'I love to hit the knuckleball.' He was the only guy I heard say that in my life."[35]

"Ernie was a very optimistic guy," says Hobie Landrith, who joined the Cubs the next year. "He was always up. Very few negative words ever came out of his mouth. In spite of playing on a team that lost many more games than they won, the next day he always showed up believing we would win. And, of course, we all looked at him as an exceptional talent."[36]

On August 2, against the Pirates at Wrigley Field, Ernie hit another grand slam. That gave him four on the season and tied a major-league single-season record shared by 10 men, among them Babe Ruth and Lou Gehrig. Two days later, he put on another power display with 4 hits, 3 home runs, and 7 RBI to propel the Cubs to an 11–10 win against the Pirates. In a game that typified the Cubs of the era, they had led, 9–2, after four innings before the Pirates came back and took a 10–9 lead. Ernie's third home run, a two-run job, came in the bottom of the eighth to put the Cubs back on top for good. In a nod that officially welcomed him to the club of elite sluggers, reporters noted that Ernie was only one game behind Babe Ruth's 1927 home run pace. On August 11, Ernie hit home run number 39 to tie Vern Stephens for the most home runs ever by a major-league shortstop. He added his 40th two weeks later in Chicago.

Teammates began noticing that not only was Ernie a great player, but also he had an inner toughness and competitive drive that was masked by his stoic demeanor. In early September, he developed a "charley horse" in the right thigh while running out a double in the seventh inning. Owen Friend replaced him and finished the final two innings (the first innings Ernie had missed all year and, amazingly, only the second and third innings he had missed in his career to that point). After Ernie was examined by the team physician, manager Hack announced he would sit a couple of days. "He pleaded with me to let him play," Hack told reporters the next day after he changed his mind and put Ernie back in the starting lineup. Hack added,

> He said if Doc Scheuneman [Cubs trainer] would tape him up, he'd be all right. I believe if I hadn't relented he would have burst into tears. You don't find that kind of spirit very often any more. The average guy would have figured it was September and the ballclub wasn't in the pennant fight, so why not take it easy on the bench for several days.[37]

But Ernie Banks wasn't an average guy. He hadn't gone through everything he had endured just to get to the major leagues and take it easy. He played on. Grand slam number five came on September 19, off Lindy McDaniel of the Cardinals. "I was just a dumb rookie at the time," says McDaniel. "Nobody had told me yet to never try to throw a fastball for a strike to Ernie Banks."[38]

The blow set the all-time major-league record for grand slams in a season (later broken in 1987, by Don Mattingly, with six).

Late in the season, there was talk of having an "Ernie Banks Day" at Wrigley Field. Initially, it was reported to be canceled because there was not enough prep time. Soon thereafter, however, reporters were told Ernie had turned it down. "I've been playing for the Cubs only two years," he said. "I don't want a day until I have proved myself. I just don't think I deserve one yet."[39] Apparently he was the only one who didn't think he had proven himself or deserved special recognition.

Ernie concluded his magnificent 1955 season with 44 home runs, 117 RBI, and a .295 batting average. To say he carried the Cubs offense would not quite tell the entire story. After Ernie, the next closest Cub in home runs and RBI was Jackson, with 21 and 70, respectively, and the next-highest batting average was Baker's .268. With little protection in the batting order, the 24-year-old Banks had turned in the best offensive season by a shortstop in major-league history. His home run total is even more impressive when viewed against that of his contemporaries: He hit one less home run than the other seven National League shortstops combined and more than all eight American League players.

Ernie also led the league's shortstops in fielding percentage, while committing only 22 errors. He was named the Associated Press Sophomore of the Year for the National League, getting 96 votes; Hank Aaron was second, with two. Ernie finished third in the Most Valuable Player voting, with 195, trailing only Campanella (226) and Snider (221) of the world champion Dodgers. The elevation of Ernie Banks from the Negro League to one of the elite players in the game in a little more than two years, without any training in the minor leagues, was stunning.

The Cubs had made a strong effort at the first division but trailed off to sixth, finishing at 72–81. Still, it was their best season since 1946, and it was cause for cautious optimism. Attendance was 875,800, the highest since 1952. Fans sensed the franchise was moving in the right direction. And their shortstop was leading the way. National magazines and newspapers ran feature stories on Ernie. Reporters speculated on an assault of all sorts of all-time records, notably the hallowed number of 60 home runs in a season. Ernie was usually patient and obliging with interviewers but seemed embarrassed by the personal attention. Occasionally allowing that, "I've been swinging the bat pretty well," was all the chest-thumping he would do. And he often quickly added that he still needed to improve his strike zone and stop swinging at so many bad pitches.[40]

Reporters trying to get the inside scoop on Ernie were left frustrated. He was referred to in print as a "speaks only when spoken to shortstop."[41] Ernie and Mollye were noted to live quietly, attend a nearby Methodist Church, and bowl or go to the movies for a big night on the town. Mollye was reported to proudly keep a scrapbook of her husband's accomplishments.[42] Another time it was written that Ernie didn't drink or smoke, had no use for the night life, liked to watch TV in his spare time, and "tries to get 10 hours of sleep a night."[43] In other words, the couple was not exactly Joe and Marilyn as far as filling up print space.

After the 1955 season, Ernie joined a barnstorming tour playing against a team of All-Stars from the Negro American League. Willie Mays and Don Newcombe had arranged a 33-game schedule throughout the South, Southwest, and Pacific Coast—reaching places where fans did not get to see Major League Baseball. The team included Baker, George Crowe, Hank Thompson, Aaron, and Sam Jones. Mays was the star attraction and thrilled fans at every stop with long home runs and circus catches. A highlight of the tour for Ernie came in Dallas on October 11, at Burnett Field. Before the game, a ceremony was conducted, led by George Allen, an African American and chairman of the citizen's appreciation committee. Ernie was given a new Oldsmobile from the combined efforts of the Dallas Chamber of Commerce and the Dallas Negro Chamber of Commerce. Mayor R. L. Thornton proclaimed the day "Ernie Banks Day in Dallas." In a brief acceptance speech, Ernie called it, "The greatest moment of my life."[44] A picture of Banks, wearing a 10-gallon hat, another gift, standing next to the car, appeared in the next day's *Dallas Morning News*.

Initially, the crowds on the tour were good, averaging more than 20,000 for the first five games, but as the temperature dropped, so did the attendance. Only 1,698 showed up in Atlanta; 2,643 in Little Rock; 1,509 in Knoxville; and a mere 677 in Asheville, North Carolina. They got a break and had a good turnout in New Orleans, which made the trip profitable, but overall it was a disappointing postseason haul. Television and a changing society were killing off barnstorming. It was the last of an era. Barnstorming would continue for Ernie and others sporadically through 1960, with diminishing results, but they would never again corral the big stars or crowds.

Ernie signed with the Cubs in late October, more than doubling his salary to $20,000. He was now making serious money. He and Baker had received the league minimum of $6,000 in 1954, as well as identical $9,000 contracts for 1955. For 1956, Baker was bumped up to $15,000.

In January 1956, Ernie was proclaimed the most popular Chicago Cubs player in a poll conducted by the *Chicago Daily News*. He received 1,434 votes, easily outpacing the second player, who got 380. "Among the Wrigley Field faithful, Banks already rivals the great Cubs of the past in popularity," wrote Tom Siler in a feature article in the *Saturday Evening Post*. Siler felt compelled to add the thought that was still on the minds of many people of the time: "Little of this seems to stem from the fact that Banks was the first Negro to play for the Cubs."[45]

The race question was never far from the surface. Ernie's younger brother Ben was signed by the Cubs in February 1956. More muscular than Ernie, Ben had been a star athlete at Booker T. Washington High School and, as a switch-hitting second baseman, followed Ernie's footsteps with the Amarillo Colts and the Kansas City Monarchs before being drafted into the U.S. Army. Ben was assigned to the Lafayette Class C team. A picture ran in the *Sporting News* of Ernie handing his brother a Cubs jersey.

But Ben Banks would not receive the welcome his big brother did in Organized Baseball. Before the season started it was announced that he was being reassigned. The Evangeline League, of which Lafayette was a member, was hit with a new antiracial edict. The Baton Rouge team had built a new stadium, and their local Recreation Commission had passed a rule stating, "No tan players are to be permitted to play in the new city park." Not only were "tan players" not permitted to play, but they were also not even allowed to sit on the bench.[46] Ben was reassigned to Twin Falls. The effect of all this can only be imagined, but Ernie later said Ben lost interest in baseball not long thereafter and moved to California, his professional baseball career over.

Ernie picked up where he left off in 1956, bludgeoning opposing pitchers. But the season did not end well. On August 11, he showed up in the clubhouse with an enormously swollen, painful hand, the result of an infection that had developed after he scraped it while sliding. The infection knocked him out of 18 games and ended his consecutive game streak at 424, which bested the old major-league record for most consecutive games from the start of a career (394) set by Al Simmons of the A's. The hand injury also caused a sharp decline in Ernie's production. Before the injury, he hit .307, with 25 home runs and 69 RBI. Afterward, in 33 games, he hit .267, with just three homers and 16 RBI.

In its preseason issue, *Sports Illustrated* had said of the Cubs, "They have the best second-base combination in either league in Ernie Banks and Gene Baker but have only hustle and high hopes to go with it."[47] That proved prophetic, and the hustle was quickly exhausted and the high hopes were unfounded. The Cubs finished last in the National League, with 94 losses, the most in team history, and attendance fell to 770,000. Whatever optimism fans held after the previous year's sixth-place finish was thoroughly dashed. Owner Wrigley vowed change. In October, he ushered Hack and Matthews out the door, and replaced them with Bob Scheffing and John Holland, respectively, who moved up from the Los Angeles Angels, where they had combined to win the Pacific Coast League pennant.

Wrigley announced that he was determined to improve the lot of his team. After essentially standing pat the previous winter, the Cubs made more moves than any team in the majors after the 1956 season, completing trades involving 13 players. Wrigley continued to claim that anyone on the roster was fair game to be traded. Anyone, he always added, except for Ernie Banks. In December, it was announced that the Cubs had turned down an offer of $500,000 from the Cardinals for Banks. "Mr. Busch called me and suggested we make a bid for Banks," said Cardinals general manager Frank Lane. "I told him it would be a waste of time. . . . He said, 'Why not offer the Cubs $500,000?'"

"'Mr. Busch,' I told him, 'Mr. Wrigley needs $500,000 about like you do. He wouldn't part with Banks at any price.' Of course, they said 'no.' and that was that."[48] It would not be the last time Phil Wrigley would refuse to trade Ernie Banks.

The new manager, Bob Scheffing, was an ex-military man, more organized and more of a disciplinarian than "Smiling" Stan Hack. The big, rugged Scheffing also took losing harder than his predecessor. Unfortunately for his disposition, the team's results were not much different.

The Bingo Bango combo was broken up in 1957. Early in the year, Scheffing moved Gene Baker to third base. Baker had slipped to .258, with 57 RBI, in 1956, and a leg injury had limited him to 140 games. He was now 32 years old, and there were concerns he might be nearing the end. On May 1, he was traded, along with first baseman Dee Fondy, to the Pirates for outfielders Dale Long and Lee Walls.

Losing Gene Baker as a friend and companion hurt Ernie, but it also signaled the emersion of his own personality. More and more, Ernie started talking and joking, both with teammates and the media. He was clearly the big name in the Chicago Cubs clubhouse and lineup. And, after three years, he was one of the team's veterans at age 26. The Baker–Fondy trade left Ernie and Walt Moryn (who had been with the team only a year) as the sole regulars from 1956 still on the team.

In his own way, Ernie was becoming a team leader. He played every game. He hustled. And he added a steady influence and attitude to the clubhouse. "I joined the team in 1956, straight out of the University of Minnesota," said Jerry Kindall, who received a large bonus. Kindall elaborated,

> Back then if you signed for more than $4,000 you had to spend two years on the major-league roster. A lot of guys resented us because of the money and because we were taking a roster spot and not really ready to help the team. Some froze us out and didn't even talk to us. Ernie was one of the few players who made me feel welcome. He was already a star by that time. The first day I took pregame infield

with him. I was a shortstop too, but, obviously, he didn't feel threatened about his job. He complimented me and was very encouraging, and gave me some tips. That meant a lot to me at the time.[49]

"He was still kind of quiet," says pitcher Don Kaiser, who played with the Cubs from 1955 to 1957. "If you asked him something, he'd talk to you. But everyone liked him and respected his manner. He was a complete gentleman on and off the field. He set the example for everyone on the team. I can't say enough about him."[50]

"Ernie had a great influence on me," says George Incledon, who was the Cubs batboy for two years, starting as a 14-year-old in 1956. Incledon further stated,

Even back then, he was always optimistic about everything, always smiling and upbeat. You never saw him get mad or say anything inappropriate—even in the clubhouse when he thought nobody was around. As batboys, we got to see everyone's true behavior away from the public. But Ernie came as advertised. And he was always so humble, even when I picked up his bat after a home run—he crossed the plate and went to the dugout—you would have never known what he had just done. He was a great role model for me to watch at that age, and I still feel his influence more than 50 years later.[51]

Every sports hero needs a sick-kid story, and Ernie checked off his in 1957. On September 8, he made a visit to South Chicago Community Hospital to visit 12-year-old Michael Fagan, who was recovering after a train accident. Young Fagan was a Little League second baseman and a huge Ernie Banks fan. He asked to meet Ernie, and the Cubs star obliged. After a 10-minute chat Ernie presented Fagan with an autographed ball. As he shook hands, Fagan said, "Mr. Banks, I'll never forget this visit, and I hope your reward for taking the time to see me will be to become the new home run king of the majors."

"I wonder if little Mike realizes the class of company he placed me in," Ernie told reporters before naming off Sievers, Mantle, Williams, Aaron, Snider, Mays, and Mathews as the premier sluggers of the game. "Really, you can't realize what a big boost the kid gave me."[52]

At the time, Ernie had 33 homers and was far back from the leaders. He soon went on a tear with eight in the next 12 games, including three in a 7–3 win against Pittsburgh. By September 18, Ernie had hit his 42nd home run and was the major-league leader. He finished with 43 home runs (Aaron got three the last week and edged him for the title, with 44) and 102 RBI. Once more, Ernie's home runs more than doubled the Cubs' next best slugger, Dale Long, with 21. Observers felt Ernie had peaked and couldn't possibly do more. They were wrong.

6

MOST VALUABLE PLAYER

Ernie reported to spring training 10 days early. He had experienced various annoying physical ailments during the 1957 season and was determined to get off to a good start. He told reporters he had been doing eye exercises throughout the winter and they had improved his vision, and he predicted a sharp upturn in his batting. He said that at times in 1957, he had been unable to see a pitched ball until it was barely two feet from the plate. Opposing pitchers, reading this and remembering his 43 bombs from the previous year, may have shuddered wondering how he could do if he actually saw the ball better.

Manager Scheffing made two changes for 1958, to improve on the team's dismal offense of the preceding season: increased batting practice and the addition of 62-year-old Rogers Hornsby as batting coach. Ernie had never had much hitting instruction—managers and coaches had wisely left him alone—but he had some holes. In 1957, pitchers had been successful working continuously on the outside as he tried in vain to pull everything. Frequently feeling he had to do it all by himself, he had enlarged his strike zone. Also, teams had been employing a shift on him, the Phillies and Pirates extremely.

Ernie spent extra time daily with Hornsby in the spring. Arguably the greatest right-handed hitter in baseball history, Hornsby lacked interpersonal skills, was rumored to have racist tendencies, frequently seemed more interested in how the ponies were running than helping young hitters, and especially didn't suffer mediocre ballplayers, but he took a special interest in Ernie Banks. They worked for hours on hitting to all fields. Hornsby also counseled him on pitch selection and knowledge of the strike zone, endlessly repeating the advice he had given to every good hitter he ever saw: "Ya gotta get a good pitch."

"Hornsby really helped me," Ernie told reporters in midseason. "He taught me to keep my eye on the ball, to hit to right, and the determination you need to be a good hitter."[1] Ernie tore up the Arizona League throughout the spring and didn't slow down once the season started. Eye exercises, good health, going to right, pitch selection—some of it or all of it—something was different, improved. He hit .435 the first week of the regular season and had 11 home runs and 30 RBI in his first 74 at-bats. After 53 games, roughly a third of the season, he was hitting .324, with 17 home runs and 49 RBI.

Ernie was now considered to be the best slugger in the game. "Banks Labeled Top Bet to Break Babe Ruth's Record," was the headline in the *Sporting News* on August 27, 1958. It was becoming a yearly watch: Jerry Holtzman noted that with 40 home runs, Ernie was only two behind the Babe's 1927 pace.[2]

As Ernie continued to rake—by the fourth week of August, he had 42 homers (just three behind the pace)—reporters continued to pound the topic. On September 3, the *Sporting News* devoted a full-page article to Ernie with the title "Banks Given Best Chance to Tie Bambino."

"He has no holes," said Scheffing. "He has the perfect swing, and now that he doesn't go for bad balls, he's the toughest man in the league to pitch to."

Ernie seemed embarrassed by the hoopla: "You can put all my homers end to end and I'd never match Ruth."[3]

New teammates were surprised at this humble attitude from a major star. "I was in awe of Ernie Banks when I first joined the Cubs," says pitcher Dick Ellsworth, adding,

> I was first with the Cubs in June 1958, right out of high school. I had heard a little bit about Ernie, and he had already won a lot of accolades, but what surprised me was how quiet and humble he was. Most great athletes are outgoing and have big egos. You could make the statement that without those two characteristics it's hard to make it far in professional sports.
>
> But I didn't see any of that in Ernie at all. He was generally quiet in the clubhouse. The only time he engaged was if someone else took the initiative. Then he would join in and laugh and talk. I ended up spending seven years in Chicago and my locker was only two or three away from his, and he was always that way: quiet and thankful for being there. I never recall him coming in after a game and complaining about an 0-for-4 or a couple strike outs or leaving men on base in a key situation. That just wasn't his demeanor. He accepted the day for what it was and looked forward to the next day.[4]

The calm nature could be misleading to those who didn't see him on the field each day. "I never saw him get mad in all the years I played with him," says

Jerry Kindall, who was on the Cubs from 1956 to 1961. "But his lack of temper shouldn't be looked at as a sign that he didn't care. He was a bear-down guy who tried exceptionally hard. His naturally mellow personality masked a truly fierce determination."[5]

"Ernie wanted to win as bad as anybody," says Ellsworth. "Nobody was fooled by his demeanor. We just accepted it for the way he was. You could see he played hard every day."

As the best player on the team, Ernie was a frequent target of brushback pitches. "There were no helmets," says catcher Hobie Landrith (Ernie would not wear one until 1962). "Nobody wore armor all over like guys wear now. Any hitter who goes into the batter's box has to have courage. If he doesn't, they find out real quick, and he won't be there long, no matter how much talent he has."[6]

"Ernie had a lot of courage at the plate," says Jim Marshall, who played first base for the Cubs in 1958 and 1959. He continued,

A lot of people don't realize that because of the other aspects of his personality. He was extremely competitive, but he just didn't show it outwardly. It took tremendous courage for him to stand in there like he did, given the aggressiveness of the game at the time. Pitchers didn't hesitate to throw at you if you were going well. And Ernie was always going well. He didn't have a lot of protection in the lineup most of the time either. There were times you just knew they were going to throw at him, and they did. But he handled that very well.[7]

"They threw at him a lot," says Jerry Kindall, "but he never got mad. He didn't complain or whine to the umpire or charge the mound. But teams later found out that it didn't help to knock him down." With the impassive face of a serial killer, Ernie let pitchers know there was a price to pay for throwing at Mr. Banks. Jerry Holtzman reported that four different times in 1958, he hit the next pitch he saw for a home run after being either hit or knocked down (against Don Drysdale, Bob Purkey, Jack Sanford, and Bob Friend).

"Teams tried to pitch around him," says Marshall, who added,

Managers were determined not to let him beat them. There were a lot of real short pitchers' scouting meetings when opposing teams came to Wrigley Field. It was, "Walk Banks four times today and we'll win." But it wasn't that easy. He never changed his mechanics, he was very consistent, and he got to where he was very selective. He knew what he hit best, and he waited on it. A lot of times in baseball, against major-league pitching, you may only get a few pitches a game that you can truly handle. Most guys might foul them off or barely miss them and make an out. But those two years, when Ernie got a pitch, he just never missed it.

"You'd think people wouldn't pitch to him, but sometimes you couldn't avoid it," says Lindy McDaniel, who pitched for the Cardinals at the time. States McDaniel,

> I remember one time the Cubs came to town and Ernie was red hot. At the team meeting, Hutch [manager Fred Hutchinson] said, "Whatever you do, don't pitch to this guy. Don't let him beat us." Well, he knocked in six runs that day, and they beat us six to two. Every time he came up, there was a guy on first, and they had to pitch to him, so the clubhouse meeting didn't do any good.

He was just such a hard guy to get out in those years," continues McDaniel. "I always threw Ernie fastballs but about a foot inside. I would throw him fastball after fastball like that." McDaniel, who had one of the best curves in the majors, rarely showed him the curve. "He would look for certain pitches. You didn't dare throw what he was looking for, because if he got it, he would kill it every time, no matter how good it was."[8]

"Ernie's hands were just so quick, it was impossible to get a fastball by him," says Pete Richert, who pitched for the Dodgers a few years later, teammates with noted fastballers Don Drysdale and Sandy Koufax. "I never saw anybody throw a fastball by him. You just hated to see him come to the plate with men on base."[9]

Ernie was clearly the top player in the league, but as the Cubs swooned once more in August and September (they had been near .500 until midseason) Chicago reporters and fans worried the team's dismal finish would hurt his chances for postseason honors. The Most Valuable Player Award had never been given to a player from a seventh- or eighth-place team in either league. Furthermore, the last five National League awards had gone to men from the pennant winners.

Ernie finished the 1958 season with 47 home runs and 129 RBI. The RBI count broke the league record for RBI by a shortstop (126 by Glenn Wright in 1930). He finished eighth in the league with a .313 average. His dominance was illustrated by the fact that he led the league in home runs, RBI, at-bats, slugging percentage, total bases, and extra base hits, and was second in runs (119) and triples (11). Retrospective statistical analysis shows he was second in the league in OPS, and his WAR of 9.4 was second to the 10.2 of Willie Mays. Ernie was also the only National League player to play every inning of the season (he had missed only four innings of play during the 1957 season).

The MVP voting was not close: Banks won with 283, well ahead of second-place Mays, who had 185. Ernie was named on every ballot and received 16 of 24 first-place votes. He received the news at home in Chicago, expressing surprise when told of the landslide victory. "Just think of all the great players in the National League," he said. He also thanked his wife, stating that she "encourages me all the time. Without her I couldn't have done it."[10]

Jim Murray, columnist for the *Los Angeles Times*, later wrote the following of Ernie's MVP season: "To win this award (MVP) on a second-division team you have to do everything but heal the sick."[11] Perhaps Murray hadn't heard about the little boy in the hospital.

It was about this time that rival manager Jimmy Dykes, now a believer, uttered the famous line, "If the Cubs didn't have Banks, they'd have finished in Albuquerque."

Even though he had been putting up big numbers for four years, Ernie's home run totals continued to amaze those who saw him up close—they couldn't help but wonder how he was able to generate the force to hit the ball so far, so consistently. He was a stark contrast to the traditional behemoths of bash, like Ruth, Gehrig, Foxx, Greenberg, and Kiner. Contemporaries Willie Mays, Mickey Mantle, and Frank Robinson left no doubt as to their power when they took off their shirts—revealing six-packs and layers of unnaturally ripped muscles. But Ernie was decidedly skinny and, other than the large hands, looked almost ordinary. No one had foreseen the prodigious slugging, not Buck O'Neil and certainly not anyone in the major leagues.

Everyone understood that the casual ease with which Ernie appeared to meet the ball without swinging hard was an optical illusion. The discussion concerning the source of Ernie's power, always a hot topic, intensified. "He hits 'em with his wrists," said radio commentator Mel Ott, himself the owner of 511 home runs as a player, voicing the most common theory.

Lew Fonseca, a former batting champ and head of the MLB motion picture bureau, concurred. He had offered a detailed analysis before the 1956 season: "Our movies show how he does the damage with the wrists and forearms . . . the bat at impact is traveling faster than the ball. . . . Many of Banks's blows start off like line drives. He seldom hits a towering home run. The level swing and the incredible wrist action does the trick."[12]

Others offered complimentary factors, for instance, swing mechanics, the lighter bat, and his unusually acute eyesight. They pointed to optical tests performed by the Cubs that showed Ernie could see at 20 feet what the average person can see at 10. Ted Williams later wrote that Ernie was "one of the best in baseball history at pulling a pitch into his power field."[13]

Rogers Hornsby, a fair judge of hitting, firmly stated it was the perfect confluence of many extraordinary factors. "It's all those things put together. Good eyes, timing, the wrists, and the follow through," he said.[14]

Ernie, himself, always gave credit to the wrists and, in the new millennium, decided it sounded good to cite the influence of picking cotton as a youth. He repeated the answer numerous times, ignoring the obvious fact that thousands of others from his time also strengthened their wrists picking cotton, but none of them grew up to hit 500 home runs.

Hornsby's explanation appears to be the best: It was multifactorial. Ernie's home runs were the result of a perfect weight-shift—an incredibly coordinated movement of the shoulders, pivot of the hips (with the belly button rotating to face the pitcher), and stride—along with wrists and lean muscles that were a natural gift of fast-twitch fibers. And world-class hand–eye coordination certainly helped. The result was a split-second explosion when bat met ball. The point of impact of Ernie's swing was the far end of a Newtonian physics equation. It was a mercurial phenomenon possessed by only a handful of men in baseball history. They could no more teach someone else how to do it than they could explain it to a mere mortal. It was just a fact of nature, like the Grand Canyon or Niagara Falls—beautiful to behold but impossible to reconstruct.

But while the talent was there to give the potential for greatness, an undeniable amount of work was required to bring forth the full realization—good, old-fashioned sweat. In 1997, in a rare instance of self-promotion, Ernie said, "I had discipline. I was very disciplined. I spent time hitting. I spent time alone. I mean hard practice and commitment . . . you have to have discipline of mind to do it without a whole lot of people around."[15]

As the reigning league MVP, Ernie was a fixture on the knife-and-fork circuit during the winter, attending banquets throughout the country. He hit St. Louis, Baltimore, New Hampshire, Boston, and New York, among other locations—23 stops in all, increasing his national exposure. He was becoming skilled at the give-and-take of mindless baseball questions and humor. He was repeatedly queried about Babe Ruth's record. Ernie laughed them off, asking, "Who me? Now you know I don't stand a chance."[16]

The man acclaimed to be more valuable than any other in the National League signed a new contract for an estimated $40,000. "He got a nice increase and appeared to be very satisfied," John Holland told the press, and Ernie agreed (although the salary was well below the $80,000 Mays was making).[17]

Ernie bruised his right knee in a collision at home plate in the spring and started the 1959 season hobbling, but he soon picked up where he left off the previous year. After 20 games, he was hitting .342, with six home runs and a league-leading 24 RBI. He had 71 RBI in the first 72 games.

He never let up. And his numbers weren't the result of a few huge games at Wrigley with gale-force winds. In fact, he hit two home runs in a game only twice and twice had five RBI. Instead, he steadily produced almost every single game. His batting average never dipped below .276 throughout the year. By season's end he would have 24 home runs and 73 RBI at home, and 21 and 70, respectively, on the road.

The fantastic hitting overshadowed Ernie's fielding. He was as sure-handed as any shortstop in the majors. "There is no superior shortstop than Ernie," said Stan Musial. "He hardly ever fumbles a normal ball, hardly ever makes a bad throw. He won't make as many great plays . . . but no shortstop is as steady and as consistently good as Banks. He's not flashy, but he's fast and he surprises you with his range."[18]

"Ernie can cover some ground," said Hall of Fame shortstop Lou Boudreau, then broadcasting for WGN. "I'd rate him among the top five fielding short-stops in the majors. Ernie's only minus point is being the middle man in the double play."[19]

"He had really soft hands at shortstop," says Ellsworth. "If he got to a ball, he'd make the play." Ernie finished the 1959 season with a record for the fewest errors (12) by a shortstop and set the fielding percentage record of .985 as well (Roy McMillan, of Cincinnati, won the Gold Glove).

The Cubs made a bid for their first finish in the first division since 1946. Despite a bruised back, Ernie hit a two-run homer to help the team to a 5–4 win against the first-place Giants on August 16, to move them into a tie with Pittsburgh for fourth place. That was typical of Ernie's way: He not only refused to sit out with injuries, but also produced in spite of them. His durability impressed and inspired teammates. On August 15, he was nailed in the back by a Jack Sanford fastball and cringed with pain but stayed in the game until his shoulder stiffened a few innings later. Doctors said he would be out for three to four days. He showed up the next day barely able to walk, but after 40 minutes of heat treatments, he suited up and played. "Watching him, I thought, 'There's no way he'll play,'" says Marshall. "He couldn't walk up the stairs to the clubhouse. He didn't work out before the next game and barely made it out to shortstop. And then he hits a home run in the first inning." Ernie homered off Johnny Antonelli in the first inning and hit another one the next day.

Scheffing was amazed. "Everybody that's human has aches and pains, but Ernie never complains about them," he said in midseason, declaring,

Last month in San Francisco, he was spiked, and the nail on the big toe of his right foot was cut in half and pushed down. I said to myself, "This is the one time he's going to have to sit down a few games." The next day Ernie had the toe taped up, cut out the top of his shoe, and damned if he didn't play.[20]

Ernie finally showed he was human the last day of the 1959 season. The day before, he had been hit in the left leg by a Johnny Podres fastball. He came to the park for the final game walking with a cane. When he didn't start the game it was the first time all season he had missed as much as an inning. Ernie made himself available as a pinch hitter and got into the game to keep his consecutive game streak going at 498. After he popped up in the seventh-inning he was given a standing ovation by the Wrigley crowd as he limped back to the dugout.

The Cubs finished in a tie for fifth place with a record of 74–80, missing the first division by four games. Ernie hit .304 with 45 home runs and 143 RBI (the highest in the league since 1937 and 18 more than anyone else in the majors). The 45 home runs tied the Braves' Eddie Mathews for the National League lead but the Braves got to play another game because they forced a play-off with the Dodgers to decide the pennant. Mathews hit a homer in that one and since playoff numbers were added to regular season totals in those days, he won the home run title.

Ernie was nearly a one-man wrecking crew in 1959. In leading the Cubs to their best record of the decade, he hit 31 more home runs than the next closest teammates, Walt Moryn and Dale Long who hit 14. Bobby Thomson was the next closest in RBI with 52—almost a hundred less than Ernie. And Ernie's RBI did not come cheaply due to a plethora of base runners: leadoff batter Tony Taylor hit .280 and no one else was higher than .270. Ernie led both leagues in intentional walks with 20, but pitchers had to throw to him sometimes and he rarely failed to pick up opportunities to drive in a run: He hit .381 with runners in scoring position overall and .433 with two outs and runners in scoring position.

Despite Ernie's stellar season, the MVP vote was expected to be close. Aaron had a great year with a .355 average, 39 home runs and 123 RBI, Mathews hit .306 with 46 homers and 114 RBI and Mays hit .313 with 34 and 104. But in November, Ernie got a phone call from Hy Hurwitz, secretary of the Baseball Writers Association of America. "This is becoming a habit with you," Hurwitz said as he broke the news that Ernie had become the first National Leaguer ever to win back-to-back MVP awards.[21] Ernie got 232 votes, Mathews 189, and Aaron 174. Later WAR calculations would show voters had made the right choice: Ernie's WAR of 10.2 was well ahead of Hank Aaron's second-place 8.6.

Eddie and Essie Banks were proud parents as they traveled to Chicago by train to attend the Annual Diamond Dinner of the Chicago Baseball Writers in January 1960. Ernie introduced them and got one of the night's loudest and longest ovations. They watched their son receive a trophy, along with Nellie Fox, as Chicago's Players of the Year (each had won their league's MVP Award). Eddie was thrilled when he met Stan Musial. "I've followed Stan through his entire career," he told reporters. "Stan spent more time talking about Ernie than he did himself. I'd waited a long time to meet him."

Essie, on the other hand, only had eyes for the "Yankee Clipper." "Joe DiMaggio has always been my favorite in baseball," she said. "I almost fell off my chair when Ernie brought him over to our table for an introduction."[22]

The Cubs wasted no time in talking contract with Ernie. He signed shortly after the season for a reported $60,000—an all-time high for a major-league shortstop. Only one Cub had ever received more money and that was Kiner—and only because it was a holdover from his Pirates contract—with $65,000 in 1953.

But it was not all awards and raises for Ernie Banks in 1959; his five-year marriage was coming to an end. The public had been unaware, but close friends on the Cubs, for example, Monte Irvin, had known the marriage was in trouble as early as 1956. By 1958, Ernie and Mollye were rarely together, and late in the year Ernie had filed for divorce. According to his attorney, Claude Holman, for most of the previous year they had "not been living as a married couple although sharing the same apartment," whatever that meant. Ernie had finally moved out six days after winning the MVP Award in November 1958 (and five days after telling reporters he couldn't have done it without her). In January, a Chicago columnist claimed Mrs. Banks would "reconcile her marital differences if Banks returns home," but she denied it.[23]

Ernie did drop the suit and they were reportedly trying to work things out, but in April 1959, Mollye filed notice in the Chicago Superior Court that she intended to seek separate maintenance from Ernie, to get payments from him while they were separated. Her attorney said he was discussing an amicable settlement.[24]

On June 30, 1959, Mollye Banks was granted a divorce on grounds of cruelty. Ernie did not appear in Superior Court with her—he was busy hitting a single and a triple in four at-bats against the Cardinals that afternoon. He agreed to pay her $65,000 over 15 years and $11,000 in attorney fees.[25] A picture of a sad Mollye, sitting alone in court, ran in the Chicago papers. It was rumored among Cubs players that the Cubs and P. K. Wrigley had helped Ernie with the divorce situation so he wouldn't worry too much, and indeed it had not affected his play on the field. The charge of cruelty against Ernie Banks might raise eyebrows when viewed now, but in 1959, it was taken with a knowing smile, if noticed at all. Illinois, like most states at the time, did not have a no-fault divorce law—irreconcilable differences was not an acceptable reason to formally end a marriage. Divorces could only be granted if one party could show that the other had been at fault, usually through adultery, through criminal behavior, or, by far the most commonly used phrase, for reasons of cruelty.

The couple had been young, Ernie 22 and Mollye 18, when they married in 1953. Mollye had occasionally entertained reporters for a domestic story on the team's star, and the couple appeared together on the cover of an April 1956 issue of *Jet* magazine above a caption that read, "Can Ernie Banks Do It Again?" But otherwise she had remained quietly in the background while Ernie's local popularity soared. The strains of moving to a new city, being thrown into an entirely new lifestyle, and the time demands of constant travel by the husband would tax any such couple. In one 1956 article, Mollye had lamented that their wedding day, April 6, "comes too close to Opening Day, I guess. Ernie never remembers our anniversary."[26]

The divorce wrangling would not be final for some time—in November 1963, attorneys for Mollye would file a petition in Superior Court asking Ernie to show cause why he should not be held in contempt of court for failing to place money in escrow and make payments on an agreed-upon $30,000 life insurance policy with her as the beneficiary. But the childless marriage would fade from memory as Mollye moved back to Dallas. Ernie would not even mention Mollye or the marriage in his 1971 autobiography. What he did mention was that after the 1958 season, he had a meeting at a public relations firm and was immediately impressed with the attractive receptionist. He returned the next day, introduced himself to the receptionist, Eloyce Johnson, and asked her out for dinner and a show. Soon they were an item. In October 1959, it was announced that Ernie had married the "beautiful Los Angeles socialite."[27]

7

BECOMING MR. CUB

Ernie Banks was born and raised a Cub and he'll die a Cub.

—Chicago Cubs coach Elvin Tappe[1]

Sandburg—the poet, not the second baseman—famously called Chicago the "City of the Big Shoulders."[2] It is somewhat ironic, then, that the player who would become the most cherished in the city's history had decidedly narrow shoulders for one who performed powerful feats. But by 1960, Ernie Banks had achieved a level of local popularity reached by few athletes in any city at any time. He was as much a part of Chicago's identity as deep-dish pizza, St. Patrick's Day parades, and shady politics.

The Cubs had possessed their share of heroes in the past—Tinker, Evers, Chance, Hartnett, Cavarretta, Sauer—good guys, good players, Hall of Famers, MVPs. Some had stuck around for 10 or 15 years and won championships, but they belonged to the distant past and none had ever touched the core of the fan base like Ernie. The previous decade, as the team lost both continuously and spectacularly, they had added veterans with big names almost on an annual basis: Ralph Kiner, Monte Irvin, Richie Ashburn, Bobby Thomson. But it was always at the end of their careers, their best seasons, not to mention healthy knees and backs, only a distant memory. They were never good enough or lasted long enough to build a following. Ernie was the one constant for the Chicago Cubs—their All-Star, their perennial hope for the future.

On the South Side, the White Sox had guys like Luis Aparicio and Nellie Fox. They were All-Stars and popular, and the Bears, Bulls, and Blackhawks had their heroes also, but no one was close to Ernie. He stood alone among sports stars in the second-largest city in the country.

There were a number of reasons for Ernie's mass appeal. Initially, it was his consistent excellence on the field. He had been an All-Star in each year after his rookie season (six times by 1960) and Most Valuable Player twice. After seven seasons in the majors, he had hit 269 home runs, an average of 38 a year. His 41 homers in 1960 made him only the third National League player in history to have five 40–home run seasons (Kiner and Duke Snider were the other two). After leading the majors in RBI in 1958 and 1959, he narrowly missed in 1960 (117 to Aaron's 126), which would have made him only the second player (behind Babe Ruth) to have led the majors for three straight years. When he led the National League in home runs in 1960, it was the second time in three years, and if not for the extra home run Mathews got in the playoffs in 1959, it would have given him three consecutive titles. From 1955 to 1960, he hit more home runs than anyone in the game.

And Ernie was reliable. From the time he started in September 1953, he did not miss a game until August 11, 1956—after two and a half seasons and a record 424 consecutive games from the start of his career. After the hand infection forced him out for 18 games, he launched another consecutive-game streak that by the end of the 1960 season had reached 654 games, the longest active streak in the majors. Ernie not only played every day, but also he always hustled. Even on those Death Valley afternoon Wrigley games in August and September, when the league leaders were a rapidly fading trail of dust far ahead, when lesser men would beg off for a day or two or mail in their games, Ernie was still sprinting around the bases, scrambling to the outfield grass trying for every ground ball up the middle, and sliding on every close play.

Many seasons when there was precious little reason for joy in Wrigley, Ernie could be counted on to provide it. Despite lousy teams, fans showed up to watch Ernie—to watch him swing, to hope for a home run. And he rarely let them down. He was a supernova in an otherwise cloudy, starless night sky.

The appreciation of his talent was quick, almost immediate. The love came more slowly, building up during a span of five, six years until it finally exploded. And it was Ernie's public persona that raised him to the pantheon of sports idolatry. He was the consummate professional, and he never lost faith. He didn't get mad or mope when the Cubs lost; he just came back the next day, convinced that the team's salvation was just around the corner, or maybe the next corner, day after day, year after year. Fans could clearly see he was enjoying himself when he played. They loved him because he loved the game they loved. And, more importantly, he seemed to love them back. He was always happy to meet and talk to fans, at the ballpark and around town.

While his personality matured a few years later than his hitting, the conversion from wordless wunderkind to the character who would become one of the most recognizable and enduring in all of sports was no less amazing and unexpected in its celestial trajectory than the league-leading home runs. Gone forever was the cautious, stone-faced young ballplayer who slunk in the background and mumbled one-word answers.

When Gene Baker was traded in 1957, Ernie lost his social safety net. And he quickly realized he needed one, a necessity demanded by the attention all those home runs guaranteed. He later admitted that public speaking was a frightening, painful experience for him when he first came to Chicago. During his first year, he rarely made statements to the press other than to assure them that he liked "being in the majors and playing every day."[3]

The following radio interview with Bert Wilson from Mesa in the spring of 1955 is classic early Ernie Banks:

Wilson: "Ernie, you look like you're ready to go for 1955."

Banks: "Yea, all ready Bert."

Wilson: "I understand that you might have gone to the New York Yankees or the Chicago White Sox, but Wid Matthews kept after somebody and got you in the Chicago Cubs organization."

Banks: "Well Bert, I think it's a fine organization and, uh, I really like playing with the Cubs."

Wilson: "It's amazing to see how you get so much power out there Ernie. . . . It's that wrist action that does it I guess. Is that natural, that wrist action?"

Banks: "Yea, it's natural. I just swing that way and I just try to meet the ball."[4]

Ernie once replied to a reporter's question about his reticence: "I didn't come up here to talk. I came to play ball."[5] How quickly things changed.

The makeover was aided by the influence of several mentors. He adopted Buck O'Neil's infectious enthusiasm and optimism. He also watched how the ebullient Minnie Minoso carried himself. Already established in the city when Ernie arrived, Minoso had been the first black Chicago baseball player for the White Sox and become a favorite of fans of all colors with his hustling style of play and friendly nature. "I followed Minnie Minoso and tried to pattern myself after him," Ernie said in 2006. "He was nice to people, he signed autographs, he talked to people. He played hard. I admired that."[6]

In 1956, Monte Irvin, then 37 years old, played for the Cubs in his final major-league season. Irvin had been a member of the pioneer generation when he integrated the New York Giants, along with Hank Thompson, in 1949. Levelheaded, hardworking, and eager to help, Irvin was the black player the other black players revered. Like O'Neil, Irvin rarely showed a public face that was not positive. On dealing with the white public, Irvin said,

> I will not say that we do not feel the history of the South around us and try to be especially good about giving the autograph and then standing around and chatting. If I can show a few little Southern boys that the things they have heard about us are wrong, I think I have made some small contribution. The hope is always in the new generation.[7]

Ernie's new image bore the unmistakable shadow of Buck, Minnie, and Monte. It was a good fit.

After his first offseason spent back in Dallas, Ernie had made Chicago his full-time home. He became ubiquitous around town. Hang around Chicago long, and it was almost impossible *not* to run into Ernie somewhere. He had regular radio sports programs during the winters beginning in 1957, with a show shared with Chicago Cardinals football player Ollie Matson on station WBEE. In addition, he worked for a soft drink firm and later a local ice-cream company, and spent many hours spreading goodwill and encouraging Chicago-area kids to use their products. Fans could easily see the man with their own eyes, and he was the same, whether at the ballpark or on the street. He walked the rail before games, offering greetings, chatting, and signing autographs. After a while he remembered the names of the regulars in the sparse crowds. On a personal level, he came across as a regular guy. He never appeared annoyed by attention from fans or acted like his talent gave him privileges.

The relaxed atmosphere of the ballpark of that era certainly helped fans learn to appreciate Ernie and aided in his transformation. Wrigley Field was much more intimate, with small crowds and easy access to players. "You could get tickets and get right down near the dugout or on the rail almost anytime you wanted," says Larry Davidson, who was eight years old in 1960. Davidson added,

> They closed off the upper deck for weekday games because nobody went. As a kid, you could get a ticket for 75 cents, and then after the game, if you went around and flipped up the seats so the guys could clean, they would give you a ticket to the next game. So you could actually get to see all the games, a season ticket, for 75 cents if you were ambitious. A lot of players would come over to the

rail for pictures and autographs before and after the games. You got to see these guys up close and personal, you got to learn what kind of guys they really were.[8]

While Ernie working the rail and signing was not unusual for the time, the frequency with which he did so and the enthusiasm he exhibited were unsurpassed. "Ernie had a personality unlike any other athlete," says Mike Filipiak who idolized Ernie as a 12-year-old fan in 1960. Filipiak elaborated,

He was very willing to talk to fans. He couldn't have been nicer. And he didn't just sign autographs; he always talked to you and made eye contact. I must have gotten his autograph a hundred times and it was always the same—never just an autograph, always a conversation. His eyes would light up: "How are you doing? Playing ball this year? How's your team? Hitting any home runs?" He made you feel that he was genuinely interested in you, even though you were just a kid. Each time you walked away feeling 10 feet tall. Nobody else made you feel that way.[9]

"I was in the Gene Baker–Ernie Banks Fan Club in the mid-50s," says Dennis Freres. "The club was started by a girl, Phyllis Kline, who had polio and had trouble getting around." Starting in 1954, Phyllis put out 36 consecutive issues of *Keystone Kapers*, the club's monthly publication. Freres continued,

There were about 20 kids in the club, and one of the things was that we would go to about 10 or 12 games a year and sit in the grandstand. After the games, Ernie and Gene would come up and talk to us for a while. It was a completely different era as far as how players and fans interacted. The first year Ernie was kind of quiet and let Gene do most of the talking, but as time went by you could see his personality coming out more and more. Ernie also appeared at my Little League banquet one year. He was very patient and kind with everyone. He talked to us individually like we were his friends. Years later, my son and I went to a Bulls game, and Ernie happened to be there. I hadn't seen him in 20 years. I took my son down and introduced myself, and told him who I was. He acted like he remembered me and was happy to see me again. I think he did that with everyone. But it made you feel good. It was certainly a highlight for my son.[10]

The good feelings didn't just occur naturally. Ernie obviously had a plan and an idea of what he wanted to become; he had an agenda. He worked on his public appeal and never turned down an opportunity to speak and interact with fans. Little League banquets, civic speeches, charity dinners, he did them all, often gratis. He made trips throughout the country on behalf of the Boys' Clubs of America. He talked to groups of high school dropouts about the importance of education. He gave baseball clinics for kids. And like his performance on the field, he never settled for a tired, haphazard appearance. He put his whole being into it each time.

"Ernie Banks may not be the best public speaker who will ever grace the platform of the Dubuque Sports of Sorts Club, but when a nicer guy comes along we want to be there," wrote the sports editor of the *Dubuque Telegraph-Herald* after a typical Ernie Banks performance at a father–son affair at the local American Legion. For more than an hour before and after, he shook hands with everyone who wanted to meet him and signed autographs "with a zestful approach that made each person feel that Ernie came just to see him."[11]

Ernie routinely signed everything stuck in his face, even to the point of suffering the barbs of his teammates waiting for him on the bus. "He was always gracious with the public, couldn't do enough for the fans," said infielder Jerry Kindall. "He was just always so accommodating and nice. Watching him, you wished you could be that nice to everybody, but it's really hard, even if you try. You know, sometimes you don't feel good or you had a bad day at the plate. But Ernie acted like he never had those days."[12]

With little natural skill at the start, Ernie had labored on his public speaking ability and honed his persona. Through trial and error, he developed his go-to expressions, which he then used liberally. In time, he became an entertaining and polished speaker, always upbeat and enthusiastic—damn glad to meet everyone. Fans walked away feeling that they not only knew the guy, but also knew him well. He was especially effective when speaking to youth groups. He told them, "When you work, work hard. When you play, play hard. When you pray, pray hard. And always tell the truth. That way you never have to remember what you said." When those words came from Ernie Banks, kids sat up and listened.

While his public appearances made Ernie fans one room at a time, the Chicago-area media made him fans by the thousands. The Cubs were one of the first teams to have all their games televised. A generation of kids rushed home from school each day trying to catch one or two Ernie Banks at-bats. An army of reporters followed the Cubs, but perhaps reconciled with years of losing, they were generally supportive, rarely got too personal, and were tolerant of the team's lack of success, possibly out of respect for the Wrigley family, possibly out of pity for the men trapped in the Wrigley clubhouse. When it came to Ernie Banks, they ate up his act. Ernie was on a first-name basis with the Chicago writers and many from out of town. He was always polite, always had time for them. He smothered them in clichés and platitudes, spoken with a smile. While he gave them not a whiff of personal info other than the tidbits he had parceled out years ago, they didn't seem to mind. They promoted his image and uniformly loved him, almost to the point where no one would dare say anything bad about him.

Whereas Ernie's social life began and ended with Gene Baker his first year, he gradually expanded his circle of friends and acquaintances, with people of all colors. He befriended several white sportswriters, and they introduced him around. He often seemed more comfortable and friendly with the members of the press who covered the team. At least they stuck around longer than players. He particularly developed a relationship with Jim Enright of the *Chicago American*.

The rotund, cigar-smoking Enright, who had campaigned in his paper for the Cubs to promote Baker and met Banks at the Pershing Hotel the day he signed, was a workmanlike sportswriter whose prose would never be confused with that of, say, Hemingway, although he did possibly introduce the phrase "March Madness" to the sports lexicon in a book about Illinois high school basketball. Enright, 21 years older than Ernie, was influential among the Chicago sporting press, contributed to the *Sporting News* and *Baseball Digest*, and worked as a college basketball referee in the winter. The two struck up a friendship that would last decades. It was not uncommon for Ernie to accompany Enright on trips to the Midwest during basketball season for games. "Almost painfully shy and completely withdrawn off the ball field," Enright explained Ernie to another reporter in 1958. "Everybody gets the same treatment until he warms up. . . . Actually, Ernie has a helluva sense of humor, in his own quiet way."[13]

Although he became more expansive to the press, Ernie remained modest to a fault. He was unable to say anything remotely self-promoting. When cornered, Ernie might admit that "things were going my way," when he had been blistering the ball, but that was all the chest-thumping he would do.

He deflected praise to teammates and peers in the league. After the 1960 All-Star Game in Kansas City, for example, when reporters crowded around Ernie and wanted to talk about the double and home run he hit to help the National League to a 5–3 win, Banks only conceded that it was a thrill, then quickly added, "But look at that Willie, how about the day he had? He was 3-for-4."[14]

"There is probably no other major-league star who minimizes and soft-pedals his achievements as Banks does," Jerry Holtzman wrote in 1958. "He almost never speaks about himself, especially when with a group. Ask him about hitting and he'll talk in surprisingly vivid detail of Stan Musial, Willie Mays, or Frank Thomas. He almost never mentions Ernie Banks."[15]

"It seems almost amazing that, in an era of highly paid, highly temperamental ballplayers, someone as outstanding as Ernie Banks should fail to acknowledge his own ability," noted a feature article in *Sport*.[16]

Ernie's reputation as a model citizen and humble hero further helped his appeal in an era when those traits were not only valued, but also the public appearance of such was almost necessary in heroes, from the Lone Ranger and Superman to Joe DiMaggio. Ernie had always done the right things. He had never had any public trouble and was a credit to the organization. He never complained about anything and was careful not to be trapped into an unpleasant quote. "Ernie was a master at handling the media," says pitcher Dick Ellsworth. Ellsworth further commented,

> In general, the media wants something controversial, something for a big story. But Ernie never gave them anything. Sometimes someone would ask a pointed question, something you knew was designed to get something negative or controversial. But Ernie always took the high road and looked at the positive of any situation.[17]

Part of Ernie's public image resulted from the need to protect himself from the onslaught of reporters. "Being such a superstar presents a problem for a natural and humble individual," says George Altman, a roommate and friend who played with Ernie from 1959 to 1962, and who shared many quiet talks. "I think Ernie changed his personality as a defensive mechanism. The demands for his attention became so great until he figured out that it would be less pressure if he controlled the conversation and mood."[18]

Ernie was first and foremost loyal to the cause. By the 1960 season, he had suffered through eight losing seasons, the best of which was the 74–80, fifth-place 1959 team. Ernie watched as the team brought in an endless parade of hotshot young pitchers, prematurely rushed to the majors, with the longevity of a county fair goldfish. No matter how many runs he knocked in, it was never enough. And yet he never uttered a discouraging word in public, no demands to be traded to a contender, no calling out teammates in the media after a tough loss, no harangues about inept front-office maneuvers—even as management bumbling kept the team irrelevant year after year, ruining his prime years. Ernie kept to the party line and did one better. He was happy to be there and couldn't imagine playing anywhere else, for any other owner, in any other city, on any other home field. And, even more impressive, he gave every indication he was sincere. It was even reported that Ernie chewed only Wrigley Spearmint gum during games—he was too perfect.

Every spring Ernie showed up predicting a pennant for the Cubs—trying to convince everyone else who knew differently that *this* was finally the year. He started making up rhymes for each year, for example, "The Cubs are gonna shine in '59." The press eagerly awaited the new season's proclamation, time-lier, yet significantly less accurate, than the groundhog's prediction of spring's arrival: "The Cubs are due in '62," "The Cubs will come alive in '65," "Wrigley Field will be heaven in '67," and "The Cubs will be great in '68." Sure, it wasn't Walt Whitman, but then Whitman could never hit a curve.

Black kids, growing up on the South Side of Chicago, had traditionally been White Sox fans. They knew without a doubt they were unwelcome on the North Side of the city, and that included Mr. Wrigley's ballpark. A trip on the "L" to Wrigley Field seemed like a trek to another country, full of foreboding and unknown danger. There had been little reason to make such a trip before. But suddenly, here was a guy on the home team who looked like them, who lived in their neighborhood, who was being cheered and celebrated more than anyone in town. And, just as important, he was doing it the right way. One of those kids, future ESPN journalist Michael Wilbon, later wrote of the local impact of Ernie Banks: "How thrilled my parents must have been that their sons' first athletic idol, Mr. Banks, was a man who embodied all the values they held dear: that he was decent and clean-cut back when that mattered, that he was approachable, downright sunny, a gentleman."[19]

Ernie's race was not insignificant in his popularity, and that, perhaps, made everyone feel even better. Many Midwestern white fans had never before had cause to cheer for a black man, or even met a black man for that matter. But Ernie was the perfect athlete to help bridge the gap. He was respectful of au-thority and nonthreatening at a time when the world increasingly seemed to be threatening. With his background, he represented what people wanted to believe about the American Dream, about hard work and patience, and being a good role model.

Ernie appeared genuinely thankful for the opportunities baseball had given him. "I can't begin to tell you what baseball has done for me," he said in a typi-cal pronouncement in 1960. "I've met so many wonderful people and had so many wonderful opportunities because I was lucky enough to make the grade in baseball. If it stopped tomorrow and I was washed up as a player, I'd have no complaints."[20]

Question: How could you not love the guy?

Sometime during the 1959 season, Ernie's nickname was unceremoniously changed from Bingo to Mr. Cub. It wasn't a sudden change, but rather a slow, inevitable realization that he had become the franchise ticket and much more. Enright appears to have originated the phrase, but little by little everyone in the press began using the new moniker. It fit.

Two other Ernie Banks trademarks emerged during this period: welcoming everyone to the friendly confines of beautiful Wrigley Field and the phrase "Let's play two." P. K. Wrigley had known for years that his team stunk, and his plan was to sell the ballpark experience, figuring fans would come out for a lovely day in the sun at the park if it provided for good family entertainment. If the team won, great; if they didn't, well, it was still a nice day to be at the park. Bert Wilson, the Cubs radio man from 1943 to 1955, loved to tell everyone, "It's a beautiful day at Wrigley Field," along with, "There isn't a bad seat in the house."[21] Perhaps Wilson originated the phrase, no doubt he was encouraged to use it by Wrigley, but regardless of the origins, which were definitely not Ernie's, Ernie picked it up and it became his standard greeting, even on those miserable days when the frigid wind blowing off Lake Michigan threatened to turn the ivy into frozen tundra.

Ernie's signature phrase, "Let's play two," would go on to become one of the most famous baseball quotes in history. The origin of this phrase is difficult to ascertain, especially since the originator, Mr. Banks, seemingly had no idea himself. Throughout the years, in response to the countless questions regarding the matter, Ernie gave at least four different stories relating to when the phrase first surfaced: 1) at the All-Star Game in 1960, in Kansas City; 2) July 1967, the first time the team started winning big; 3) Opening Day 1969; and 4) mid-season 1969, when the team was lagging and needed a pickup. As Ernie aged, number four became his preferred answer, perhaps because it felt and sounded better, and because the 1969 team and its fate became so legendary. But which one is correct?

Although in mid-1968, Ernie was quoted after a doubleheader at Wrigley as saying, "Great day to play three,"[22] an apparent play on his expression, there was little mention of "Let's Play Two" by the media until 1969, when everyone turned their thoughts to Ernie as the Cubs raced for the pennant. The phrase was printed often when writers praised Ernie upon his retirement, then exploded in print leading up to his Hall of Fame induction in 1977. Thereafter, the phrase was omnipresent. But it cannot be found in print before March 14, 1969. Two early season magazine articles, in *Jet* and *Sport*, mention the phrase, however, which easily eliminates numbers three and four from contention.

What about the memories of Ernie's contemporaries? Don Kaiser, who played with the Cubs from 1955 to 1957, says, "I don't recall him ever saying, 'Let's play two' while I was there. He was still pretty quiet around the guys then."[23]

Hobie Landrith, who played one season with the Cubs, 1956, remembers that Ernie would be particularly enthusiastic the day before doubleheaders. "Almost every time the day before a doubleheader he'd be running around to all the guys saying, 'Tomorrow's gonna be a long day, better bring your lunch,' with a big smile on his face." But there was no, "Let's play two."[24]

On the other hand, Jerry Kindall, who played with the Cubs from 1956 to 1961, distinctly remembers hearing Ernie say it while he was there. Moreover, one of Buck O'Neil's favorite stories involved Ernie and the phrase. O'Neil, who served as a Cubs coach from 1962 to 1965, told of one particularly hot day, usually placed in August 1962, when the Cubs were playing a doubleheader against Houston in old Colt Stadium. Ernie scurried about the place before the first game, proclaiming it to be a beautiful day and encouraging everyone to play two. Unfortunately for Ernie, the mind was willing, but the body was weak—he fainted in the sweltering Texas heat between games. After the game, O'Neil laughed, "Beautiful day Ernie?"

"They're all beautiful days, Buck." Ernie replied. "Just some days are more beautiful than others."[25]

George Altman, who played with the Cubs from 1959 to 1962, relates a similar story in Houston, most likely the same day, when Ernie passed out after uttering the phrase.[26] So this narrows the origin to sometime between 1957 and 1962. It is possible that Ernie did say it at the 1960 All-Star Game, or it is possible it just popped up and, liking the way it sounded, Ernie made it part of his routine without fanfare but later, amid continuous questions, felt there should have been a monumental first time.

Ernie Banks had achieved an exalted level of adoration in the city of Chicago, and the feeling of mutual love would only continue to grow. In late 1964, with Mr. Cub nearing the completion of his 10th full season with the team, P. K. Wrigley decided the time had come for a formal show of appreciation. August 15 was designated as Ernie Banks Day at Wrigley Field, the first such honor given to a Cubs player. There had been suggestions by the club in the past for similar events, but Ernie had always turned them down, stating he hadn't done enough yet. Now, closing in on 400 career home runs, feeling he had finally earned it, he agreed, provided that monetary proceeds from the day be dedicated to the underprivileged youth of Chicago.

No expense was spared in the planning—Wrigley said he wanted it to be "such a day in Ernie's life that he'll never forget it."[27] Some of Chicago's most prominent citizens were named to the Ernie Banks Day Planning Committee: the president of the Chicago Museum of Science and Industry, the president of the Serta Mattress Company, the president of Montgomery Ward and Company, the vice president of U.S. Steel, the president of Northwestern University, and the CEOs of several of Chicago's most prestigious banks and law firms.

Wendell Smith and James Enright represented the local media, and retired millionaire banker and personal Wrigley friend Phillip R. Clarke was the chairman of the committee.

Jack Brickhouse emceed the pregame ceremony. Ernie's father, wife, and twin sons, outfitted in matching Cubs uniforms with "14" on the back, were present with him on the field. More than 3,000 area Little Leaguers, clad in their own uniforms, ringed the infield and lined the outfield six and seven deep.

The Saturday afternoon Wrigley Field crowd of 20,000 was treated to an elaborate pageant of affection on the baseball field. Clarke told them, "We are saluting Ernie Banks with stirring words as not only one of the all-time greats of baseball, but as a great American." A procession followed, with adoring subjects offering their gifts to the royalty. The Cubs organization gave Ernie a ring containing 14 diamonds arranged in his uniform number, 14. A plaque was presented by National League president Warren Giles, and a framed commemorative front page was given by the *Sporting News*. There was a top-of-the-line 11-transistor, heavy-duty, Trans-Oceanic portable radio from WGN and a sterling silver tray inscribed "To Mr. Cub" from the players. Each of the Banks children was given a $50 savings bond from the Chicago chapter of the Baseball Writers Association of America. Ernie was presented with a new Dodge station wagon from the fans. Also, there was a five-foot cake decorated with bats and baseballs, and topped with a statue of Banks, along with a handmade card with 216 signatures from the Rehabilitation Institute of Chicago, where Ernie had visited almost two dozen times to cheer up patients. Fund-raising for the day came from the sale of 25 cent buttons and raised more than $5,000, which was given to the Better Boys Club of Chicago in Ernie's name.

After the gifts were presented, the man of the hour stepped in front of the microphone. Ernie told the crowd, "I want to thank God for making me an American and giving me the ability to be a Major League Baseball player."[28] The applause was deafening. It was definitely such a day that Ernie would never forget. The relationship between Ernie, the city of Chicago, and the Cubs had existed for more than a decade, but now it was formally consummated. Ernie even had the ring. No matter what the future brought, they would never be torn asunder.

8

THE OLD
COLLEGE EFFORT

The saga of the Chicago Cubs took a bizarre turn in January 1961, when P. K. Wrigley announced, in an unprecedented break with baseball tradition, the club would make their way through the coming season without a manager. Instead, they would employ a panel of coaches dividing their time between the Cubs and their minor-league farm teams, taking turns acting as head coach. The plan was given the ostentatious name the "College of Coaches."

Like all great ideas, and a lot of terrible ones as well, this was not a precipitous decision; the stage had been set for more than a decade. So many managers had jumped on and off the Cubs' carousel that vertigo was an occupational hazard. Charlie Grimm had started the 1949 season as Cubs manager. A member of the organization since beginning as a player in 1925, and manager since 1932, "Jolly Cholly" was a good-timer, liked by most. After a poor start in 1949, Grimm announced he'd had enough of managing and stepped down. Hall of Famer Frankie Frisch was brought in. Frisch was an irascible fellow, chronically dyspeptic because none of his charges could play the game nearly as well as he had. His team had little success and was let go in mid-season 1951.

Phil Cavarretta, Ernie Banks's first manager, then assumed the mantle. He lasted until just before the 1954 opener, when he was relieved due to intolerable honesty. The good-natured Stan Hack took over and made it through the 1956 season. Keeping to the time-honored owner playbook, Wrigley had replaced a tough guy with a nice guy, then went back to another tough guy, going to disciplinarian Bob Scheffing. Although the team appeared to be improving and Scheffing led them to a record of 74–80, and a fifth-place finish, their best season in seven years, he was fired after the 1959 season. The rumor among players was that his wife had said something at a team function, within earshot of Wrigley, about the poor level of talent on the team (this fact seemed to be apparent to everyone except Wrigley, but no one was allowed to say it publicly).

The year 1960 brought the Cubs management drama to new heights. Grimm, who in the meantime had mismanaged the great Milwaukee Braves of Aaron, Mathews, and Spahn out of a few pennants, took back the reins. After a 6–11 start, however, Wrigley made the startling move of trading Grimm to the broadcast booth for announcer Lou Boudreau. A knowledgeable baseball man, Boudreau could only forge a 54–83 record but was enthusiastic about the team's future with newcomers Ron Santo and Billy Williams in the lineup. Unfortunately, Boudreau had the audacity to express his desire for the security of a two-year contract, which was something Wrigley opposed as a matter of principle. They amicably agreed to part ways.

For those keeping score at home, that's seven managers in 11 years: five seventh-place teams, three eighth-place results (last), and zero first-division finishes. And Ernie Banks had played for five managers in the first seven years of his career.

This is when Wrigley decided to take the path less traveled—actually, never before or since traveled. Historians would later credit 32-year-old part-time backup catcher and coach Elvin Tappe, a Wrigley favorite, with the idea. While Tappe pleaded guilty to suggesting a panel of coaches, for unified teaching throughout the system, he would go to his grave denying he had anything to do with the lack of a major-league manager and the rotating head coach part of the plan. That, indeed, was P. K.'s baby.

Wrigley had always detested the term "manager." For years, he had referred to his chief of baseball operations (called general manager everywhere else) by anything *but* general manager. He went to great lengths to avoid the "m" word. He told the press he had looked up the word in the dictionary and the closest synonym was dictator. "We don't need a dictator," he stated.

"Since we've attempted just about everything else possible trying to improve our lot, I think the time has come to assemble the soldiers and sergeants before turning them over to a brand-new general."[1]

He explained he had tried "every type of manager, from inspirational leader to slave driver,"[2] and had come to the conclusion that no single manager would work. "Managers are expendable. I believe there should be relief managers just like relief pitchers."

Everyone on the executive team (surprise!) bought into the system and enthusiastically promoted it to the press. "We couldn't hire a Durocher or Stanky, although they're good baseball men," said vice president John Holland. "We didn't want the type of guy who wants it done his way or else. We needed harmony, men who can be overruled and not take it personally."[3]

According to Wrigley's plan, a rotating team of coaches would take turns being the "head coach." He did not offer, and apparently there was no set plan for, what the criteria would be for the selection of the head coach on any given day or when a change would be made. The College of Coaches for 1961 included Elvin Tappe, Harry Craft, Vedie Himsl, Rip Collins, Goldie Holt, Charlie Grimm, Verlon Walker, and Bobby Adams. Most had been long-term members of the Cubs system at various levels.

Predictably, Wrigley's project was met with skepticism. Armed with almost a century of well-established practice patterns, critics opened fire mercilessly and with much mirth. One wag suggested, "The Cubs have been playing without players for years. Now they're going to try it without a manager."[4] The coaches were called the "Enigmatic Eight," and the team was labeled the "Unmanagables." It was said the reason the Cubs went with eight coaches was so there would be more room to spread out the blame for their inevitable failure. Rumors circulated that Wrigley was going to install a rotisserie grill at Wrigley Field to keep the revolving coaches hot.

Once the season started, it didn't take long for everyone to learn that the College of Coaches was a disaster. Players, who had been skeptical from the start, rapidly found that the system was killing the team. There was a tremendous void of leadership—in the dugout and the clubhouse. Several of the coaches were good baseball men, but no one, absolutely no one, knew who was in charge.

Confused players were told one thing by one coach and the opposite by another. When the head coach changed, players didn't know where they stood with the new guy—their status changed without explanation or cause. The coaches became territorial and defensive; suspicious of undermining by others. Some coaches did nothing to help the current head coach, but merely watched until their turn came. Others openly stabbed their fellow coaches in the back.

The lack of leadership was especially evident when the team was on the road. There were loud whispers among the media that an absence of discipline among players was leading to excessive after-hours shenanigans (evidenced by the 40–37 home and 24–53 road records in 1961). "Nobody is going to want to be the tough guy who cracks the whip and becomes unpopular," said an unnamed former manager in a September 1961 *Sporting News* article entitled "Bruins' Teddy Bear Road Act Traced to Slipshod Discipline."[5]

With such a deficiency of direction from the top, an outspoken, forceful clubhouse leader among players would have been helpful. But the Cubs didn't have one of those either. "Ernie Banks was very quiet," pitcher Ed Bouchee said later, speaking of that season. "He was a good person to have around because he kept everybody loose, but he'd just go out there and want to play two games every day."[6]

That had been the lone negative charge against Ernie Banks for years. "If any attribute is missing from Banks's catalogue of baseball virtues, it is that of take-charge guy," Tom Siler wrote in the *Saturday Evening Post* in 1956. "He is not the holler type. His seemingly effortless style of play and his expressionless demeanor convey an impression almost of indifference. Banks rarely shows any emotion on the ball field or off it, for that matter."[7]

"Ernie Banks is the logical fellow to take charge of the infield, since he's the big guy on the ballclub," Scheffing had said in 1958. "But Ernie just doesn't do it. He isn't the assertive, aggressive type to take charge."[8]

"I never felt Ernie was the leader of the Cubs," said Dick Ellsworth years later. "I sensed that he didn't want to be. He was comfortable in his role, which was to play every day and drive in a lot of runs."[9]

There was a lot of private griping among players, who were unanimous in their disdain for the system, but few dared speak out in public due to P. K. Wrigley's well-known policy of tolerating no negative comments from his ranks. Ernie's response when questioned was typical and as expected. "I think it's wonderful," he said in April 1961. "All the fellows seem to enjoy it. All the coaches have been helpful in giving advice on hitting and fielding. I'm well satisfied. . . . We're going to do all right. Just wait and see."[10]

The one player who openly disagreed with the plan was fireplug second baseman Don Zimmer. On a radio interview with Lou Boudreau, Zimmer said the system was especially harmful to young players who were getting too much conflicting advice. Zimmer, previously on the protected list for the upcoming expansion draft, was soon made available and found himself a member of the New York Mets. Pitcher Don Cardwell, whose 15 wins topped the staff, commented to Holland at the end of the season that he didn't like the rotating coach system, and he was traded. The other players took notice and kept quiet.

Among the turmoil of the coaching situation, there were signs of hope for the future. Ron Santo had joined the team in June 1960. Santo was aggressive, confident, and obviously had a much brighter future than almost everyone else on the team. It showed and was resented by many. It was an era in which hazing of rookies was commonplace. "I was pretty well isolated," Santo later said of his first year. "To give you an idea, at breakfast nobody would sit with me. Nobody. The only guy who would talk to me was Ernie Banks."

Santo continued,

> I remember the first day I came to the big leagues, June 26. . . . I was sitting on the bench [before a doubleheader with the Pirates], and Ernie Banks was sitting next to me and he said to me in his joyful way, "Are you nervous?" I said, "Oh boy, am I nervous." He said, "Lookit, kid. Think of [Pirate pitchers] Bob Friend and Vernon Law as minor-league pitchers when you go to the plate."

Santo went 4-for-7, with five RBI, and the Cubs won both games. "That was the kind of person Ernie was. . . . That first year, Ernie Banks was tremendous to me. He was the only one."[11]

This was nothing unusual for Ernie. He was the unofficial welcoming party for the team. New players were often surprised at how friendly and approachable he was. "I was in awe of Ernie Banks when I joined the team late in 1964," says Don Kessinger. "I think all the young guys were just because of who he was and his stature, and what he had done in the game. And you found out very quickly that he was just a great guy, very relaxed, always optimistic. He immediately made the young guys feel welcome and a part of the team."[12]

One of those young guys was Lou Brock, a man with immense physical talent, who became a regular for the Cubs in 1962. Most observers felt Brock had been rushed to the big leagues by the Cubs, and he was almost ruined by the College of Coaches. One coach would tell him to swing for the fences, one would tell him to bunt more, one would give him the green light to steal, another would castigate him for being thrown out. And all of them confused him in the outfield.

Brock's one island of sanity was rooming with Ernie Banks on the road. Ernie tried to separate Brock from the stress that was eating him from the inside out. "The harder you try, Lou, the worse you're gonna get," he would say, adding,

> When you walk up to the plate, there's really only three factors involved: you, the pitcher, and the ball. Once the ball is released, there's only two factors: you and the ball. And hell, Lou, the ball is just a round, hard piece of horsehide, but you are a man with a bat in your hands and good eyes in your head. So whaddya mean, you can't hit Koufax?[13]

Coming from Ernie, it oddly made sense.

Left alone by coaches, Brock would eventually relax and turn into a Hall of Famer. Unfortunately for Cubs fans, that would not occur until after he was traded to the Cardinals in 1964.

In addition to the stress of the unorganized losing team, Ernie found a new frustrating experience in 1961. His body began to break down. During spring training, he was sidelined a week with a swollen left knee. He described it as a chronic ailment that had been aggravated. This surprised many team followers because he had never complained of knee problems before. It was referred to in the press as loose cartilage. At times, Ernie attributed it to an old football injury; other times he related it to an injury he sustained while in the army. He played on Opening Day, despite pain and swelling in the knee, and kept his consecutive-game streak alive. He received heat treatments and walked with a slight but noticeable limp for the first month of the season. Meanwhile, the team limped to a 5–21 start. Ernie was switched to left field on May 23—replaced at shortstop by Jerry Kindall—in a bid to take some pressure off his knee, which had become especially balky and painful on the quick starts and sudden turns required at short.

On June 16, Coach Elvin Tappe switched Ernie to first base. Before moving to first, Ernie had played 1,057 games at shortstop, 54 at third (a bad experiment in 1957), and 23 in left field. In his first game at first base, Ernie was knocked down in a collision with the Giants' Joey Amalfitano. Soon thereafter, he hurt his knee running into a box-seat wall chasing a foul ball.

Still Ernie refused to sit out a game, even an exhibition like the All-Star Game. Although Maury Wills was voted as the All-Star starting shortstop, Ernie showed up and played as a reserve.

Prior to the injury, Ernie had been one of baseball's iron men, playing in every game on the Cubs' schedule for six of his seven seasons. But the knee gradually worsened. Every time he bumped it or turned hard, it swelled again. He had it drained several times—the last time a pint of blood was taken off. Finally, with no relief in sight, he voluntarily removed himself from the lineup on June 23; his five-year, 717 consecutive-game streak was over, sadly within striking distance of Stan Musial's then-National League record of 805. Ernie told reporters the team doctor had said that there was no need for surgery at the time but that it could be seriously aggravated in its current weakened condition and then surgery would be required. Ernie sat a few more days, serving as an occasional pinch-hitter, and then he was back in the starting lineup.

Later in the 1961 season, it was revealed Ernie had also been battling a mysterious eye condition that affected his depth perception. Again, he had not complained, and the news was broken by the press. Ernie explained to questioning reporters that he had developed a blind spot in the left eye and often couldn't track the ball after it left the pitcher's hand. He termed it a Charley horse of the eyes. In an effort to compensate for the eye facing the pitcher, Ernie had changed his batting stance, opening it up to allow him to track the ball more with his right eye. He had been taking daily corrective exercises in hopes of improving—carrying a stethoscope-looking instrument on the road with him. The stereoscopic device, which cannot be found in any modern ophthalmology textbook, may or may not have helped, but Ernie felt it did and that was all that mattered.

Ernie struggled to the finish, playing in only 138 games, getting 80 RBI and 29 home runs. The home runs barely edged George Altman's 27 for the lead on the Cubs—the first time any teammate had been within 21 since 1956. It was a startling drop in production—the first time in five seasons he had less than 40 home runs and 100 RBI.

Ernie was officially moved to first base on a full-time basis for the first practice of the spring of 1962. The move was big news. Ernie had obliterated all previous standards for offensive production from a shortstop. While never considered to be a top-fielding shortstop—he was a few steps short in range and made fewer flashy plays than McMillan, Reese, Aparico, or Wills—Ernie had been reliable. In his last complete season at shortstop, 1960, he had led the league's shortstops in putouts, assists, double plays, and fielding percentage, and was rewarded with his only Gold Glove.

But playing shortstop was felt to be too much of a strain on his knees. The move to first would undoubtedly extend his career. While Ernie did not appear to be overjoyed at the idea (during the winter, when questioned, he had said, "I would rather play shortstop because I feel more natural there, but I'll play any position they want me to as long as it's somewhere in beautiful Wrigley Field"[14]), he accepted the move without complaint. His usual answer in the spring to the multitude of questions regarding how he liked first base was, "Fine, fine." The transfer across the infield at that stage of his career was a sign of Ernie's overall value to the team, the need to keep his bat in the lineup. Few shortstops had ever been worth keeping around without the benefit of their glove in the middle of the infield.

At 31 years old, Ernie's body suddenly seemed to be aging in dog years. Still, he played every exhibition game except one and kept in good spirits. As the only player in the Cubs lineup older than 29, he was now officially the old man of the team. The move to first base had an unforeseen consequence for the Cubs: They couldn't shut him up now. Whereas he had previously been quiet in the field at shortstop—to the point of never walking to the mound to talk to the pitcher unless others were there first—now he was a nonstop noisemaker, constantly yapping, to the pitcher, other infielders, baserunners, and the opposing team's dugout. He never stopped talking in the field.

In May 1962, Ernie was hit in the head by a Moe Drabowsky fastball and fell unconscious. He was carried off the field and spent two nights in a hospital with a concussion. Drabowsky, a former teammate, was distraught after the pitch and visited Ernie in the hospital to beg forgiveness, which was quickly bestowed. Ernie told reporters he was sure the pitch had been an accident, that he had seen it but just couldn't get out of the way in time. Ernie returned to the field three days later and smacked a double in his first at-bat, while wearing a helmet for the first time in his career. Then he hit three consecutive home runs. "You can call them headache homers," a smiling Banks told reporters after the game. "After hitting a double my head started aching again. So, in the third inning before I went to bat, I took a couple of aspirin . . . but my head still ached a little."[15]

The Cubs, meanwhile, were in pain throughout the year. The 1962 team fared worse than the year before: 59–103. Even more embarrassing, they trailed the first-year Houston Colt .45s by five games. Ernie rebounded to have a solid season, with 37 home runs and 104 RBI. But there was more trouble ahead, for Cubs fans and Ernie Banks.

Ernie played with the Kansas City Monarchs in 1950 and 1953. He missed the two seasons in between for Army duty. *Negro Leagues Baseball Museum*

The 1953 Kansas City Monarchs, champions of the Negro American League. Ernie is sixth from the right. Buck O'Neil is on the right end. *Negro Leagues Baseball Museum*

September, 1953. There is no sign of the character who would become Mr. Cub. His face says it all: apprehension and doubt. *National Baseball Hall of Fame and Museum*

Bingo and Bango; Ernie and Gene Baker. Baker was an invaluable companion and mentor for young Ernie Banks. *National Baseball Hall of Fame and Museum*

September 1953. Cubs manager Phil Cavaretta (center) is flanked by new arrivals Gene Baker (left) and Ernie Banks (right) and teammates. *National Baseball Hall of Fame and Museum*

Ernie towers over traditionally sized All-Star shortstop Pee Wee Reese. *National Baseball Hall of Fame and Museum*

Twenty-seven-year-old Ernie Banks on a visit to his hometown of Dallas in 1958. In a few years, he had transformed himself into a polished public speaker. *From the collections of the Texas/Dallas History and Archives Division, Dallas Public Library*

The National League MVP in 1958 and 1959, Ernie hit more home runs from 1955 to 1961 than anyone in baseball. *National Baseball Hall of Fame and Museum*

Ernie was reunited with Buck O'Neil in 1962, when O'Neil joined the Cubs coaching staff. O'Neil helped Ernie learn the finer points of playing first base. *Negro Leagues Baseball Museum*

Stan Musial checks Ernie's "Nice Guy" award for ticking, 1968. *National Baseball Hall of Fame and Museum*

Ernie flashes the famous Mr. Cub smile. *National Baseball Hall of Fame and Museum*

In 1972, Ernie was now a coach, but that didn't stop him from picking up a bat whenever he got the chance. *National Baseball Hall of Fame and Museum*

Ernie signs for a couple of lucky kids at Wrigley Field, 1962. *Courtesy Larry Davidson*

Schmoozing at Cubs Convention, 2003. *Courtesy Stephen Hullcranz*

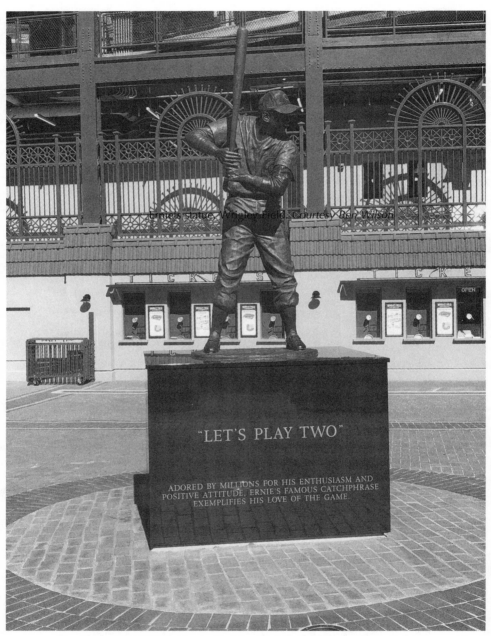

"LET'S PLAY TWO"

ADORED BY MILLIONS FOR HIS ENTHUSIASM AND
POSITIVE ATTITUDE, ERNIE'S FAMOUS CATCHPHRASE
EXEMPLIFIES HIS LOVE OF THE GAME.

Ernie's statue, Wrigley Field. *Courtesy Ben Wilson*

9

WINDMILLS

The young candidate woke up early; dressed sharply in a sports coat, white shirt, and pencil-thin brown tie; helped get his toddlers ready for day care; and set out for another day of campaigning. He walked through the frigid Chicago weather, ringing doorbells, shaking hands, and handing out literature. He made cold calls to businesses and school officials, chatting about taxes and juvenile delinquency and listening to suggestions about such concerns as blacktopping playgrounds and the need for a sewer at the corner of 83rd and St. Lawrence. He walked into a crowded pharmacy and introduced himself to the entire establishment. Few people gave him a second thought—just another guy stumping for election—until he said, "Hello, I'm Ernie Banks. I'd appreciate your support."

Ernie's success in baseball had opened doors and allowed him to meet with important people—to do things he could never have imagined 10 years earlier. Personally, he seemed determined to better himself and become a factor for change in society. Ernie had made more than 50 appearances speaking to juvenile groups in 1962. He proudly wore the title of head of 9,000 Boy Scouts on the South Side and spent many hours, eventually becoming a member of the board of directors, with the Better Boys Foundation, an organization sponsored by the Chicago business community that fought delinquency and encouraged boys to give up membership in gangs. He gave talks to high school dropouts to stress the importance of education. He took college classes in sociology, economics, and business at Northwestern and the University of Chicago. By all appearances, Ernie Banks was a man on the way up and a credit to his community.

Still, both the baseball and Chicago political worlds were stunned by the December 20, 1962, announcement that Ernie Banks, Chicago Cubs first baseman, was running for alderman of Chicago's Eighth Ward. While many former baseball players have had successful political careers—from local sheriff to U.S. senator—and active players often held such positions as deputy in the offseason in small towns back home, this was different. This was one of the best players in the game, still active, seeking a leading position in the second-largest city in the country.

While vacationing in California, Ernie had been contacted by an aid to U.S. senator Everett Dirkson, a powerful downstate Republican and the current Senate majority leader. Dirkson wanted to boost the meager total of Republicans in Chicago's City Council and thought Ernie's name recognition could compete with Democratic incumbent James A. Condon. Ernie appeared enthusiastic about the idea. "It's a wonderful opportunity," he said. "I don't consider myself a politician. All I want to do is help the people in my community."[1] Ernie noted that before officially registering, he had gotten consent from his primary employer. P. K. Wrigley had agreed, with the stipulation that the duties wouldn't interfere with baseball. Ernie proudly added that Mr. Wrigley had even contributed money to his campaign.

The Republicans soon double-crossed Ernie by backing another candidate, however, and let it be known that they hoped he would bow out gracefully. No reason was given publicly for the change of heart. "I don't understand this political game too well," Ernie said. "They try to strike you out before you even get a time at bat."[2]

But Ernie would not strike out looking. He liked the idea of becoming alderman and wanted to see it through; he stayed in the race as an independent. Banks maintained this was not a stunt. He stated he wanted to get into politics "to do everything in his power to help youth."[3] Ernie's motivation appeared to be entirely altruistic. He told reporters his goals were to combat juvenile delinquency, improve police protection, lower taxes, increase street lighting, and create more recreational programs for youth. He even promised to return his $10,000-a-year alderman salary to the ward to be used for improvements.

Despite Ernie's pronouncements, the media and political observers had a hard time taking his run seriously. The opportunity for baseball-mixed insults proved irresistible. John Baspar, in the *Chicago Daily Calumet*, said, "Ernie Banks should be right at home as alderman of the Eighth Ward. After all, the Cubs have been wards of around eighth place for some time."[4]

Benjamin (aka Duke, aka Big Cat) Lewis, a notorious alderman of the slum-ridden West Side 24th Ward, said, "He's a major-league ballplayer, but he's a minor leaguer as far as politics is concerned."[5]

The Honorable Richard J. Daley, the final word on any political conversation in the city, stated that Banks would finish the alderman race "somewhere in left field."[6]

Ernie Banks was indeed out of his league—and out in left field. He was honest and agreeable to everyone and reflexively avoided conflict—not exactly the type for Chicago city politics. Alderman, one of 50 men who formed the City Council and governed the city of 3 million, was a coveted position of power and influence that often brought both political and financial benefits. City Council meetings sometimes turned nasty and degenerated into shouting, threatening chaos. The risks to unwanted local candidates were real. Coercion, intimidation, and even beatings were not unknown for Chicago political wannabes. Benjamin Lewis, who flaunted an extravagant lifestyle that, according to reports, was much out of proportion to his known income, was found the morning after the 1963 election in his office, handcuffed to a chair with three close-range bullets fired into the back of his head. It is a crime that remains unsolved to this day. Chicago politics—not a business for the faint of heart.

Condon, an experienced politician, well aware of the impregnable Democratic organization of the ward, told reporters he was not worried. And he had good reason not to worry: He knew things that Ernie Banks, despite his local popularity and good intentions, did not.

Ernie knew absolutely nothing of true city politics; of everyone making a buck; of ward committeemen who plotted and planned the next decades' worth of candidates; of precinct captains who made sure the votes tallied out just right, one way or the other; of the multitude of city jobs handed out to keep the masses happy and votes coming; of other candidates who had worked years to get where they were politically—climbing the ranks of the party, starting at the bottom with the dirty work, getting out the votes, buying and selling tickets to the ward boss's golf outings and $25-a-plate dinners. Ernie knew none of these things, and worse for his chances, he had done none of the activities on the working-up-the-ranks-checklist that were a prerequisite for aldermen consideration.

Most likely, Ernie also knew little of the true power and invincibility of Richard J. Daley and his political machine, against which he would be competing. Daley, who as mayor presided over the City Council, had been mayor since 1955 and would hold the office until his death in 1976. By the early 1960s, the City Council was viewed as a rubber stamp for Daley proposals and had little actual influence on decisions. In fact, little occurred anywhere in the political arena of Chicago without Daley's express consent. Ernie couldn't even count on his own people for votes. Daley's machine, through deals, favors, and intimidation, controlled the black vote—which was usually counted on to come in at 95 percent or better for his candidates.

"We need someone with a little independence in this ward, someone who doesn't jump every time Daley says something," said one local businessman.

Ernie's campaign manager, the son of a local undertaker (insert your own symbolism), promised, "Ernie will be a vocal spokesman for all the people in the ward."[7]

These were nice sentiments, but an independent has a hard time winning an election for county clerk in Idaho. There was no chance against a veteran candidate backed by Daley, particularly in a ward like the Eighth, with its strong Democratic organization. A Chicago election board leader once said of independents' applications for election, "We throw their petitions up to the ceiling, and those that stick are good."[8]

By all appearances, Ernie knew none of these things. He seemed to actually believe he lived in an honest-to-goodness representative republic. He was an ideologue, a political neophyte who had no special interest group support, offered no one undue influence in exchange for votes, and didn't even have a sugar daddy. In other words, he never had a clue, or a chance. But that didn't stop him from trying; long odds were nothing new to Ernie Banks. Having no chance had never prevented him from showing up at the corner of Addison and Sheffield with a huge smile on his face and playing his heart out every day of every long, hopeless summer. He refused to acknowledge that anything other than good existed, in every person and every situation. He was a true-life Don Quixote de la Mancha, seeing the world not as it was, but as it should be, climbing aboard his trusted steed, ready to charge windmills to undo wrongs and bring justice to those in need.

"We're gonna win it," Ernie told a visiting reporter. "The Eighth Ward and the pennant."[9]

Ernie and his wife Eloyce had lived with their three-year-old twin boys, Joey and Jerry, and infant daughter, Jan, in the neighborhood for three years. Their house, a roomy brick two-story home with a front balcony and gabled attic on a corner lot, was bought in 1960 for $20,000. In earlier days, it had probably been the number-one house in the neighborhood. The young family lived comfortably, not lavishly, on a quiet, tree-lined street in the West Chesterfield section of Chatham on the South Side, about 12 miles from Wrigley Field. The population of 93,000 in the ward included 46,000 registered voters, 45 percent black, 55 percent white. It had originally been an all-white, mostly European neighborhood, but the whites had begun fleeing in the 1950s, and it was in the process of converting to a strongly middle-class African American area. Daley's successful strategy in such wards had to be to stick with the white alderman, like incumbent Condon, until a ward was almost 100 percent black, then bring in a black.

Campaign headquarters, on South Cottage Grove, had a big picture of Ernie in baseball uniform in the window. Above it a red and blue sign announced, "South Side Committee to Elect Ernie Banks Alderman, Eighth Ward." His campaign slogan was, "We need a slugger in City Hall."[10] Ernie averaged about four speeches a day while campaigning and told reporters he did not use a speechwriter, instead just talking about things he knew. He said he had consulted some political veterans and gotten advice in planning. While he eventually had a group of 65 volunteers, it was not nearly enough to cover the 83 precincts.

The election was February 28, the day before Ernie was scheduled to leave for spring training. "I'll be leaving for the Cubs spring training camp in Mesa, Arizona, Wednesday as alderman," he said cheerfully.[11]

But it was not to be. Ernie came in a distant third in the four-man race, with 2,028 votes. Condon had 9,296, while Republican Gerald Gibbons had 4,264. Coleman Holt, another independent, got 1,335. An Associated Press headline read, "Ernie Banks Strikes Out in First At-Bat in Politics."[12]

The results were not entirely disappointing, wrote Red Smith in his syndicated column: "Ernie Banks is the only ballplayer who ever finished a race higher than his team in the standings."[13]

Afterward, Ernie told reporters, "I learned a lot. I learned that those professional politicians are a lot tougher than the National League pitchers. Those boys don't leave much to chance."[14]

He added that he was not sorry he had tried and that he enjoyed meeting the public and discussing issues. There was one hurdle: "My toughest job was making these people believe I was serious. . . . When it came time for questions, most of the people asked about the Cubs."[15]

Ernie also commented, "It was an experience. Friends kept asking me, 'What do you want to get into politics for? It's a dirty game.' I had to tell them, 'The answer's easy, isn't it? If it's as dirty as all that, then we'd better try and get some decent people in it.'"[16]

Ernie initially said he was anxious to try his luck again in 1967, but he never did. In 1968, in answer to a writer's question, he said, "The only thing I'm running for is first base."

Years later, he would sum up his political career with, "My timing was a little bit off," but he added, "I don't regret doing it."[17]

The failed attempt at politics would not be the only frustration for Ernie Banks in 1963. Before the season, after two years of abject failure with the College of Coaches program, P. K. Wrigley struck again. He hired former U.S. Air Force colonel Robert Whitlow to run the team, giving him the working title athletic director of the Chicago Cubs. The 43-year-old Whitlow was a recently retired West Point graduate who had no baseball experience whatsoever. Yet, Wrigley announced he would be given complete control of the organization, at both the major-league and minor-league levels. The story that accompanied his hiring was that he had stopped by the Wrigley Building to visit an old friend, a nephew of P. K.'s, and somehow met the big guy and talked himself into a job. In any other organization, the story would have been difficult to believe, but with the Cubs, somehow it passed without much question.

An unimaginative man with a likable smile, Whitlow announced in the pre-season, "We're going to win a few, lose a few, and there will be some games rained out." He also told reporters he thought the Cubs had a chance to "take all the marbles."[18] Whitlow stated that he had been reading up on stamina tests and quick-energy release foods, and would make appropriate training changes for the team. Also, positive thinking only would be tolerated for the organization, and the word "fear" would be struck from the organization's vocabulary.

Initially, there was a positive move, as Whitlow and Wrigley decided to stick with one man, Bob Kennedy, as head coach for the entire 1963 season, abandoning the much-hated rotating-head-guy scheme. But players quickly became annoyed by the inexperienced Whitlow and his attempts to treat them like a bunch of college kids or military recruits. They especially resented the formal, lined-up calisthenics and jumping jacks in spring training, led by the colonel himself in uniform.

Ernie, as usual, predicted big things from the 1963 Cubs. While appreciating the hopefulness, teammates sometimes were left to ponder how he could remain so upbeat in the face of constant failure. "Ernie was always so optimistic, it was unbelievable," says pitcher Lindy McDaniel, who joined the Cubs before the 1963 season. McDaniel elaborated,

> It was always win one game in a row and now we're going to win the pennant. You wondered how he could be that way all the time, knowing how bad the team was. My first spring with the club, the manager, Bob Kennedy, held a meeting, and he got a rookie to stand up and he told us to all get a good look at this kid. He said that the last time the Cubs had finished in the first division, this kid wasn't even born yet. That's how bad things were there.
>
> But Ernie kept thinking things would turn around any day. I remember talking to him one day in the outfield before a game, and he just couldn't understand why

we couldn't win. I was surprised—I thought everybody knew. You know, Mr. Wrigley wouldn't spend a lot of money to go out and get players. We just never had enough good players. It takes 25 men to win. I said, "Ernie, we have some good players, but not enough." But he honestly didn't know why we weren't winning. He actually expected to win.[19]

The Cubs responded to the single manager with a record of 82–80, the first time they had broken even in a decade. Things were looking up for the team, as Billy Williams and Ron Santo were maturing into All-Stars, second-year man Ken Hubbs proved to be one of the best second basemen in the league, and the pitching staff was solid with Dick Ellsworth winning 22 games and getting help from starters Bob Buhl and Larry Jackson and relievers Lindy McDaniel and Don Elston. The team drew 980,000 fans, just short of reaching 1 million for the first time in Ernie's career.

But Ernie Banks did not share in the warm glow of helping his team break .500. Instead, he was saddened and frustrated by wondering what might have been of the team's chances—six more wins would have put them in third place—if he had turned in a typical Ernie Banks effort. Instead, he suffered through the worst season of his career—an endless procession of slumps and physical ailments. As late as June, he was still struggling to keep his batting average above .200. For the first time anyone could remember, teams began pitching to him with runners on base, even as he hit fifth in the lineup with only light hitters following him.

Ernie was encouraged in June, when he hit five home runs in a seven-game span. Three came against the Dodgers on June 9 (the first two off Sandy Koufax), the fourth time in his career he had hit three in a game. Unfortunately, that was to be the high point of his year. He was soon mired in another slump, this one even worse than the last. Amazingly for Banks, he would not hit a home run at Wrigley Field after June 19.

Reporters and fans alike continually asked, "What's wrong with Ernie Banks?" It was openly speculated that his career was coming to an end. On July 27, he was removed for a pinch-hitter for the first time in his career—Bob Kennedy pulled Ernie from the on-deck circle and sent up left-hander Merritt Ranew when the opposing manager brought in a righty. There were a few boos from the Wrigley crowd, then a hush as Ernie strolled back to the dugout, halfheartedly swinging his bat.

Other than the badly bruised right knee, which caused him to limp at times, Ernie denied there was anything physically wrong throughout the year, but he lost weight, didn't have an appetite, and appeared listless. For the first time anyone could remember, Ernie was down mentally. He later admitted that for the duration of the summer, he feared that he had leukemia—thinking of Syracuse Heisman-winning running back Ernie Davis, who had recently died of the disease. In early August, with only two home runs in his last 38 games and a season's batting average of .226, Ernie entered Wesley Memorial Hospital, a teaching hospital of Northwestern University, for a thorough checkup. He missed eight games while tests were being run, but everything returned negative. After the season, Wrigley would pay to send him to the Mayo Clinic in Rochester, Minnesota, for another week of tests. The only thing doctors found was evidence of a viral infection they termed subclinical mumps. They prescribed nothing more than rest during the offseason.

Ernie finished the season hitting a miserable .227, with only 18 home runs and 65 RBI. "I was tired all the time," he said during the winter. Banks continued,

> And I realized there was something wrong with me. I desperately wanted to do something to help them [the team], and I couldn't do it sitting on the bench. . . . I do know that I was a disappointment to the Cubs and myself. They had a great season, and I wasn't a part of it. . . . I know I tried to force myself beyond my physical capacity and that didn't help either.[20]

It was also revealed that Ernie's wife had major surgery and extended hospitalization in May, and at one point there was concern for her life, which also affected his state of mind.

Ernie was only 32 years old, but the sharp decline in production during the past two years had been as startling as his early success. In a show of confidence, Wrigley presented Ernie with a contract for 1964, at the same salary as 1963, when he returned from the Mayo Clinic, refusing to cut his pay, as was customary at the time after a bad season. Ernie recovered and bounced back to play in 157 games in 1964 and 163 in 1965, hitting 23 and 28 home runs, with 95 and 106 RBI, respectively. He was good but no longer an automatic All-Star selection and no longer on the short list of the best in the game. The Cubs, meanwhile, returned to their usual ways with two-straight losing seasons, eighth-place finishes both years.

As the 1965 season ended, Cubs players didn't realize it, but the days of summer slumber, monotonous mediocrity, and quiet acquiescence to losing were over. A storm was about to descend on Chicago—a noisy, blustery, lippy storm. And Mr. Cub would need all his powers of patience and optimism because the storm was headed directly for him.

10

LEO FEROCIOUS

The Cubs shocked the baseball world on October 26, 1965, when they announced the hiring of Leo Durocher to run the team. Robert Whitlow had resigned in January 1965, saying he was never taken seriously by baseball men throughout the league (surprise!), and Kennedy had been replaced by Lou Klein during the 1965 season. But the free fall continued as the team lost 90 games. Wrigley and company felt the time had come for a new management plan.

Durocher was a baseball legend, an oversized caricature who dominated every scene by sheer force of personality. His baseball career had started with the Yankees of the late 1920s, where as a hustling, good-field-poor-hit shortstop, he famously had trouble getting along with Babe Ruth, who called him the "All-American out." And he either did or did not steal the Babe's watch, depending on whose version you're willing to believe. As a manager, Leo had taken over losing teams in Brooklyn and New York, and turned both into pennant-winners.

Leo Durocher was a master of the dark arts of baseball. Flinging dirt in infielders' faces, kicking balls out of their gloves, stealing signs, beanballs, intimidation—nothing was too much if it helped him win a game. He would say virtually anything on or off the field to give his team an edge. When he yelled to his pitcher from the dugout, "Stick one in his ear," no one doubted he meant it with all his heart.

No fan of sportsmanship, Durocher said, "Show me a good loser in professional sports, and I'll show you an idiot." And, "I believe in rules. Sure I do, if there weren't any rules, how could you break them?" He wanted "scratching, diving, hungry ballplayers who come to kill you," on his team. He freely admitted

---

111

that if his mother was rounding third with the winning run he would trip her—but he did offer that he would pick the old lady up and brush her off afterward.[1]

Durocher was a Jekyll and Hyde. He could be a soft-spoken gentleman with polish and charm, a clear-thinking, intelligent, glad-handing life-of-the-party. But flip a switch and he was a rude, impulsive, cussing, gambling tyrant. Learning at an early age that yelling was the way for him to get the upper hand in life, he had an explosive temper that begged for anger management therapy. Branch Rickey had famously said Durocher "had an infinite capacity for making a bad situation worse."[2]

But few managers could get more out of a ball club than Durocher. He knew baseball, and he knew how to win. Possessing a voice with the commanding ring of a marine drill sergeant and a snarl savage enough to give even the toughest of badasses pause, Leo had the ability to captivate a group of men and enforce his will. Brutally frank and decisive, if the square-jawed, steely-eyed Durocher ever had a doubt about anything he did, it never showed. Confidence exuded from his pores and enveloped him like a bad cologne. He was absolutely certain deep in his heart that there was no man whom he couldn't bluff out of a pot while holding a handful of nothing, and there was no dame he couldn't talk out of her pants with a few well-chosen words and a fistful of charm.

It took a certain toughness of character, and luck, to be able to play ball for Leo. His past was littered with the carcasses of players for whom he had no use, men he had broken. He loved letting his team know that no one's job was secure. His favorite expression was to "back up the truck," as in loading up the unwanted players and carting them away.

Although he had not managed a baseball team since 1955, the 59-year-old Durocher was still very much a dynamic, forceful, dominating personality. He had remained in the public eye by coaching with the Dodgers, expounding on televised games and being a general celebrity. He was perhaps the only man who could boast of achieving the 1960s cultural trifecta of appearing on the *Mr. Ed*, *Munsters*, and *Beverly Hillbillies* television shows (as himself, of course). When Fred Flintstone was wooed by a tough-talking big-league manager named Leo Ferocious of the Boulder City Giants, there was little doubt who the cartoon character represented.

After years of sitting on the sidelines, Leo was ready. His impact on Chicago was both immediate and seismic. At the introductory press conference, someone asked what Leo's title would be since the mimeographed announcement handed out avoided defining it. In fact, the announcement included this bit of Wrigley-ism: "We have found from long experience that it doesn't make any difference what title a team leader has as long as he has the ability to take charge."

Leo was having none of that. "If no announcement has been made of what my title is, I'm making it here and now," his voice boomed. "I'm the manager. I'm not a head coach. I'm the manager. . . . One man has to be in complete authority. There can be only one boss."[3] And just in case anyone was wondering, Leo informed them, "I'm not a nice guy. I'm still the same SOB I always was."[4]

Leo's arrival signaled a significant change for P. K. Wrigley: a reversal in his thinking in terms of the operation of his ball club. Not only was the salary, north of $50,000 a year, the most money he had ever paid a manager, but also the three-year deal marked the first time he had given anyone anything other than a single-year agreement. It also meant the elimination of the all-coach system and the introduction of a strongman to the picture—something P. K. had assiduously avoided in the past. The man who famously disliked the term "manager" was now firmly in the manager sweepstakes.

Leo set the tone immediately with his first speech to the team in spring training. In no uncertain terms, he let the entire club know that he was the man. Period. There would be no doubt about where to go in the future for any problems or questions. He summed up by saying he wasn't there to win any popularity contests and that Mr. Wrigley did not hire him to lose. He also added, just in case anyone hadn't gotten the memo, that no one's job was secure.

Then Leo set about making sure everyone got the point. He jumped on longtime clubhouse man Yosh Kawano for not having certain things ready for the players. Then he loudly prevented Charlie Grimm from coming in the clubhouse—he wanted no interference and no bad vibes from previous failures.

Next, he turned his wrath on Ernie Banks—something no one had ever done before. He nagged incessantly about little things, like throwing the ball back to the pitcher without tagging a runner on a pickoff throw: "Dammit, when the pitcher throws the ball to you, I don't want you to throw it right back to the pitcher. I want you to tag the runner at first. I don't give a shit if he is standing on the base or not."[5] He quickly added complaints about Ernie not taking a big enough lead as a baserunner.

This was standard operating procedure from the Leo Durocher manual. He was making a statement, installing a Leo the Lip–type attitude. In getting on the senior clubhouse man, the senior management person, and the senior player, Leo was letting everyone know that he was indisputably the alpha male.

But in publicly chastising Ernie Banks there was also a more sinister motive. "Pitching, defense, and speed, that's the kind of ballclub I like," Leo had told the media before the season. "And that's what I'm going to be working toward with the Cubs. Hit-and-run, bunt, steal. You can't win with those big, slow-footed guys even if they do hit one out of the park for you once in a while."[6] Shortly after taking over the Giants in 1949, as part of his master plan to produce two pennants and a world championship in five years, Leo traded 30-something-year-old All-Star sluggers Johnny Mize and Walker Cooper—less than two years removed from combining for 86 home runs—peddling them to open space on the team for the kind of guys he liked. He wanted to do something similar in Chicago, and there was one obvious, slow-footed target who could no longer run, bunt, or steal: Mr. Cub.

Initially, Durocher had said, "As for Banks, he comes with the franchise, and I'm glad to have him on my side for a change."[7] But anyone with even remote knowledge of the game could see Leo had other plans for Banks. He talked of trading him to the Giants for Orlando Cepeda but quickly learned what every other manager, director of player personnel, and general manager had learned: The chances of P. K. Wrigley agreeing to any trade involving Ernie Banks depended entirely on the weather—just in case hell *did* freeze over.

Since Leo could not trade Ernie, he did the next best thing: He began to plot a way to shame him off the field. Leo was merciless in pointing out Ernie's deficiencies, both to Ernie and, more embarrassingly, the rest of the team and the press. He constantly harped on the lack of speed and publicly called him a "rally killer."

"Mr. Cub, my ass," became one of his pet phrases, often snorted in loud disgust after Banks made an out, or when he told reporters, "Mr. Cub, my ass. I'll give Mr. Cub $100 anytime he even attempts to steal second."[8]

Cubs players knew what Leo was trying to do. Pitcher Fergie Jenkins later wrote,

> One thing that drove Durocher nuts was that, at that point in Ernie's career, when he was 35 or 36 years old, you didn't have to be Einstein to know he wasn't going to steal any bases. So Ernie took tiny leads off first base, like three inches. He wasn't going to steal, and he sure as heck wasn't going to let himself get picked off. Durocher screamed to the first-base coach, "Get him off! Get him off!" Meaning he wanted him to make Ernie take a bigger lead. . . . That went on the whole year. The rest of us, sitting on the bench, watching and listening, just wanted to turn to Leo and say, "Give it a rest." But nobody did that. Ernie was just the greatest guy. . . . Durocher seemed to be the only person on planet Earth who had trouble getting along with Ernie Banks.[9]

While Leo later grudgingly conceded that Ernie had been a great player in his time, "Unfortunately, his time wasn't my time," he wrote. Durocher continued,

> He couldn't run, he couldn't field. . . . As a player, by the time I got there, there was nothing wrong with Ernie that two new knees wouldn't have cured. He'd

come up with men on the bases, and if he hit a ground ball they could walk through the double play. . . . I've got to have somebody there who can play. Balls are going by there this far that should be outs or double plays. . . . But I had to play him. Had to play the man or there would have been a revolution in the street. Ernie Banks owns Chicago.[10]

Ernie Banks owning Chicago seemed to be significant. "It was just that Ernie was too big a name in Chicago to suit Durocher," wrote Jack Brickhouse, who, like most media members in Chicago, came to despise Leo. "I am positive Leo objected to Ernie's tremendous popularity with the fans. He did his best, I felt, to break down Ernie's spirit, but no man can break a spirit like that."[11]

In Leo's defense, inheriting an aging star is one of the least pleasant tasks for a new manager—a political quicksand for any polite leader concerned with social etiquette. And Leo was never accused of politeness or social etiquette. Also, Leo loved to play amateur psychologist. He was making a statement to the entire team that no one was above reproach.

A conflict between the two had been inevitable. In the course of human events, rarely have two more disparate people been thrust together by circumstances. It was smiling Ernie Banks, the perpetual line drive of sunshine, who searched for the good in every situation, even when there was none to be found, versus Leo Durocher, the consummate tough-talking, rule-bending wise guy, who never hesitated to break any person in his way and often went out of his way to break people just for the hell of it. Leo's professional life seemed to be dedicated to his self-promoted motto, "Nice guys finish last." And Ernie Banks was universally acknowledged as one of baseball's nice guys.

Leo was a walking camera magnet. While he hated media personnel individually, he loved having a microphone in his face or a photographer nearby. He created stories where there were none. Ernie, on the other hand, could not be forced to talk about himself by any means. By the mid-1960s, Ernie had perfected a smiling two-step whenever a writer got too close: "Thank you, thank you, it's a beautiful day for baseball here at the friendly confines," he would say, while walking the writer to the other side of the clubhouse. "And the guys you want to talk to are right here, Donnie Kessinger and Glenn Beckert, two of the next stars, the best young double play combo in baseball." And when the writer turned around, Ernie would have vanished. It was a polished, seemingly effortless move and always left Ernie looking like a good guy, while both giving the young players some exposure and saving Ernie from any prying questions.

While Leo was known to nurse grudges for three and four decades that had started over impossibly trivial transgressions, Ernie allowed monumental slights to roll off his back like raindrops off an infield tarp. Whereas Leo spent a lifetime refining how to get what he wanted by climbing in faces and forcing uncomfortable situations, Ernie was a perpetual conflict-avoidance seminar. He was constitutionally, almost pathologically, unable to have a forceful face-to-face disagreement with another human being. Typical was the time Ron Santo, frustrated the day after another in a string of losses, entered the clubhouse and flew into a rage. Ernie pleaded with him, saying, "Don't let the past influence the present."

Santo turned on Banks and exploded, yelling, "What the hell's wrong with you? You like losing?"

Ernie merely walked away while saying something about it being a lovely day—the fact that it was cloudy and drizzling at the time did not matter—and that it was time to "beat the Pirates, beat the Pirates."[12] That day, the Cubs did beat the Pirates, winning 8–4, and Ernie's two doubles and Santo's home run accounted for four RBI.

Whereas Ernie almost never lost his temper and rarely said a foul word, Durocher was a volcano whose vocabulary of four-letter words was encyclopedic. He routinely used every vile invective and slur against both opponents and his own players. Jews were Kikes, Italians were Dagos, and blacks were, well, called much worse. And according to the grammatical rules Leo preferred, the slurs were most often used as adjectives, surrounded by other less-than-endearing terms, for example, when he often referred to Cubs pitcher Ken Holtzman—to his face and in front of teammates—as a "gutless Kike bastard."

In early 1966, Leo told Ernie, "I can trade you if I like. And don't be surprised if your black ass is moving out one of these days."[13]

Some have suggested race as a factor in Leo's treatment of Ernie, but it could not be accurately said that Leo was a racist. He was an equal-opportunity hater. He despised everyone—regardless of race, religion, or belief—who stood between him and victory. He had taken a stand for Jackie Robinson during Jackie's first spring with the Dodgers, saying at a late-night meeting of the team, "I'll play an elephant if he can do the job, and to make room for him I'll send my own brother home."[14] With the Giants, he had helped ease Monte Irvin and Hank Thompson into the clubhouse, and he had been a father figure to Willie Mays, who adored him.

But whatever the reason, Leo never let up on Ernie. In mid-May, with the 35-year-old Banks hitting .188, Leo pounced on his opportunity. The Cubs traded pitcher Ted Abernathy to the Braves for first baseman-outfielder Lee Thomas. "I'm going to give him [Thomas] every chance to play regularly at first base," Durocher told the press. "Ernie Banks hasn't done it for me, so I'm going to give Lee every chance to show me."[15] Initially, Durocher moved Santo to shortstop and Ernie to third, and put Thomas at first—an experiment that lasted four days and weakened all three positions. Then he benched Ernie outright.

By June 1, Ernie was back as the regular first baseman, and he launched an eight-game hitting streak. On June 11, the old man legged out three triples in a game—all pokes to right field. But the good times didn't last. A month later, Ernie was on the bench again. This time Durocher announced that the first-base job had been given to 25-year-old John Boccabella, who had hit 30 homers in the minors in 1965. With the Cubs locked in the cellar, Durocher added, "The future of this team has to be with the young fellows."

Edgar Munzel wrote that Banks took the news with "impeccably good grace. He has the unfailing gift of always saying the right thing." Ernie told reporters, "There comes a time in every player's life when he must face up to this sort of thing. As we get older, we have to make way for the younger players. . . . I won't say it doesn't hurt because it definitely does; however, I simply have to adjust to it."[16]

"Ernie was such a gentleman despite the way Leo Durocher treated him," says Lee Thomas. Added Thomas,

> When I came in, I was in awe of Ernie. You had to respect all those homers he had hit. He was a great player, and by that time, everyone knew he was going to be in the Hall of Fame. And he was just an incredibly nice guy. Even though the papers said I was coming to take his job, he showed no hard feelings. He welcomed me to the team. We ended up playing quite a few card games together. The way he treated people—you had to love the guy. But Leo really treated him badly. He would ignore him; he wouldn't play him. Sometimes he would say things in front of the team or in the papers. It bothered me, and I know the other players didn't like it either. But Ernie was always upbeat. Every day.[17]

"The stuff with Leo did hurt Ernie," says shortstop Don Kessinger, who continued,

> He might have acted like it didn't, but it hurt him a lot. Ernie wanted to please. He wanted people to know he played hard. And he did. Ernie was never a guy to come in and throw a helmet, but some people mistake that for meaning he didn't play hard or didn't care as much as someone who does that stuff. I think Leo misread Ernie from the start. You have to remember they were two very different people.[18]

Contrary to superficial appearances, Ernie proved to be Leo's equal or better in terms of tenacity. As per his custom, he played the long game; content to absorb short-term defeats, he ignored some insults and swallowed a little pride, confident that in the end he would prove victorious by taking the high road. Reporters, knowing what he was going through, continually hoped for a juicy quote from Ernie on the subject—to fill column space and create controversy. They continually dangled the lure, but Ernie refused to nibble. "Leo Durocher is the greatest manager I've ever seen," became Ernie's standard answer to questions, inserted into interviews so often that nearby teammates would snicker when they heard it.

"Kill 'em with kindness," Ernie said in 2014. "I'd sit by him in the dugout, on the plane, in the dressing room."[19] And always with a smile on his face.

Time and again, before the last shovelful of dirt could be tossed on his grave, Ernie came back. Inserted in the lineup after Boccabella failed to produce, he finally started hitting like Ernie Banks. From the All-Star Game to August 11, during a five-week period, he hit .359 (37–103). He ended the season with 15 home runs, 75 RBI, and a .272 batting average.

The Cubs, meanwhile, fought through another miserable season. They finished in last place in the 10-team National League with a record of 59–103. But it has been said that the 1966 Cubs were perhaps the most promising 100-loss team in history. There were plenty of encouraging signs. Twenty-one-year-old left-hander Ken Holtzman was 11–16. The young keystone combo of Glenn Beckert and Don Kessinger improved throughout the year. And the team had picked up catcher Randy Hundley, as well as pitchers Bill Hands and Fergie Jenkins, in trades. Along with holdovers Ernie Banks, Ron Santo, and Billy Williams, the seeds were planted for success.

"The year 1966 was a long, long year," says Kessinger. "But we knew we were building something for the future. We felt good about the team. We could see we would be good very soon. So, it was an exciting time to know we were going to be a part of something special."

Good times, and heartache, were coming.

11

RESPECT

Throughout the offseason Leo Durocher repeated that he was sticking with the youth movement and that John Boccabella would be given a full shot at first base. At one ceremony, Durocher called Ernie Banks "Grandpa." Liking the sound of that, he used the term liberally the rest of the winter.

Leo also came up with a new strategy to deal with Mr. Cub. On February 28, 1967, it was announced that Ernie had been named to the Cubs coaching staff. Leo stated that he would do a " lot of playing for us, the only difference is that Ernie now will be able to teach our kids. He'll have as much authority as any of the other four coaches."[1]

The move was a complete surprise, and the new coach seemed as surprised as anyone (Durocher admitted Ernie hadn't been consulted until 9:30 a.m. the morning of the announcement). Behind the grand proclamation, handshakes, and congratulations, it didn't take much analysis to see the meaning: Durocher was trying to push Ernie off the field—since he couldn't trade him and failed to shame him into leaving, maybe he could make him retire comfortably by giving him other duties. Durocher, of course, publicly stated this shouldn't be construed as a move to end Banks's playing career. He emphasized that Ernie still had a chance to fight for playing time, but his tone left little doubt that the first-base job was Boccabella's to lose. For his part, Ernie smiled, noted that he would become just the fourth African American major-league coach (after Buck O'Neil, Gene Baker, and Junior Gilliam), and said, "It's all very gratifying."[2]

The exhibition season opened with Ernie sitting on the bench while every other regular from 1966 was in the lineup. Leo proceeded to play Boccabella, Clarence Jones, Norm Gigon, and Lee Thomas at first base the next month, while feeding rumors of other first-base candidates being brought in by trades. Ernie didn't get any regular playing time until about 10 days before training camp was over.

Leo reacted angrily when writers suggested Banks was being ignored. "Why don't you knock off that Mr. Cub stuff?" he snarled. "The guy's wearing out. He can't go on forever."[3]

When Ernie continued to hit ropes in the batting cage, Leo acted like he didn't notice and instead raved about the young prospects at first base. It became a running gag in the press box whenever Banks hit a home run or knocked in a key run: "Do you think Durocher will acknowledge that?"[4]

Despite the near-daily criticism and suggestions he was through, the 36-year-old Banks seemed exactly the same to observers. He never let on that it was anything other than a typical, glorious spring camp in the Arizona sun. He showed up every day with a smile on his face, singing to the pregame music, welcoming one and all to the ballpark, and cheering on opposing teams in their warm-ups. Then he got into the cage and flicked line drives with his still-magnificent wrists.

Near the end of the exhibition season, with Ernie hitting .419, Leo conceded that the first-base job probably belonged to the old-timer. The press loved the fact that Ernie had proven Leo wrong by beating out the young challengers. Ernie never let on, but he had worked hard for the victory. Determined to bounce back from his disappointing 1966 season, he had begun intensive workouts in January at the Southtown YMCA, exercising two or three hours at a time, running, playing handball, and going through calisthenics. Then he arrived in camp a week ahead of everyone else and continued the regimen. Never one to gain too much offseason weight, Ernie had lost almost 10 pounds, back to his playing weight of the 1950s.

The Cubs got off to their best start in 10 years and were soon the talk of the major leagues. And Ernie Banks was one of the main reasons. He hit safely in each of the first seven games. In May, he began driving in runs in bunches. Except for two second games of doubleheaders (he played both games in six others), Ernie was on the lineup card every day from April 28 to June 20. He hit .315, with 14 home runs and 42 RBI in his first 61 games.

Teams once again learned there was a price to pay for not respecting Mr. Banks. June 9, in the bottom of the ninth inning at Wrigley Field, the Cubs had two on and one out in a 5–5 game against the Mets. The New York manager ordered his right-handed pitcher to walk left-handed Lee Thomas to load the bases to face Ernie, who then lined a game-winning single to left field. Ernie carried a .300 average into the All-Star break and was picked as a reserve by Walt Alston.

In late May, the Cubs were 18–15 (they had lost 42 times in 1966, before winning their 18th game), but instead of fading, as was the team tradition, they got better. A June spurt of 14 wins in 15 games moved them to 17 over .500 (46–29). Suddenly, people started noticing that something was up in the Windy City aside from crime and cholesterol levels. Chicago was buzzing for baseball on the North Side; fans began turning out with an enthusiasm that hadn't been seen in a generation. Actual traffic jams occurred outside Wrigley Field on game days. Cub players were now mobbed as they walked to their parking lot across Waveland Avenue beyond the left-field fence. There was free access to players and little security because, quite frankly, it had never been needed before—no one had cared. Now, they were rock stars.

The change was startling in its abruptness. "In 1966, when I came up at the end of the season, there were so few people in the park for some of those week-day afternoon games that you could see all the vendors, but it was hard to see any fans," says pitcher Rich Nye. He continued,

> You just saw rows and rows of empty seats. But all of the sudden, 1967 was exciting. Every day you came to the ballpark and people were already lined up around the stadium, waiting to get general admission tickets. The bleacher bums were starting to get famous. They would respond to cheers and things the guys in the bullpen would do to get them fired up. The whole atmosphere of the park changed. It was electric.[5]

On July 1, the Cubs beat the Reds in front of a full house at Wrigley Field to move to within one game of first place. The next day, more than 40,000 fans, many of them left standing, packed into Wrigley Field. There were rumors of 10,000 more being turned away without tickets. Ernie Banks watched the carnival atmosphere while wearing street clothes in the broadcasting booth. The day before, he had been spiked in a close play at first base by Pete Rose. The deep gash on his right heel caused him to leave the game, amid vicious boos directed at Rose.[6] He was taken to the hospital, where 10 stitches were required to put him back together again. Unable to get a shoe on his foot due to the swelling the next day, he was forced to sit out the game.

Ernie was a guest on Lou Boudreau's pregame show and explained to the listening audience exactly why the Cubs were going to win the 1967 pennant. He asked if he could remain in the booth and then spent the rest of the afternoon sitting between Boudreau and play-by-play man Vince Lloyd. Ernie led cheers throughout the game, at one point standing up and waving his arms like a conductor to whip the fans into a frenzy. When he leaned out of the booth, nearby fans swarmed to shake his hand and pat him on the back—almost pulling him out. Only the quick hands of Boudreau and Lloyd kept him from joining the mosh pit.

While the Cubs were beating the Reds, 4–1, the delirious crowd kept watch on the scoreboard and cheered madly for each run posted for the Mets, who were playing a tight game with the first-place Cardinals. When the scoreboard announced that the Mets had won in extra innings, the place exploded. After the Cubs victory, an amazing thing happened—no one went home. Fans stayed in the park, chanting, "We're number one, we're number one." Cubs players, half-undressed in the clubhouse, heard the commotion and went back out onto the field and witnessed fans going berserk as the scoreboard flags that marked the league leaders were changed. Players stood, drinking in the surreal scene. For Ernie Banks, who had been playing in the major leagues for 14 seasons, 1958 was the first time he had ever seen the Cubs flag on top later than May 7.

Although the Cubs finally faded, they remained respectable to the end; they played four games over .500 in September and ended in third place, at 87–74, their best finish in 21 years. Ernie Banks had been a key part of the turnaround. Playing in 151 games, he had 23 homers and 95 RBI. The RBI total was second on the team to Santo's 98 and trailed only MVP Orlando Cepeda among National League first basemen. "In my opinion, he [Banks] was the most valuable player on the Cubs," said Dodgers manager Walt Alston. "Without the fine year he had, they don't finish in the first division."[7]

Ernie refused to rub his personal success in Durocher's face, even though reporters continually teed it up for him throughout the winter, practically begging him to take a swipe. Unbelievably, he *gave Leo* credit for his good season. The extensive time on the bench in the spring had been the plan all along, you see, to allow the aging star to get ready on his own, to take his time getting in shape. "That undoubtedly was a good break for me," Ernie explained with a straight face, "because if I had tried to compete with the young fellows, I would have been struggling, really struggling . . . [by the time he started playing at the end of spring] I was ready."[8] The digging-for-a-horse-in-a-pile-of-manure line must have sounded good to Ernie because he repeated it throughout the fall and winter to inquiring writers.

Durocher, for his part, admitted that perhaps he had been premature in predicting Ernie's demise: "Frankly, I had resolved a couple of times even before last spring that Ernie had about reached the end of the road, and I was going to retire him. But he has cured me."[9]

And Coach Banks? The coaching duties never seemed to materialize. Ernie continued as he always had. While he had initially told reporters it would be great to work with youngsters as a coach, he later admitted that all along, in the back of his mind, he thought, "I know I can still play regularly."[10]

The drama between "Leo the Lip" and Mr. Cub would continue to play out during the next four seasons: an ebb and flow of vitriol and passive-aggressiveness. Ernie would continue to maintain the upper hand by bobbing and weaving, slipping Leo's jabs and parrying his haymakers. "Ernie knew that Leo didn't like him," said Fergie Jenkins."[11] But he never let on in public.

"Leo hated Ernie," traveling secretary Blake Cullen recalled. Cullen further commented,

> I'll never forget this scene in spring training. Ernie was playing first base during infield practice, and Leo shouts, "Hey old man, ever play shortstop?" "Well," Ernie says, "I useta play a little . . . nine years at Wrigley Field," and Leo says, "Get over there. Ten balls for a Coke."
>
> So Ernie goes to shortstop with his hat on backward, somebody throws him an infield glove, Leo grabs a bat, and they start. Leo hits one to his left four steps. Leo hits one to his right five steps. Then Ernie backhands one. Now he scoops a slow roller. Finally, he's damned near third base, and Leo is hitting him shots. There isn't a sound in the park. Everybody is watching. Ernie goes 10-for-10, throws the mitt into the air, and runs off laughing.[12]

But it was no laughing matter for Leo. He wasn't known as Leo the Lip because of his trumpet-playing ability. Even after they were no longer together, Leo couldn't resist firing shots. In his 1975 autobiography, he devoted an entire chapter to Ernie, entitled "Mister Cub." It is not a nice chapter. Determined to tear down the Ernie Banks myth, Durocher spent much type listing Ernie's shortcomings and implying a lack of intelligence, writing,

> There are some players who instinctively do the right things on the basepaths. Ernie had an unfailing instinct for doing the wrong thing. . . . To do me any good he would have had to hit 70 home runs and knock in 200 runs. . . . But did anybody in Chicago ever write that Ernie Banks couldn't get off a dime? Never. Criticizing Ernie Banks doesn't sell papers. The best it's going to get you is a ton of abuse.

Leo remained mystified at the goodwill Ernie had built up in Chicago. He continued,

> How does he do it? You could say about Ernie that he never remembered a sign or forgot a newspaperman's name. All he knew was, "Ho, let's go. Ho, baby-doobedoobedoo. It's a wonderful day for a game in Chicago. Let play twooo."

We'd get on the bus and he'd sit across from the writers. "A beaooootiful day for twoooo." It could be snowing outside, "Let's play three."[13]

Ernie was much more charitable in his own autobiography, published in 1971. He wrote, "It was misinterpreted that Leo disliked me. He made my life better, he made me a better player."[14]

When goaded by reporters, Ernie frequently reframed questions and talked about the team and its success rather than broach their personal relationship. "All I can say about Durocher is that the time he was manager was one of the happiest of my career," he said in 1975. "During that period we began to gain respectability, not only in Chicago, but all around baseball.[15] Sure he got mad at us and yelled a lot of times, but I'll say one thing about the time when Durocher was managing—it wasn't dull."[16]

In 1977, *Jet* magazine ran the suggestive title "Banks Finally Tells of Durocher's Many Insults" on the front cover. The article, however, proved to be overhyped. The author wrote of several alleged insults, but Banks himself spoke no evil. All Ernie said for the article was,

> I learned long ago that when you say derogatory things about people it stays with you. Everybody remembers it, especially if it's written. You can't retract those things. Of course, you have those feelings. You'd like to say, "I hate that guy," or "I'd like to kill him," but suppose that tomorrow you feel he's a nice guy again.[17]

Ernie maintained that stance throughout the ensuing decades. "Leo wasn't jealous of me," he said in 1985. "I think he was just trying to push me. You know, when you're in the latter stages of a career like I was, sometimes you get lackadaisical. I understood what he was trying to do."[18]

"In Leo I saw a man in his 60s," he said in 1989. "Actually, it was joyful to see him so involved. How many men in their 60s can get that involved in something? And it couldn't have been easy for him, with all the travel. So, when he got cantankerous, I figured that most of the time he just didn't feel so good."[19]

By 2014, however, Ernie was finally ready to come clean. "That man hated me," he told author Rich Cohen. He continued,

> I never understood that. So, what did I do? Did I challenge him? Did I take him on? No. He was the manager. The boss. He was allowed to hate me. My response was the same as it always has been—put my head down and play the game. That's all you got. The game. . . . That for me was dignity—the fact that I went out there and played as well as I could every day.[20]

And play Ernie did. He responded with three-straight solid years after his career had been given up for dead.

While bringing unwanted drama, there was no denying the effect Leo Durocher had on the team. The 1967 season was a watershed year for the Cubs franchise. The whole thinking of the players had changed in less than a year. Pre-Leo, the Cubs had been an embarrassment to themselves and their fans. They knew when they stepped onto the field that other professional players recognized the disorganization. The popular view of the Cubs was summed up by Jim Murray when he wrote, "The Cubs are less of a team than a comic-opera in baseball suits. They have more generals and less troops than a South American revolution. They come to a game like a bull to the plaza; the best they can hope is that someone doesn't cut off their ears."[21]

Suddenly everything was different. Leo had indeed backed up the truck. Only five players (Kessinger, Beckert, Williams, Santo, and Banks) were left from 1965. Everyone was a believer now. Leo had ingrained in them that they could win any game. "The one great thing Leo brought was there was absolutely no doubt about who was in charge," says Don Kessinger, who further commented,

> Leo didn't have to answer to anybody. He did what he thought was best. I will always be grateful that he played me and Beckert when we were kids, even though we might not have been ready yet. But he stuck with us. Maybe he could see what we would become. We all knew, and appreciated, what Leo had done for our team.[22]

The players felt it. They were no longer satisfied with losing. They expected to win. They demanded to win. From the end of the 1967 season until the spring of 1968, the entire city changed its attitude toward the Cubs. Now, the Cubs had respect.

While the Cubs were finally achieving respect on the field, Ernie continued to wage his own private battle as a black man striving for respect in American society. By 1967, the racial climate of baseball and the country looked nothing like what Ernie had experienced when he started in the game. Among active baseball players, only Willie Mays and Hank Aaron remembered those days firsthand along with Ernie.

When Ernie had broken in with the Cubs in 1953, there were 20 black players on seven of the 16 major-league teams. Within a decade, every team had integrated, and there were 85 black players, taking 19 percent of major-league roster space. In the 1950s, eight of the 10 National League MVP Awards had gone to black players. The old argument of whether blacks could play the game at the highest levels was now as much a reminder of former stupidity as believing that the earth was flat.

Progress was not confined to the field. Monte Irvin declared in 1957,

> Baseball has done more to promote goodwill and to open up doors—literally and figuratively—for the Negro than all the political speeches and diplomatic conferences . . . once we [black ballplayers] are accepted, the average colored man, traveling through the city on business, is presumably accepted, too.[23]

Ernie had witnessed that progress himself. Whereas in his rookie year, he and Gene Baker were forced to find other accommodations in St. Louis, by 1957 black players could stay with their white teammates in every National League city (but they still couldn't use the pool or hotel bar in St. Louis). Most of the abuse from the stands had died away, other than from a few rednecks.

In the May 1957 issue of *Ebony* magazine, Branch Rickey commented on the status of race in baseball 10 years after his great experiment. "I would say a Negro can today play a good game of baseball without carrying his race on his shoulders," he stated. While acknowledging that the "problem has not been solved," he added that African American players should strive to remain vigilant of maintaining good conduct on and off the field at all times. He urged patience on other matters and concluded, "There is no problem at all [for an African American in baseball] if he's a gentleman and can play the game."[24]

Sam Lacey, who wrote mostly for the *Pittsburgh Courier* for 73 years and was considered the dean of African American sportswriters, concurred that progress was being made. In 1960, he wrote, "Certainly the last decade has been the most productive in racial understanding and tolerance our history encounters. Especially is this true in the story of our advancement in sports."[25]

It seemed important for the establishment to let everyone know that integration was a complete success in the baseball world. By 1960, some insinuated in national articles that the only complaint African American baseball players possessed concerned the lack of commercial deals. The conservative *Sporting News* particularly liked to trumpet the fact that equality among the races had arrived and that all was well, stating, "The social relationships of major-league players, Negro and white, absolutely are unaffected by color."[26]

This was a nice thought, but it was entirely untrue. Although there was little outward hostility and players mixed on the field, most teams remained segregated socially. While Rickey's statements seemed positive, on closer inspection, one could conclude that they were somewhat condescending and implied a double standard of tolerated conduct between the races, illustrating the type of unspoken attitudes still present and showing that the problem certainly had not been solved to that point.

More troubling, this was a time when players of color still could not eat at certain establishments in many cities throughout the league, and they continued to be prohibited from staying at the same hotels as their teammates in Florida during spring training. During the 1960s, the progress that had been made was offset by the burning desire for more—and faster—and less tolerance for racial slights of any kind. Baseball players would be caught in the storm of political and social unrest.

Wendell Smith wrote a series of scathing reports in the *Chicago American* in January 1961, informing the sporting world that African American ballplayers resented spring in the South and demanded an end to housing discrimination during spring training. Such headlines as "Negro Ball Players Want Rights in South" and "Negro Stars Find Themselves 'Caged'" let the public know that fairness and harmony did not exist within the game, despite pronouncements otherwise. "Beneath the apparently tranquil surface of baseball there is a growing feeling of resentment among Negro major leaguers, who still experience embarrassment, humiliation, and even indignities during spring training in the South."[27]

Ebony magazine added in June 1962, that while players like Mays, Banks, and Aaron were now well paid, "Money has not ended spring camp bias. . . . Money did not buy complete equality of treatment for them at all of the 14 spring training camps in Florida." Although some teams were now allowed to stay together in hotels in Florida, "Negro players with the New York Mets 'understood' they were not to 'congregate' in the lobby of their team's hotel." And, obviously, pools were off-limits.[28]

White mainstream journalists soon picked up the story. Joe Reichler of the Associated Press ran an interview with St. Louis All-Star Bill White, who said, "How much longer must we accept this without saying a word on our own behalf? These things go on every day and yet they advise us to take it easy, we're making progress, don't push too fast, it will come. How much longer are we to wait?"[29]

African American players on the Cubs faced less institutionalized discrimination during the spring in Arizona, but there were still regular slights. In the early 1960s, black players and their wives were still forced to stay in a shabby hotel, referred to as the "hut," in Tempe rather than join with teammates in more plush accommodations in Mesa. There were places they couldn't eat in the Phoenix area as well; players were assured by staff, "We don't mind, but our clients mind."[30] It was embarrassing for everyone concerned, demeaning, and just plain stupid. More insults waited after camp broke, as the team played its way north in such places as Mississippi, Louisiana, and Texas.

When National League teams were added in Houston and Atlanta, the slights were not just confined to the spring. "I clearly remember one uncomfortable situation all these years later," says Dick Ellsworth. He added,

> In 1962, on our first trip into Houston, we landed at the airport, got on a bus, and went to the Rice Hotel, where we had been booked. When we all walked into the lobby we got some funny looks. There was some confusion and then we were told by management that the blacks couldn't stay there. At the time, we had Ernie and Billy, George Altman, and maybe one other guy. We just stood there, but Ernie was quick to understand the situation; obviously he had dealt with it before, growing up in Texas. He told the rest of us, "You fellas check in and we'll find someplace else to stay."
>
> But we rallied around and agreed we were staying together as a team. The traveling secretary found us a hotel on the outskirts of town where we could all stay. I thought, "What a tragedy. What a tough thing to have to deal with all the time." Most of us never really thought about it because we weren't faced with it. I was from California, and it didn't come up there. You know it had to be tough for those guys. But Ernie was just so good about deflecting negative things like that. I really came to love the guy.[31]

Black Cubs, like their counterparts on other teams, were disappointed that the owners did not stand up for their rights. While it took the federal enforcement of the 1964 Civil Rights Act to end discrimination in spring training hotels and restaurants, some owners did act on behalf of their players individually. In the early 1960s, the Cardinals' management, backed by the powerful deep pockets of the Busch Beer empire, assisted Bill White when he wanted to buy a house in a white neighborhood but had been refused.[32] Black players on the Cubs had always been forced to live south of Chicago's infamous red line and make a miserable drive through traffic—a half hour on a good day, an hour or more on a bad day—to commute to work. It would have been nice for P. K. Wrigley to throw some of his Wrigley muscle around and assist his players with housing. Perched in his eponymous towering building, which dominated the north side of Michigan Avenue, he certainly had the political and economic clout to take a stand and make a difference. But he never did; he remained silent, content with the status quo.

The Cubs' black players were left to ponder the paradox of progress when they watched the Buck O'Neil coaching fiasco. O'Neil, who joined the Cubs organization as the Negro Leagues were fading, initially functioned as a scout, leading the team to an abundance of talent. He was named to the Cubs coaching staff in June 1962, becoming the first African American to coach on a major-league team. The move inspired such national headlines as "Cubs Sign Negro as Coach" and could have made Wrigley a true innovator. But once again, Wrigley missed a golden chance, and it turned into another sad episode for the team.

O'Neil was universally respected for his baseball knowledge. With his enthusiasm, deep bass voice, and tremendous presence, he was a natural leader of men. When he was added to the coaching staff, O'Neil thought he would get a chance to manage someday. "I soon found out there was no chance of that happening," he later wrote.[33]

Lest there be any confusion on the elephant in the room, O'Neil's hiring was accompanied by the following official pronouncement: "Buck O'Neil will serve in the capacity of an instructor and as such will not be considered a potential head coach or manager under the club's rotation plan."[34] O'Neil, the man with more professional managerial experience than anyone else on the staff other than Grimm, was the only one to have that stipulation. Why? The answer to the question was obvious—and disappointing.

Buck's presence was initially gratifying for Banks, Altman, Williams, and Brock, who had all either played for him on the Monarchs or known him from his scouting days, as well as African American players throughout baseball. But it also brought more frustration. "O'Neil should've gotten an opportunity to manage that year because of the fact that he was the best manager of the group," Altman said later. Altman further commented,

> He had experience and knowledge, and all the players took to him. He was a fiery guy. In the dugout you could hear his booming voice giving encouragement to players and so forth. Everybody loved Buck. . . . I thought he was going to get his chance. . . . The rest of us thought Buck . . . would at least get a brief shot at it, but it just never happened.[35]

Under orders from above, O'Neil coached from the dugout and was not allowed to set foot on the field during games. On July 15, 1962, head coach Charlie Metro was ejected from a game, and Elven Tappe, the third-base coach, took over. When Tappe was later ejected, Lou Klein, who had moved from first to coach third base, stepped up. Rather than have O'Neil, the obvious choice, coach third the rest of the game, the pitching coach was called in from the bullpen and O'Neil remained in the dugout. "I think by that point in my life I knew how to wave a guy around a base. . . . Not going out there that day was one of the few disappointments I've had in more than 60 years in baseball," the eternally optimistic O'Neil wrote years later.[36] O'Neil eventually understood that the Cubs had no intention of ever giving him a chance to advance, and he went back to scouting.

As the Civil Rights Movement gathered momentum, many questioned why the biggest black sports stars did not use their popularity as a platform and stand up for the cause. In 1964, the *Pittsburgh Courier* wrote that black players had "voluntarily acquiesced to racial segregation and discrimination in certain instances."[37]

But the response was complicated for everyone. It was generally understood in baseball that marginal players of any color had best keep their mouths shut on controversial topics—be it long hair, the emerging war in Vietnam, or even wearing turtlenecks under their sports coats—otherwise they might find themselves looking for a new job. This was also true of black baseball players, even superstars. The Branch Rickey definition of "gentleman" included keeping quiet on social issues—no one wanted an angry black man on their team. Players without a college education and no other means of employment clearly understood the tenuous nature of their situation. Billy Williams later wrote, "Even though black Cubs players such as Banks, Fergie Jenkins, and I were future Hall of Famers, we knew that somehow our livelihoods were at stake if we made a big public commotion in that era."[38]

"It was tough for us," Ernie said in 2004. "We had to stand back. We had families to support."[39]

The general feeling is that Chicago, and the Cubs' management, would not have tolerated open dissent. "It's interesting that the three biggest African American stars on the Cubs, Ernie, Billy, and Fergie, were all laid-back guys who didn't rock the boat," says Chuck Shriver, Cubs public relations director from 1967 to 1975. He added,

> I don't think that's a coincidence. None of them ever spoke out about the racist things they had faced or current conditions. In 1968, we got Lou Johnson, who was much more outspoken. He caused some problems. After Martin Luther King Jr. got shot, Johnson made a big deal that he thought the team should cancel the games. I know he got upset at Ernie and those guys when they didn't back him up. He ended up getting traded away pretty quickly.[40]

For his part, Ernie almost never mentioned race issues in his early years in Chicago. In 1960, for a national magazine feature, the writer stated that Banks "feels fortunate to have escaped the segregation problems of the South and his hometown of Dallas [the writer's words, not Ernie's]." Ernie, on the other hand, was quoted as saying, "Conditions are getting better all the time in sports for the colored players, and I don't have any gripes. . . . I've never had it so good, I can do practically anything I want to, so what's there to complain about." He declared that the United States is a great country and raved about "all the opportunities there are in Chicago, where everyone is equal."[41]

There were those who would disagree with Ernie about the equality of Chicago. As the city's black population had grown from 8 percent to 22 percent between 1940 and 1960, their voting power had increased as well. Yet, overall living conditions had dramatically decreased. Mayor Daley's machine counted on, and usually received, near-unanimous black votes. But he and the city gave little back in the way of jobs, housing, and opportunities. Chicago blacks were crammed into ghettos, unable to escape. They were only able to buy houses on the edges of the slums—allowing the ghetto to extend by amoeboid movement—but were not permitted to vault into nicer parts of the city. Civic services, such as transportation and education, were scandalously inadequate in the black parts of Chicago.

As tensions exploded throughout the country in the 1960s, Chicago became one of the tinderboxes of the Civil Rights Movement. In 1966, Martin Luther King Jr. took his Southern Christian Leadership movement north for a highly publicized visit to Chicago. King, who was appalled at the conditions in the West Side slums, met with Mayor Daley and led demonstrations at Soldier's Field and in white neighborhoods, calling for jobs, open housing, and improved education. He and his marchers were met with a rain of bottles, spit, and insults. Unable to cause any meaningful change, King eventually withdrew from the city in disappointment. When frustration in the ghetto boiled over with riots in 1967 and 1968, Daley's only answer was pools and spray fountains to placate the masses in the hot summer weather. Yet, Ernie always spoke of Daley, and the city, in only respectful tones, even admiration.

As the 1960s progressed, some black athletes began coming forward with calls for progress. The Cardinals' Bill White, who later became National League president, was one such outspoken baseball player. In a 1964 *Sport* article, White expressed his impatience for what he called the "equality of all people." White, who grew up in a small town in northern Ohio, had been one of the few baseball players to speak out against the housing issue in spring training in Florida. He commented,

> I've been aware of our problems from the start. I've always fought to solve them. . . . Many players who'd been in the league long before me never said a word about housing segregation in spring training. . . . I think that all of us in the big

leagues should say and do more. . . . I don't think we've said enough as ballplayers. We've become part of the 1 percent of American Negroes who've done well.
When you're part of the 1 percent, there is a tendency to forget the 99 percent.[42]

Even though he was long retired from the game, Jackie Robinson was constantly pushing, agitating, and moving the bar. Robinson called on the best
athletes to take a stand. In a 1966 article in *Sport*, he acknowledged the financial
risks they faced, saying, "If he is any kind of a Negro, he can forget it (opportunities after career). If he is willing to try to fight the masses of people once his
playing days are over, his job is over, too." Nonetheless, Robinson felt the stars
were obligated by their talent and stature to take a leadership role and was particularly critical of Willie Mays as "not willing to stand up on the race issue."[43]

He later called Mays a "do-nothing Negro in the area of race relations."[44]

Willie defended himself, saying, "We all have our own ways of approaching
things. Each man has to take the path that is right for him. . . . I like to feel that
just by coming up, being lucky to have better than average ability, conducting
myself in a good manner, I have made progress for our people." Mays refused
to bring up past slights and, in fact, would never talk about the race issue even
long after he retired. "I don't want to bring up all that stuff . . . baseball has been
great to me. I owe it a lot."[45]

Similarly, Ernie never wanted to bring up "that stuff," and when cornered,
he only focused on the positives. He pointed to the good changes that had occurred during his career:

> In 1954, in St. Louis, we could stay at the Chase Hotel, but we couldn't eat in
> the dining room. Also, certain movie theaters wouldn't let us in. And when we
> did some barnstorming through the South, we had to change clothes on the train
> and use segregated facilities in the stations. But that's all a thing of the past now.[46]

Sam Lacey, disappointed that not enough had been accomplished after the
initial positive steps of the 1950s, wrote an article in 1970 titled, "What Has
Baseball Done Lately," in which he commented on those statements. He wrote,
"Both Ernie and Willie are, shall we say, the 'diplomats' among major-league
ballplayers of our acquaintance. Ironically neither Ernie nor Willie had much to
do with the improvement. . . . Efforts to enroll both in the battle, when it was at
its peak, were met with silence."[47]

African American players who had been raised in the North tended to react
much more emotionally to the racism, often responding with hate and anger.
Those from the South, like Ernie and Willie, were used to the way things
were; they had long ago learned how to deal with it and learned the often-

necessary trait of how to hide the frustration and rage. "I think black players who grew up in the South had a different way of coping," says Nate Oliver, who would be a 1969 Cubs teammate and whose father played in the Negro Leagues. Oliver continued,

> I grew up in St. Petersburg. By the time we got to the major leagues, we had all seen much worse things growing up. And back then our communities prepared us and taught us how to handle it. We learned and understood about bigotry and prejudice, and how to deal with it. We were surrounded by family and the neighborhood, and everybody looked out for you because they knew what we were up against. They prepared us so later we didn't feel so bad with all the things, all the slights and insults. We had learned how to deal with it without letting it eat you and destroy you.[48]

In private conversations with Bill White, Willie Mays had voiced a similar sentiment.[49]

While appearing disinterested and avoiding the topic publicly, Ernie was very concerned about civil rights and the plight of his people. By virtue of his stature in the game and the city of Chicago, he moved in high circles. He was acquainted with virtually all the prominent blacks in politics, entertainment, and sports at the time, and he frequently took part in conversations regarding the movement. He later said he "didn't get involved in the marches and demonstrations because we were in baseball. Our life was baseball. We knew [racial strife] was going on but had no involvement in it." Black entertainers of the 1950s and early 1960s, like Nat King Cole, Lionel Hampton, Eartha Kitt, and Pearl Bailey, urged Ernie and other sports stars to lead by example. Said Ernie, "Their message to those of us in baseball was to keep playing baseball. 'People are watching you, [so] just keep playing, just keep hitting the ball.'"[50]

Perhaps the major factor in Ernie's approach was his obvious distaste for conflict and optimistic way of viewing life—he preferred to focus on the positives of change rather than dwell on insults of the past or what more needed to be done in the future. "There is nothing you can do to me to make me angry enough to do something or say something back to you," Ernie said in 1989. "I've been criticized for that—by my wife, by my children. 'Why don't you stand up and fight?' they ask. 'Why don't you speak out? What's wrong with you?' But it isn't me."[51]

Ernie's efforts to help those of his race were constructive and frequently behind the scenes, and rather than trying for a touchdown on one big play, he focused on short runs into the line, moving the chains 10 yards at a time. In addition to the time spent with the inner-city Boys Clubs and Boy Scouts, the antidelinquency and antigang programs, in 1955 and 1956 he and Buck O'Neil were the only instructors for the first two years of the Capitol City Kids Baseball Clinic, a program for African American youths started by a friend in Baton Rouge, Louisiana, on the campus of Southern University. By 1958, Hank and Tommy Aaron had joined; later Earl Wilson, Curt Flood, and Lou Brock helped out. By 1966, the clinic had drawn more than 5,000 kids. Ernie took time out for a similar program in urban East St. Louis.

He served as general chairman of the 1957 membership campaign of the Chicago branch of the NAACP, telling reporters he was "more than happy to make home runs on behalf of civil rights and first-class citizenship for all Americans."[52] In January 1967, he was named, along with Gale Sayers, Bill White, and Bill Russell, to a national sports committee formed to raise $100,000 for the legal defense fund of the NAACP.

Ernie supported aggressive efforts to improve employment and opportunity, but he was critical of violence. "Some people feel that because you are black you will never be treated fairly and that you should voice your opinions, be militant about them," he said, adding,

> I don't feel this way. You can't convince a fool against his will. He is still going to hold to his opinions, so why should I tell him, "Look, you are prejudiced. You don't like me because I'm black." If a man doesn't like me because I'm black, that's fine. I'll just go elsewhere, but I'm not going to let him change my life . . . we can't use prejudice as an excuse or as a crutch. . . . It is important to be yourself, be a man, accept things as a man.[53]

Ernie also commented,

> There are certain things that you have to fight for, but not by looting and burning, but by letting society know that you will demand your rights and use every legal means to get them. I don't agree with the guys that say in order to find your pride in your blackness you have to hate everything that is white. That's just plain wrong. We shouldn't hate anybody. If you want to get a good job, or get into business, you've got to live with other people, including the white ones.[54]

Ernie was truer to his word than most people knew, especially the part about living with white people. In 1963, pitcher Lindy McDaniel came to the Cubs in a trade from the Cardinals. McDaniel, who became a minister after retiring from baseball, was one of the straightest arrows the game has ever known, a man whose lips never touched alcohol and who was never heard to utter a word stronger than "dog-gone-it." McDaniel, who is white, became friendly with Banks, and they noticed they led similar lifestyles on the road. "On every team you have the group of guys who go out every night and get rowdy, drink, chase women, and drag in at three in the morning," McDaniel says. He further commented,

> Usually, you try to room with someone who keeps your hours, so there's no problems. Ernie didn't go out drinking, and he didn't chase women—if he did, I never heard about it. One day, he came up to me in the outfield and asked, "Why don't we room together?" I said, "That's fine with me." So Ernie said, "Good. I'll go tell the front office."

This was several years before Gale Sayers and Brian Piccolo famously broke a barrier of sorts by being the first Chicago Bears of different colors to room together. Ernie and Lindy would have been big news. "But then I never heard anything else," McDaniel says. "That was before blacks and whites roomed together, and I guess the front office turned it down. It's kind of disappointing. I think we would have gotten along well together as roommates."[55]

Part of Ernie's appeal to fans was that he got along with everyone and didn't make people uncomfortable. This was especially true of white fans. Ernie became a bridge between white and black Chicago. Thousands of white youngsters from the era learned about diversity and equality from the example he provided. He conducted himself as a gentleman, always seemed thankful for what he had, and never complained. Where some saw the exploitation of black labor by white owners and continued racism, Ernie chose to see the opportunity to rise from the ghetto—opportunity only baseball had given him. He was quoted in print saying things like, "The sudden association with so many white people often left me speechless and wondering why they were so kind."[56]

In 1964, when asked by a reporter if he ever encountered any race problems in baseball, Ernie answered, "The only race we have in baseball is trying to beat the throw to first for a hit, or to second, trying to steal a base."[57]

There was a method behind Ernie's supposed head-in-the-sand approach. "If you play on the racism, if you're black and feel unfairly treated, bringing it up creates more tension," says pitcher Rich Nye. "With Ernie, by always being up, you knew he wasn't going to cause waves. That lessened the tension for everyone. And I think that was his way of surviving, to ignore bad things."

When Ernie did mention racism he had faced, it was usually veiled in generalized analogies, and one is forced to read between the lines to catch the true meaning and depth. One example is the story he told for his autobiography, in which he said, "My naiveté gave Gene [Baker] a good laugh." While on a team spring trip through Mobile, Alabama, Ernie wandered into the downtown bus station to buy a candy bar and a newspaper. He was quickly chased out of the shop by the owner, who was "shouting a string of four-letter words and threatening to call the police." Ernie hurried back to the Cubs bus. "I see you just learned the facts of life about Southern hospitality," Baker told him while laughing.[58]

To believe the story at face value requires the reader to accept that 23-year-old Ernie Banks, who had grown up in Dallas, spent three summers traveling across small-town Texas playing on an African American baseball team, spent two complete seasons traveling throughout the country on a Negro League team, and undoubtedly fully understood the rules of Jim Crow better than anyone on the Chicago Cubs, including the Iowa-raised Baker, was surprised and even disappointed when he was refused service in Mobile, Alabama, in the mid-1950s. Really? Alternatively, the story could have been Ernie's attempt, with a nonthreatening, seemingly humorous story with himself as the butt of the joke, to illustrate the daily forces he and others faced at the time.

Ernie's approach made him popular among those in the establishment who favored order and undoubtedly helped him financially. Because of what they viewed as cooperation and acceptance with the current status, many young blacks considered Ernie to be an Oreo[59] or an Uncle Tom. It was openly insinuated that he was not loyal to the cause; that when the great struggle occurred, Ernie took a quiet seat or, worse, allowed himself to be bought off by the Man. The charges hurt. "I care deeply about my people," Ernie said in 1969. "But I'm just not one to go about screaming over what I contribute. I'm not black or white. I'm just a human being trying to survive the only way I know how. I don't make enemies."[60]

He also commented, "They [militant blacks] think their way is the only way. They don't understand my way. I believe in getting along with people, in setting a good example."[61]

But despite the tranquil, satisfied, get-along-with-everyone façade, there was disappointment and anger. He never forgot the pain from his youth in Dallas, and this would always color his opinion of his native city. He had seen plenty of bad things in his life—unexplainable hatred and prejudice. "Today's black athletes and major-league players have no idea what we had to endure," Ernie allowed in 2011.[62]

"Ernie went through a lot," says Kessinger. "By the time I got there things weren't as bad, but he still went through a lot. And I know it bothered him. He just never spoke out. If you talked to him, he would let you know. But he never wanted people to feel sorry for him."

Ernie was rewarded for his stellar 1967 season with a two-year contract containing a raise to $65,000 a year. Although he was no longer the highest-paid Cub (Ron Santo was making $80,000), the multiyear deal was the first Wrigley had ever given to anyone other than Leo Durocher. And while Ernie was still listed on the roster as a player-coach, there was little suspense at first base in the spring of 1968; Leo had been converted.

The Cubs showed that 1967 had been no fluke. The home crowds continued to grow, and the team broke the 1 million mark in attendance for the first time in 16 years. In the "Year of the Pitcher," 37-year-old Ernie Banks hit 32 home runs, his most since 1962, only four behind league leader Willie McCovey. On May 26, 1968, he became the 11th major-league player to hit 450 home runs. The Cubs finished in third place with a record of 84–78, the first time since 1946 they had completed two-consecutive winning seasons.

After the 1968 season, Ernie turned his eyes to the other source of great social discord of the decade: Vietnam. He and a contingent of baseball men left for a 16-day goodwill tour of U.S. troops. The trip was the third annual effort to bring baseball players to Vietnam to help with the morale of GIs. After the 1966 season, the USO and the MLB commissioner, retired U.S. Air Force general William Eckert, had united to send a rolling thunder team of Hank Aaron, Harmon Killebrew, Stan Musial, Joe Torre, and Brooks Robinson—more than 2,000 home runs' worth of baseball royalty—into the combat zone. In 1967, it was Pete Rose, Joe DiMaggio, Tony Conigliaro, and Jerry Coleman. The 1968 group was not quite as luminous but no less enthusiastic: Ernie; Larry Jackson of the Phillies; Pete Richert of the Orioles; Ron Swaboda of the Mets; Bing Devine from the Cardinals front office; and Al Fleishman, a personal friend of August Busch and public relations consultant for the Cardinals.

The group met in San Francisco, experienced the obligatory army hurry-up-and-wait of 16 hours, and then flew to Saigon on a charter jet with 160 GIs. In Saigon, they were issued fatigues and combat boots. They were told they would be under tight security—the Viet Cong knew of the visit and would have enjoyed nothing more than to ring up a handful of American baseball stars as trophies. While the men were assured that every precaution had been taken for their safety, they couldn't help but feel a little uneasy when the officer in charge instructed them on how to get down on the floor and cover their body with a mattress in case of incoming fire.

They separated into two groups: Ernie, Richert, and Fleishman went north, the others south. They made the rounds, sometimes appearing before large numbers in mess tents, showing baseball films and giving prepared speeches, but most often meeting the men in small groups. Much of the trip was spent visiting isolated firebases that were not accessible by the usual larger USO tours. Transported in combat helicopters, with a kid barely half Ernie's age sitting next to them scanning the ground with a 60-caliber machine gun, they hopped from base to base, sometimes visiting six or seven installations in a day, occasionally dropping in on mountaintops where the men hadn't known the safety of a base for more than a week. Once they met a patrol coming in and worked their way down the road, shaking hands and chatting with the GIs resting on the trail. They also entertained South Vietnamese children and visited numerous military hospitals.

Many of the stops were uncomfortably close to the enemy, allowing the baseball players to experience the sights, sounds, and smells of men in combat. Richert had served in the U.S. National Guard, and Ernie had done his two years in the U.S. Army, but that did little to prepare them for live fire in a hostile environment. They marveled at the dangers the kids faced on a daily basis. On one visit to troops of the airborne command at Camp Eagle, a forward base north of Da Nang, they learned that the base had been hit with rockets the night before. Another night, Banks and Richert were awakened by shell fire when the Viet Cong tried to breach the perimeter at Dang Tam. They stepped out to witness the sky being lit up by white flares and tracers of gunfire leaping out of American bunkers—only 250 yards away.

The ballplayers met with the men, talked, joked, and answered baseball questions. Most of all, they chatted about things back home. Enthused to see major-league stars, the young soldiers were also happy just to receive news of the real world and know they were not forgotten. The baseball players received an overwhelming response.

Ernie was the obvious headliner in the group, and he embraced the role and stepped up his game. "We'd be walking along and I'd hear, 'Hey, that's Ernie Banks!'" says Richert, continuing,

> Then some guy would say, "Nah, you're shitting me. He wouldn't be out here." And Ernie would wave. He was immediately recognizable. That's how popular he was then. Everybody knew him. Of course, wearing his Cub hat with his army fatigues helped. But Ernie was a special guy. I enjoyed getting to know him on the trip. There was just a beautiful aura about him. He was special but didn't think he was special. He was very humble and never went out looking for special treatment. It was a pleasure to be around him.[63]

"If anybody batted 1.000 on the trip it was Banks," Fleishman told reporters back home. "He is absolutely the greatest man I've ever seen. When we walked into a hospital or mess hall, Ernie simply took the place by storm. . . . No one could generate the appeal of Banks."[64]

A half-century later, memories of the trip are still fresh. "One day, somebody broke out a ball and gloves, and I pitched some to Ernie in front of the men in the middle of a swamp," says Richert. At another remote outpost, Ernie heard of a kid from Illinois who had been a good pitcher in high school. Ernie produced a ball and gloves, and watched the kid pitch, complimenting his curveball and assuring him he would have trouble hitting it.

"They fed us real well," continues Richert. He elaborated,

> A lot of evenings we were eating with generals or colonels. We had a lot of steak. Other times, we ate with the guys and had what they ate, but we didn't get served anything on a shingle, let's put it that way. We went into one firebase, and there was an area marked off with barbed wire. I asked someone what that was, and they said, "The Green Berets, special forces. Nobody messes with them." They had their own area. That night, there was a big reception for us, and we answered a hundred questions and talked to the troops, then four Green Berets walked in and said, "Richert? You guys are coming with us," and they took us out.

Richert, who had set up a program back home where he visited injured vets at Walter Reed Hospital, had befriended some severely wounded Green Berets in a special ward there called Ward One. He continued,

> I later found out my buddies from Ward One had called ahead and arranged a special welcome for us. They whisked us away—you don't argue with Green Berets—and we spent the whole night with them, talking and telling stories and stuff. Ernie didn't drink much so I had to take up the slack for him, to hold up the honor of Major League Baseball. It was rough, but by morning me and Ernie had earned our Green Berets.

The baseball players were touched by their reception and also by the pleas from officers to pass the word and let everyone know how much their presence meant to the men and to send more groups. Watching amputees in a military hospital brighten up and ask for an autograph brought the men close to tears. "You couldn't help but be moved by this experience," said Fleishman. "This trip did more for us than the men over there."[65]

"It was important just to talk to the guys, to make personal contact," says Richert, adding,

> You could see how much it was appreciated. Me and Ernie both took a pad and wrote down names and numbers of the families of the guys who lived near us.

When we got back we made 40 or 50 calls each to parents. Just to tell them we saw their sons and they were all right, and said, "Hi." That was a huge deal to those folks. You can't imagine the emotion when they heard from us.

Soon after the group returned, a letter was printed in the *Sporting News* from Staff Sergeant M. E. Blais. It read as follows: "Today I met Ernie Banks as he and his group visited this part of Vietnam. I found Ernie just as friendly and personable as I had heard he was. The troops here really enjoyed meeting Banks and Pete Richert."[66]

But, in general, the tour was not celebrated as much back home as the previous tours had been—this came 10 months after the Tet Offensive, and public opinion for the war had sharply turned negative. While conservative periodicals feted the trip and remarked how high morale was among the men, critics complained that it was conservative baseball management's efforts to militarize the American game and glorify the war.

The men themselves made no political statements, for or against the war, but confined their comments to the U.S. soldiers, risking their lives on the other side of the world. "Those guys were just doing their jobs," says Richert, further commenting,

It was the least we could do to try to make them happy and bring a little bit of home back into their lives, at least for a little while. It put things into perspective. Regardless of how you felt about the war, we were there to let the kids know they were appreciated and that we supported them. It was all about the U.S. soldiers. They were all true American heroes in my book. It was the most meaningful thing I ever did as a baseball player.

For his part, Ernie, as expected, said all the right things. He claimed he enjoyed the trip and gained a new respect for the dedicated U.S. soldiers, so surprisingly young. "It really proved to me that young people, when they're called upon, can do the job. It was a pleasure meeting them," he reflected.[67] Ernie returned from the trip looking forward to the start of the 1969 season. He had no way of knowing how monumental the year would turn out to be.

12

THAT SUMMER OF '69

There were early indications that the 1969 baseball season would be unlike any other. The nascent baseball players' union had been gradually growing in strength, and union leader Marvin Miller felt the time had arrived to make a play. At the end of the 1968 season, Miller had negotiated his first collective bargaining agreement between the players and baseball owners. Everything was agreed upon except for a pension plan to replace the one due to expire in March 1969. Miller wanted the owners to increase their contribution in an amount proportionate to their rapidly increasing revenue from television and also to balance the fact that four new teams' worth of players would need to be covered due to expansion. The owners refused.

In early December 1968, Miller met with player reps from every team and laid out his bold plan: to encourage players not to sign a contract for 1969 until a new agreement was made, boycotting spring training if necessary. Miller called a press conference and stated that support was unanimous. To add emphasis, he trotted out the names of those who supported the union action: Aaron, Mays, Rose, Robinson, Stargell, Clemente, Banks . . . all the major stars of the day. The message was clear: they were in it together.

By February 17, the day baseball camps were set to officially open for pitchers and catchers, the owners still refused to negotiate. Almost every veteran player kept his word and refused to report. The most notable exception among the roughly dozen players to show up at camps throughout Arizona and Florida was Ernie Banks.

Although Ernie had indicated he supported the union plan in December, he arrived in Mesa early as usual, walking out onto the field with arms spread and a huge smile on his face as he drank in the sunshine. He then proceeded to work out with veteran backup catcher Gene Oliver and 16 rookies and minor leaguers. Ernie explained that, as a player-coach, he was management. Also, he was technically already signed because he had been given a two-year contract before the 1968 season. In reality, it would have been highly uncharacteristic for Ernie to do anything that could have been remotely viewed as opposing owner Wrigley.

Ernie was, and would remain throughout his life, absolutely loyal to P. K. Wrigley. Their relationship was one of employer and employee, but it was solid, based as much as possible on mutual admiration and respect (although some later critics would use the nasty "plantation" word). During the losing years, Ernie had never uttered a negative word—even in private—about his boss or the organization—or the lack of organization.

In Ernie's early years, he was rewarded with regular salary increases that had soon placed him, if not in the top tier, at least near the top of all baseball players. After his decline in the mid-1960s, his salary leveled, while the still-productive Henry Aaron and Willie Mays had salaries that soared past that of Banks. While others openly insinuated that Ernie should be paid more (he never made more than $65,000 a year in baseball), he appeared happy. If the thought of holding out, or even negotiating mildly, ever occurred to Ernie, he hid it well. "I've never known an athlete as cooperative as Ernie," said John Holland in 1967. "I can't remember a time we've ever spent more than five minutes talking contract or terms."[1]

Discussing salary disputes and holdouts in 1966, Ernie said, "Money is not what baseball is all about. It's a business to the owners, but to us it's a joyous privilege to be out here in the major leagues."[2] Coming from a baseball player today, that statement would draw eye rolls and hearty laughs, if not stifled coughs of "bullshit." But at the time, Ernie pulled it off without so much as a smirk.

In 1977, he added, "I know large sums of money are very attractive, but my philosophy is that there are other things you have to think about, like your association with the owner and the general manager. Team work and togetherness are important."[3]

By all accounts, Ernie was sincere in those statements. He was well aware of how far he had come in life, how improbable that ascension had been, and the fact that everything he owned was the due to the grace of America's pastime.

But this attitude did more than just warm the hearts of fans and reporters. Other major-league players may not have been fully aware at the time, but every lowball contract offer Ernie accepted without negotiation took money out of their pockets. Although it was forbidden for players to discuss salaries, owners freely shared the information, and they were all happy that a player of Ernie's stature never topped $65,000. The Cubs used this as negotiating ammo. As late as 1970, Billy Williams, after an MVP-caliber season, was told, "We can't give you $100,000; Ernie Banks never made that much."[4]

The presence of Ernie Banks in a major-league camp was significant. While his loyalty to Wrigley and simple statements of love and appreciation for the game pleased fans (what else did they expect from Mr. Cub?) and played well in the media (which, for reasons of self-preservation, was almost uniformly pro-owners), it was a blow to the union. Lack of solidarity was the one thing that could doom the union's efforts, in 1969 and the future. Owners were counting on it. While no one publicly complained about Banks (those who knew him felt it was just Ernie being Ernie), his actions had to hurt the men who had staked their careers on union cohesiveness, men like Joe Torre, Milt Pappas, Gaylord Perry, Jim Lonborg, Jim Fregosi (who would soon be traded), and several others who would lose their major-league roster spots because of their labor involvement.

Ernie was not the only Cubs star to profess loyalty to Wrigley, however. Santo and Beckert, in Mesa and working out on their own, told reporters they would report to camp soon, regardless of the union, because they felt they had always been treated fairly by Wrigley. They were spared the difficult choice, however, when new commissioner Bowie Kuhn convinced the owners to negotiate, and the deal was soon concluded, without a significant loss of training time. The baseball business would proceed as usual for one more season.

For years, one of the annual spring rituals in Mesa, Arizona, was the unveiling of the Ernie Banks slogan of the year at the Cubs' camp. Ernie did not disappoint for 1969; if anything, he was more optimistic than usual. He greeted newly reacquired reliever Ted Abernathy in the clubhouse, singing, "Dear Abby, I'm glad you are here. We're going to win the pennant this year."[5] He told one and all that his prediction for the season was (surprise!) a Chicago Cubs pennant. And feeling extra confident this year, he had multiple sayings: "Everything will be fine in '69!"[6] and "The Cubs are gonna shine in '69."[7]

The difference this year was that people didn't laugh behind Ernie's back when he said it. After two-consecutive solid seasons, with almost everyone back, the Cubs looked like they were indeed ready to shine.

Expectations were high in Chicago for Opening Day. Despite frigid temperatures, fans began congregating at 8 a.m. outside Wrigley Field, lining up for the bleacher and general admission tickets available. A total of 40,796, the largest Opening Day crowd in team history, crammed into the park. They would not leave disappointed.

During pregame introductions, Ernie received a standing ovation, as did 73-year-old Eddie Banks, who was seated near the field. Eddie had barely gotten comfortable when his son hit a three-run home run in the first inning, touching off another standing ovation. Ernie added a two-run homer in the third inning, which was career number 476, to pass Stan Musial for 10th place on the all-time list. By day's end, George Langford of the *Chicago Tribune* had counted nine ovations for Ernie. The Phillies tied the game in the ninth inning and took a one-run lead in the 11th, but the Cubs came back and won the game in the bottom of the 11th on a Willie Smith pinch-hit home run, touching off hysteria in Wrigley Field. It was a sign of things to come.

Before anyone could say, "Hey, Hey, Holy Mackerel," there was no doubt about it—the Cubs had won 11 of their first 12 games and were on their way. By mid-June, they were 41–19, and held a nine-game lead.

It was a solid team. They had arguably the best all-around infield in baseball: athletic, smart shortstop Don Kessinger; gritty second baseman Glenn Beckert; Santo, the emotional leader, at third base; and Banks. The entire infield, plus catcher Randy Hundley, would be named to the All-Star Team that July. The outfield had Billy Williams and Jim Hickman. The starting rotation included Ken Holtzman and perennial 20-game winner Fergie Jenkins, as well as Bill Hands, a tough competitor who would win 20 in 1969. The only weak spot on paper was center field and depth in the bullpen. Leo looked like a genius.

As important as talent on the field, there was unity. After a decade of a revolving door on the clubhouse, Ernie Banks's Cubs were finally a team— brothers who knew and cared about one another. Ernie, Billy Williams, and Ron Santo had now been teammates for almost a decade; Beckert and Kessinger had been together since 1965; and Jenkins, Hands, and Hundley had been teammates since 1966.

It became the summer of love in Chicago for Cubs players and fans. "It was a very close team," says Don Kessinger. "The most close-knit of any team I've ever been a part of. We just all got along so well. After a few years we had developed a core. There was very little change. We would go to spring training every year knowing who was going to be there and what the lineup was going to be."[8]

"When I joined the team in 1969 that entire clubhouse was different," says utility infielder Nate Oliver. He added,

Everybody was collectively on the same page. I was welcomed with open arms from day one. You know, sometimes going from one club to another is hard; you don't know any of those guys, don't know how you'll fit in. But they were all great guys who really enjoyed being together. You could go out with any of the guys on the road after games. Sometimes a bunch would go together. Everybody had fun. They would feed off each other. Whatever came up each day, practical jokes, anything, we would just go with it, and all the guys joined in.[9]

"And it wasn't just the closeness of the players," Kessinger continued. "It was the relationship between the players and fans. It was very special."

Excitement had been building among North Side fans for two years, and now it exploded. With each passing week the Cubs remained in first, fans admitted, yes, this is finally the year. The Cubs were the number-one topic of conversation in the city. T-shirts and bumper stickers sold wildly. Bleacher bums in yellow hard hats ruled the outfield. Attendance soared.

And at the age of 38, Ernie Banks, creaky knees and all, was leading the charge for the front-running Cubs. On April 13, he knocked a two-out, bases-loaded single to climax a three-run, ninth-inning rally to beat the Expos, 7–6. On May 13, he hit two homers and a double for seven RBI in a 19–0 win against the Padres. The next day, Banks led off the bottom of the ninth with a home run to tie the game (the Cubs won four batters later). On May 24, his grand slam provided the winning margin in a 7–5 win. Beginning on June 4, he homered in his first at-bat in three-consecutive games.

The big hits came almost daily. After 53 games, Ernie was leading the league with 50 RBI. And it wasn't just his bat that was amazing. Since switching to first base in 1962, Ernie had been among the league leaders in fielding percentage at the position annually, beginning with his first season there, when he finished second, with .993. "The thing about Ernie in the field by then was that he had such fabulous hands," says Kessinger. Added Kessinger,

As an infielder throwing to first base, that was such a pleasure. He didn't move too well laterally at that point and maybe wasn't too good coming off the bag and making plays, but anything in the dirt was caught. He may have been the best I ever saw at digging balls out of the dirt at first base. It was those ex-shortstop hands. He saved me a lot of errors.

Ernie would make only four errors himself all season.

The winning, the hits, the camaraderie—Ernie was on top of the world. Suddenly national newsmen were falling all over themselves at Wrigley Field trying to get to him. Everyone wanted to do a feature—the feel-good story of good things coming to nice guys who had been patiently waiting, and waiting. After all those years in the wilderness, never losing faith, the old man was finally set to be rewarded with the promised land. It was an irresistible angle, and everyone wanted in on it.

For a decade, Ernie had been acknowledged, along with Stan Musial and Brooks Robinson, as a member of the holy trinity of baseball's nice guys. National writers wrote of Ernie as they would their favorite childhood dog: with aphorisms, exaggeration, and love. "Lots of guys can see the silver lining in every cloud," wrote Jim Murray of the *Los Angeles Times* in 1965, "but Ernie can't even see the cloud."[10]

"Ernie makes Rebecca of Sunnybrook Farm look like an old grouch," Murray added in 1967, ladling it on thick. "He's captain of the good ship Lollipop. Life is just one big rock candy mountain. . . . He's the kind of guy who would hang curtains in a dungeon or bring a lunch to the electric chair. If he could be bottled, Ernie would be a cure for mental illness."[11]

Ernie had been winning nice-guy awards for years. In 1965, he received the first annual Ken Hubbs Memorial Award, presented by Chicago baseball writers to the baseball player "whose conduct is exemplary both on and off the field." It was presented by Willie Mays. "When the writers picked the first man to get the award, it had to be Ernie," said Mays. "Nobody has done as many great things on and off the field as Ernie, and he's never got the recognition he deserved."[12]

In 1967, it was the Lou Gehrig Memorial Award for the player who "best exemplifies in playing ability and in personal character the attributes of the late Hall of Fame first baseman of the Yankees." In 1968, Ernie was honored as YMCA Athlete of the Year.

As the accolades piled up, sports fans were saddened by Ernie's magnified plight of doggedly playing on a losing team for almost two decades. He was now recognized as the greatest player in any sport to never make the postseason. And writers uniformly viewed this as one of life's great injustices. "If ever a guy deserves to be in a World Series, it is Ernie Banks," wrote Murray. "If ever a guy is less likely to make it, I can't think who."[13]

By mid-season 1969, however, all that seemed about to change. Reporters flocked to Ernie's locker and converged around him on the field before games. He knew exactly why they were there and what they wanted: Mr. Cub. And he obligingly gave it to them in heaping handfuls.

Before games, he hammed it up for everyone who came by. Spreading his arms and singing with a tattered tenor voice, "Younger than springtime, am I, dee-dee-dee-dee-doo-dee-doo"; he exulted in the sunshine; whether the sun was actually shining that day was completely of no consequence. Standing behind the batting cage, he announced loudly to no one in particular, "It's great to be a major leaguer, isn't it? What a life."[14]

"The area around the [batting] cage is Banks's stage, where he performs like some aging vaudevillian," Mark Kram wrote in a *Sports Illustrated* feature. Kram further commented,

> He sings, jabs at some down-home philosophy, and jabbers in a weird patois that dwarfs those ordinary apostles of boosterism. If he is in St. Louis, he will say, "St. Louis! Home of the mighty Cardinals and the great Stan. St. Louis! Great city. Meet me in St. Looie, Looie. . . ." If he is in New York, he will say, "New York, the Big Apple, the melting pot of the world. . . ." In Chicago, he overflows.[15]

"At every park upon arrival it's, 'Hey, hey, let's play two today,'" wrote Bill Libby in a June 1969 *Sport* article entitled "Why They Call Ernie Banks Baseball's Beautiful Man." "Coming out of the dugout at home, he greets the opposition with 'Welcome to beautiful Wrigley Field, where the sun shines bright in my old Chicago home.'"[16]

Ernie was a one-man sound machine, full of life and enthusiasm. Talking to everyone, talking to no one. Just talking. "Yessir, yessir, the Cubs are gonna shine in '69. And how are you Mr. Billy Williams? And how are those four children? Four children! My, my. I have to hurry up and catch up. And at my age. My, my."[17]

Singing to whatever music was playing over the ballpark loudspeaker, he frequently added his own versions of popular songs: "If I ruled the world, every day the Cubs would win a game."[18] Everyone at the park had something to say to Ernie: groundskeepers, guards, kids, newsmen, opposing players. As one writer noted, he indulged in "verbal exchanges—not to be confused with dialogue," as he fired away. He frequently switched from Yiddish greetings, "Shalom, shalom" (a particular favorite), to French or Japanese—enthusiastically rendered. "It's another lovely day—let's play three games today." Phrases and greetings rolled off his tongue, repeated with an eye-sparkling smile, and then he moved on without waiting for a reply or even an acknowledgment that the intended target had heard.

One visiting writer noted, "Although he appears to be in conversation with the fans, he is actually giving them the Ernie Banks spiel, which is kind of like a used car dealer's TV pitch. It is all to the glory of the Chicago Cubs. . . . Thanks for coming to see the Cubs win today."[19] Everyone loved it. For fans and media members, just being around Ernie Banks for a few minutes made them feel better. They didn't mind that he rarely said anything of substance.

Ernie answered endlessly the one question every reporter was waiting to ask. Sometimes, just to get it over with, he beat them to the punch: "More than anything else, I always wanted to play on a championship team just once before I quit. There's a feeling of pride and love on such a team, I'm just beginning to feel with the Cubs for the first time." He spoke of getting a game-winning home run in the World Series: "Yessir, yessir. What kind of pitch did you hit for your home run, Mr. Banks? Oh, a mediocre fastball, Mr. Newspaperman."[20]

The act Ernie performed for visiting journalists was similar to the one he had been laying on his fellow players for a decade. He was constantly singing in the shower. In the clubhouse, he would walk around and say things like, "Do you have change for three cents?" Or "The weather will be cold, the weather will be hot. There will be weather, whether or not."[21] More or less to himself.

"Ernie was always talking," says Kessinger. "He would talk all game at first. He'd yell over at us, 'Hey, you okay?' That was his way of relaxing and getting into the game."

Sometimes, the talking wasn't particularly welcome. Billy Williams, who probably became the closest to Ernie of any teammate, roomed with him for three weeks when he first came up. Williams asked to change roommates because he couldn't get any sleep; Ernie never shut up. One time before a game, smiling Ernie, in the midst of his usual jovial verbal flood, kept telling Bob Gibson that Billy was going to hit a home run off him that day. Gibson, famous for his lack of civility with opponents, as well as his nasty disposition on the mound, just glowered. Apparently unaware of the growing menace, Ernie joyfully continued poking the tiger. Finally, fearing for his life in the knowledge that he would have to face Gibson four times that day, Billy pleaded with his friend to stop: "Ernie, don't make him meaner, man."[22]

"Guys would always ask me, 'Is [Banks] always like that?'" Williams said in 2015. "I'd say, 'From the minute he wakes up to the minute he went to bed.'"[23]

Not content to entertain only his teammates, Ernie endlessly woofed at visitors to first base, the opposing first-base coach, the umpire, or the other team's dugout. Most opponents enjoyed it.

"I knew Ernie Banks years before I got to Chicago in 1969," says Nate Oliver, who played for the Dodgers and Giants from 1963 to 1968. Oliver added,

> When we would play the Cubs, Ernie made such an impact because of his enthusiasm and passion. He really meant all that enthusiasm too. That's just the way he was. He truly appreciated that he got the opportunity to play Major League Baseball. He understood what a privilege that was, and he appreciated the opportunities baseball gave him in life. He was just so happy to be there he couldn't contain himself.

"Ernie loved to talk," Oliver continued.

He would talk to anybody or anything. He'd talk to the wall if there wasn't anybody around. He just had so much fun. If you got a hit and went down to first
base, it'd be, "How ya doing? How's your family?" He acted like he cared about
you. If the next guy got a hit, you almost were torn about running because Ernie
hadn't stopped talking to you yet.

Even though he held an exalted place in the clubhouse, Ernie was still not
the team leader in the classical sense. He could not be the guy to stand up and
charge out of the dugout with an arrow through his heart. That was Ron Santo's
role. Ernie's leadership style was more by example. But he was respected and
appreciated by teammates.

"He's happy just when he walks into the clubhouse," said Holtzman in 1969.
"He has such a wonderful attitude about everything. Nothing gets him down.
If I had a son, I'd like him to be like Ernie. I couldn't think of a better model."
Santo added,

If I'm on second and he's on first, he'll yell over to me, saying I better put on the
steam. He'll say, "Now Ronnie, don't let me pass you." He's the only guy who
knows how we all feel. He takes time and trouble to know everybody. . . . If he has
something to say, he asks you a question, and then he answers it. He really wants
to give the answer, but he's not that blunt. So instead, he makes it seem like he's
asking you a question.[24]

"Ernie was the best goodwill ambassador for baseball ever," says Kessinger.
He further commented,

He genuinely loved the game, loved coming to the ballpark every day, loved the
Cubs and loved the city of Chicago. Of course, nobody can feel that good every
day, but he put on that face. Every day he came in: "It's a great day, let's play two.
It's a Cubs day." Whether he believed it or not that day, he always put in that
positive attitude. It was true optimism he brought to the park. And it meant a lot
to us to be around a guy like that.

"He was the first one in the clubhouse every day," says Rich Nye. Nye added,

He was always up. For new guys, he would come up and shake your hand, ask
about you, if you're married, do you have kids, is your wife traveling with you.

He was interested in you. And he was always talking to the younger guys, "You look good out there." He wouldn't let you get down or feel bad no matter what happened. He made a point to go out of his way to compliment you and make you feel better.[25]

While enjoying the positive vibes Ernie put out each day, teammates occasionally exchanged a knowing glance after some of his statements in front of the press, for instance, when he told reporters in 1969, "I can't find anything to complain about. People look at me and say, 'Why are you so happy?' It bothers me that everybody can't be as happy as I am."[26]

"Ernie occasionally would say the odd thing," said Fergie Jenkins, who roomed with him for two years in the late 1960s, "a little bullshit here, a little bullshit there."[27]

"He had me confused the first five or six years I was with the club," said Santo in 1969. "Then I finally caught on."[28]

"Ernie gave you, 'Let's play two' and all that stuff, and we knew that a bunch of it was B.S.," said Randy Hundley. "You've got to know Ernie. You have to know what the heck he means when he opens his mouth."[29]

"You'd go back to Chicago from the nice weather in Arizona," said Glenn Beckert, "gray, overcast, 32 degrees in Wrigley . . . start snowing about the sixth inning, and Ernie says, 'Isn't this a great day. We'll keep nice and cool so we don't get overheated!' I mean, he'd actually say horseshit like that!"[30]

Ernie had taken the time to become educated about the different towns and historical places his baseball travels had allowed, still behaving like a kid on a field trip. "One time we had to fly to Tacoma, our Triple A team at the time," Beckert continued. "We had finished a night game in San Francisco, and the plane was delayed. We didn't get into Tacoma until three in the morning." With the prospect of losing sleep and giving up a precious day off for an exhibition game, the players were not happy. Added Beckert,

> And Ernie said, "You guys, tomorrow morning at eight, Tacoma, Washington, has the biggest totem pole in the world, and for all you young guys who have never seen it, I'm taking a tour out there tomorrow morning." Can you imagine? Who wants to see a damn totem pole at eight in the morning after two hours sleep?[31]

"Ernie knew about everything in every city," says PR man Chuck Shriver. He added,

> I don't know how he found out about all that stuff because it was the days before the internet, but, in a way, he was almost childlike in his enthusiasm for seeing

stuff in big cities. I remember on the first road trip I took with the team, we flew to Philadelphia. On the plane he came up and sat down next to me and said, "Ever seen the Liberty Bell?" I told him I'd never been to Philadelphia, and he said, "Well, we'll have to go see it." I thought he was kidding, but the next morning there was a knock on my door. "Ready?" So he takes me around to see all the sights, the Liberty Bell, Independence Hall. It was great because I didn't know where any of them were.[32]

Ernie always had an inquisitive nature, eager to learn about places and things. "I never did see him read a book," said Billy Williams. "But he knew about everything."[33]

Players on the team often ribbed Ernie about his optimistic approach, but most of them silently admired his attitude. "A lot of fellows idolize this guy," said Billy Williams in 1968. "Because when he makes an out, it's just like he's hit a home run. He stays the same way. By doing this, and keeping calm, he's always relaxed."[34]

"I never saw Ernie get mad," says Rich Nye. "No matter what happened. If he popped up, he'd come back, take his hat off, and lay it down."

But what kind of a guy was he? Here was someone who had played in as many losing games as anyone in baseball history—so much so he could be considered a serial loser—and yet each day he showed up and acted like he didn't remember the score from the day before. Didn't it bother him? Why didn't he scream, throw bats, and break clubhouse lightbulbs? Some people had trouble with that, mistook it for softness or that he didn't care. But behind the happy façade, there was surprising steel when it came to the game. "Ernie was competitive," says Oliver. "He had a determination deep down—you weren't going to take anything from him. He had a fire. He just didn't show it. I think that helped with his leadership. You never felt like we should panic, because you watched the way he acted."

"He loved to win," says Kessinger. "He was a tremendous competitor. He hated to lose, but he never made an issue of it. He just came back the next day. But he certainly cared about winning. Baseball is a very difficult game. You don't play as long and play as good as he did without being a competitor."

"It was remarkable how he was able to control his emotions," said Jerry Kindall. "I don't ever remember Ernie losing his temper, on the field or in the clubhouse. He was very competitive, but he was always in control."[35]

Jerome Holtzman, who covered the Cubs throughout Ernie's entire career, said the only time he ever saw Ernie upset was when a Philadelphia columnist described him as having pencil-thin shoulders.[36]

"I've never heard him say anything bad about anybody," said Santo in 1969, "but I do remember once when he was mad. But he didn't say anything. It was, I think, in 1962,[37] when Jack Sanford hit him with a pitch for about the 12th time. When Ernie got back to the dugout, you could see he was upset. He just sat there, looking down, without saying a word."[38]

The incident must have been memorable because Ernie himself mentioned it several times throughout the years when asked if he ever got mad on a baseball field. "I got excited one time, and I regret it," Ernie said in response to a question in 1977. "Jack Sanford . . . hit me in the back with the ball. I was really burning up and churning inside." In this version, Ernie added that he came back to hit a grand slam later in the season off Sanford; however, a check of baseball-reference.com reveals that Ernie hit two home runs the next day against Sanford's teammates and later hit a grand slam in a game Sanford started, but the blow came off reliever Stu Miller; Ernie did hit a solo homer off Sanford on September 2 of that year.[39]

Sanford was a hard thrower with a reputation as a hothead. He routinely threw at Ernie from 1956 to 1965, hitting him on three occasions (less than the players seem to remember). One of the times he hit him was the episode on May 2, 1961, when Ernie was forced to leave the game after Sanford nailed him in the back. Ernie's roommate at the time, George Altman, says Ernie had privately mentioned to teammates that he thought Sanford's actions were racially motivated, but, of course, he never publicly admitted such.[40] Either way, it's obvious hard feelings were involved. In the version Santo told in his book, "Ernie sat down on the bench and made a simple declaration: 'I'll give $100 to the guy who gets him,' Banks announced. At that moment, 24 other guys were ready to jump off the bench to get Sanford."[41]

Away from the ball field and the clichés, Ernie could prove to be a deep thinker, although he kept that part of his personality away from most people. Ernie had always maintained a certain distance from the majority of teammates, preferring his space. In 1960, Rogers Hornsby had told a reporter,

> Actually, I think Ernie enjoys being alone. He usually eats alone, unless he's with a sportswriter. I see him taking walks by himself, sitting in the hotel lobbies by himself, or watching TV in the corner, usually alone. He seems to like it that way, I guess, because he's certainly very popular with the other players.[42]

Ernie often took his meals in the solitude of his hotel room.

"I never did see Ernie after games when we were on the road," says Rich Nye, a teammate from 1966 to 1969. The 1969 team, particularly, was famous for the closeness of the players, with the majority of the team often going out together after road games, sometimes partying with fans into the night. But Ernie, by far the oldest member of the team by that time, never participated. "I'm not sure what he did after games," continued Nye.

Ernie let only a few long-term teammates see the other side of his personality. "I never did really talk to Ernie deeply," added Nye, a Berkeley grad who enjoyed a long post-baseball career as a renowned exotic bird veterinarian. "When you started a serious conversation with him, maybe ask about him and how he felt about something, he would come back and ask you about yourself. He'd turn the conversation around."

"There was a side to Ernie that was much more serious that you don't hear about," says Kessinger, who, while playing with Ernie for nine years, was able to reach a level of familiarity not approached by many. Related Kessinger,

> He covered it up with all the other stuff. There was the side he wanted to be out there—fun-loving, gregarious. But there was also a deep side. You could sit down and have a serious conversation with him. You might have to look for it. He wasn't happy all the time. I've seen him when he wasn't happy.

"Ernie and I had several long and extended conversations during road trips, which were very revealing about his inner goodness, intelligence, and strength of character," said Ken Holtzman, a man with an eclectic intellect who played with Ernie for seven years. "I got to see his serious side, as well as his honesty and knowledge."[43]

The "public Ernie" was almost too good to be true. And he was rarely caught breaking character. "I put my glasses on him one day during the national anthem, and he was singing and crying at the same time," said James Enright in 1971.[44]

"Ernie is the St. Francis of Assisi of baseball," an unnamed "insider who has been around the Cubs for years" told a reporter for *Sports Illustrated* in 1969. "I used to think he was giving everyone the most fantastic put-on, but I've seen him in good years and bad years, and this is the way he is. He is for real."[45]

But not everyone felt Ernie was ready to be canonized. Some complained he was superficial, or that he just said things that put him in the best position. Or that his entire image was an act. "I used to hate you," Tim McCarver told Ernie on his radio show in 2006. "I always thought, 'How can one guy be so happy all the time?'"[46] McCarver was laughing when he said it, but others undoubtedly felt the same way.

Don Zimmer, discussing Ernie defending the Cubs after Zimmer blasted the College of Coaches, said, "Ernie's a fine player and a great guy, but he's a politician. We all know that."[47]

Dodgers catcher John Roseboro, who played against Ernie for 11 years, delivered the most eloquent statement for the prosecution when he wrote,

> Ernie Banks was just too good to be believed. Maybe it's sacrilege, but I believe Banks was a con artist. He was always smiling and always telling you what a great day it was for baseball, and what a great game baseball was and how lucky we all were that we were getting to play two today. No one smiles all the time naturally unless they're putting it on and putting you on. Every day of our lives isn't a good one, and there are even times when we don't want to play baseball, especially doubleheaders. I used to say to Ernie, "Jesus, look at the dark sky. It's cloudy. It's not a great day." And he'd say, "There's a sun behind those clouds, my man." . . . [He was] a great big pain in the ass. I can't believe he believed all that shit he spread around, but that was his image and it made him a kind of folk hero in the game. It made me sick.[48]

"Some of the players may have thought it was an act, but I don't think so," said Jerry Kindall, continuing,

> He genuinely loved the game of baseball, loved his teammates, and loved the Cubs. Seeing him up close and personal for that many years, traveling together, as teammates you hear comments in the clubhouse, you hear if guys have bad things going on or if there are problems. You never heard any of that with Ernie. It was all real. You can't keep up an act like that for that long.

The 1969 All-Star Game was played in Washington. Although Ernie was having a good year, his inclusion in the game caused some controversy. Willie McCovey and Lee May had better numbers and were selected as the first-base starter and backup, respectively. National League president Warren Giles suggested to manager Red Schoendienst that it would be nice if Ernie could be added to the team. Schoendienst agreed, but since lifetime achievement additions to All-Star Teams were not handed out as they are now, he was forced to drop someone from the roster. With so many Cubs already on the National League squad, Schoendienst picked Fergie Jenkins, who had 13 wins and was leading the league in strike outs, as the All-Star to be replaced. While happy to be included in the game, Ernie felt bad about taking his roommate's place and publicly apologized.

Ernie accompanied other All-Stars and reporters to the White House to meet President Nixon in a two-hour informal reception. In the greeting line, the president remarked that Ernie was having a fine year for someone who was 35. When Commissioner Bowie Kuhn corrected him, stating that Banks was actually 38, Nixon said, "Well, he looks 35, and don't tell any of these other fellows, but this man deserves a pennant."[49]

Away from others, Nixon also gave Ernie some encouragement, hoping he would indeed win a pennant after all the tough years. "Then he said, 'I can understand. I went for a lot of stuff I didn't make either,'" Ernie said in 1989. "'I never mentioned that until now, but it was nice of him, wasn't it?'"[50]

After the All-Star break, the Cubs continued their charge to the pennant. "It was the most happiness any of us had ever enjoyed in our lives," Ernie said years later. He added,

> I feel more identified with the '69 team than any of the others, even though my career was almost ended. Winning constitutes love and togetherness that lasts forever. Everybody talks about money, the rings, and publicity, but fellowship you develop during that time is worth more than all of that.[51]

For most of the year, life was great for the Cubs; it couldn't have been better. The players loved one another and knew they couldn't lose. Until they did. The feeling actually started changing as early as July.

Despite fantastic outward appearances, all was not entirely well with the Cubs. Like cheap mortar on a massive dam, there were weaknesses, not visible during the good times early on, but definite structural flaws that would ultimately prove fatal. Leo Durocher was a constant sideshow, a totally unpredictable wild card that hung over everything. His incessant feuds with the media sometimes interfered with the product on the field. His endless mind games wore on the players. Both players and reporters walked lightly in his presence, wary of any idle comment inciting an explosion. The tension was distracting. As the season progressed, Leo totally lost confidence in the bench and shuttled a parade of inexperienced young players and old men to fill the bottom half of his roster, giving each little chance to play before being sent out for the next batch.

While the regulars knew that after a Leo tirade, the next day the slate was clean, the bench players had no such luxury—one mistake could and often did mean the end. Leo ran a total of 41 players through his clubhouse in 1969, and 17 of them played either their first or last major-league season that year. He essentially tried to win the pennant with 15 players. Also, twice during the season Leo went AWOL from the team and was discovered in embarrassing situations, causing further distractions for those men who merely wanted to play winning baseball.

There were also diversions brought on by the attention and newfound celebrity. With hucksters suddenly popping up to pitch schemes to cash in on the craze, a business agent, Jack Childers, was hired to represent the players as a whole. He appeared almost every day in the clubhouse discussing new ideas and showing the players how the money was adding up. Childers, who had worked with Ernie on several earlier projects, used him as an entry to the clubhouse. Through Ernie, Childers was introduced to player rep Phil Regan and then won over the team with his presentation. They made records and commercials, wrote newspaper columns, did special radio programs, and made appearances throughout the city. The players established a money pot from the endorsements and appearances. The loot was to be split up after the season and eventually totaled more than $100,000. Although the players would forever deny it, outsiders questioned whether the players' business deals might take focus away from their regular jobs.

And there was suddenly an unforeseen threat to the Cubs' success coming from the nether regions of the league standings. In the seven seasons of their existence, the New York Mets had never been worthy of a serious thought in the National League, never finished higher than ninth out of 10 teams, and never won more than 73 games in a season. But a 22–9 rampage in late May and June vaulted them into second place. They had the type of pitching that forced teams to take them seriously now—guys named Seaver, Koosman, Gentry, and Ryan, young guns who could knock the bat out of hitters' hands. And their fans were going just as crazy as those at Wrigley Field.

For years, Ernie never said anything remotely negative about individual teammates or the team as a whole, always giving cryptic or bland answers when asked about the fate of the 1969 squad. But in an interview a year before his death, he said he knew much earlier than anyone else that the team was in trouble. The Cubs went into New York in early July up by five and a half games. Ernie said that before the team left for New York, he called the players together and told them, "There'll be more media in New York . . . than you've ever seen in your life. . . . Remember that and be careful . . . and stick together."

"It all came down to that one series, and not just that, but to one game in that series, and, even more, to one inning in that game," he said. The fateful inning was the ninth, on July 8. It was a tight game all the way, a pitcher's duel between Jenkins and Jerry Koosman in front of ravenous fans. The Mets took a 1–0 lead in the fifth. An Ernie Banks home run tied it in the sixth. The Cubs added runs in the seventh and eighth to go up 3–1 heading into the bottom of the ninth. But the last inning did not go well for the visiting team. Twenty-three-year-old rookie center fielder Don Young, by all accounts a quiet, sensitive type, failed to catch two crucial fly balls. Although he was not charged with an official error on either, observers felt he should have had both. The Mets won, 4–3.

After the game, the Cubs still had a three-and-a-half-game lead, but wild-eyed, panicked chaos reigned in the clubhouse. Leo screamed for everyone to hear that his three-year-old kid could have caught the two balls Young missed. Most damaging were comments by team captain Santo, roundly published, to the effect that Young was only thinking of himself, that he had his head down because of frustrations at the plate and took the team down with him.

Ernie was disheartened. "It was never the same. We just stopped being a team. . . . Was it Don Young's fault? No, it was not Don Young's fault. All of us have made big errors. The question is: Do your teammates pick you up? 'Cause it's really about the group, not the guy."[52]

Rich Nye, Don Young's roommate, agrees, commenting,

> That seemed to be the point when there was a change in the mentality. There was much more stress. The focus was on protecting the lead, not on playing and winning. Everyone was walking on egg shells. Leo didn't really make you feel comfortable and part of the team anyway if you were a reserve. It really became two squads—the regulars and the bench players. There wasn't as much camaraderie as you always hear, not from the point of the guys on the bench.

Ernie knew what was coming. Not long thereafter, on a road trip in which they had added to their lead, he invited Ken Holtzman to share a few drinks. "Kenny," he told the 23-year-old pitcher, "we have a nine-game lead, and we're not going to win it . . . because we've got a manager and three or four players who are out there waiting to get beat."

Holtzman was stunned. "I'll never forget it," he said 20 years later. "It was the most serious and sober statement I'd ever heard from Ernie Banks."[53]

The Cubs were soon sensing a kind of pressure they had never felt before. Every day they watched the scoreboard as they played, and every single damned day the Mets were winning. Ernie and some of the other players found themselves staying up late to catch the scores when the Mets were playing on the West Coast, hoping someone would knock them off, but the results were the same. Getting great pitching with obscure role players having career years, the Mets were a runaway train, confident and unbeatable, gaining steam. "It really is hard when you don't have anyone who's ever been through it," says Oliver, who played with three pennant-winners in Los Angeles. "Me and I think Phil Regan and Leo were the only ones in the whole clubhouse who had ever been in a pennant race. Phil was a reliever and I was a utility player, so we weren't the guys to stand up and say something in front of the whole team."

Still, the Cubs played well throughout August. They continued to show resiliency, for instance, the game on August 24, against the Astros. Trailing

8–3 after six innings, they battled back to score seven runs in their last two at-bats to win, 10–9. The final runs were courtesy of a two-run home run by Ernie, his third hit and second home run of the day. The Cubs won their last four games of August to make their record 18–11 for the month. Next, they swept a doubleheader September 2, to go up by five games. But then, suddenly, tragically, inexplicably, it was all over. On September 11, the Cubs fell out of first place for the first time in 156 days. A week later, they were a dead team walking. By October 2, there had been a 13-game shift—the Cubs went from five up to eight down.

Cubs hitting, great throughout the year, had mysteriously stopped. Only Billy Williams (.294) hit better than .265 during that time. Ernie hit .209. In addition to the offensive slump, the normally sure-handed infield developed leaden gloves. Each day featured a new disaster, a new way to lose: an untimely error, a bad call by the umpire on a key play at the plate, a picked off runner, a late home run by the other team. The season exsanguinated so abruptly that no one, least of all Leo, was able to grab a tourniquet. Dazed players drifted in and out of the clubhouse wordlessly, thousand-yard stares all around. Gone were the happy days of the first half of the season. The burden of expectation had crashed in on them; the confidence of six months vanished in a week.

Although the Mets did not officially clinch until September 24, the race was over much sooner. The final three weeks of the 1969 Chicago Cubs season resembled the fall of Saigon. The Cubs had a record of 8–18 for their last 26 games, the worst record in the majors other than the last-place Cleveland Indians during that period.

After the Cubs were officially eliminated, Ernie slowly drove home along Lakeshore Drive, plodding south while trying to put the season into perspective as the chilly waters of Lake Michigan splashed to his left, heralding the onset of another wet, frigid, disappointing Chicago winter. Finally overcome with emotion, he pulled off and parked by the lake. Ernie Banks, the most cheerful, optimistic man the game of baseball has ever known, sat in his car alone and wept.

13

IMMORTAL

The "collapse of '69" would be remembered as one of the most frustrating, inexplicable late-season breakdowns in baseball history. Cubs fans would remember the year with both sadness and questions of what might have been. How did a team with four future Hall of Famers (Banks, Santo, Williams, and Jenkins), a team that seemed so invincible the first half of the season, fail to win it all? The year would be added to the collective pathos of the fan base, along with goats and curses, to be passed on to future generations. Despite the disappointment of not winning it all, however, the 1969 team, by sheer force of personalities and fun, earned a place in the hearts of Cubs fans, and the adoration would only grow during the next four decades.

Throughout the winter everyone ran an autopsy on the team, looking for the explanation. P. K. Wrigley stated that outside interests played a role. The fans "made big heroes out of all of them and undoubtedly idolized the players too much. Most of the players are young and they weren't used to being celebrities. It was something new to them, and they just didn't know how to handle it."

While some players disagreed, Ernie, as expected, parroted the owner's sentiment: "I think Mr. Wrigley is right. We got carried away and probably got overconfident. I know that I'm not going to have a newspaper column next year."[1] Years later, Ernie, like his teammates, would deny that off-field interests were a factor in the team's finish.

Overall, 1969 had been a good year for Ernie Banks, with 23 home runs and 106 RBI. Only two other first basemen in the league had been more productive in driving in runs: Willie McCovey (123) and Lee May (110). The offseason was busy as he enjoyed the demands and perks of his renewed fame. In January, he was presented with the Chicagoan of the Year Award for 1969, by the Chicago Press Club. He also received the "Mister Baseball" award from the Milwaukee baseball writers and was given a trophy naming him the "Greatest Cub Player of All-Time" as the result of a poll conducted by Commissioner Kuhn's office in connection with baseball's centennial. Next, he headed south early as he had been invited to play in the Astrojet celebrity golf tournament in Phoenix before spring training.

The Astrojet was an offseason highlight in those days, an extravaganza thrown by American Airlines for the country's hottest athletes, hundreds of spectators, and dozens of the airline's big-paying customers. The all-expenses-paid trip was a chance for athletes to see and be seen in the early year sunshine, and paired a football and baseball celebrity from each city. Ernie's partner was Bears 26-year-old running back Brian Piccolo, who was recovering from lung surgery in December for the cancer that would soon take his life. True to form, Ernie enthusiastically predicted victory. "Partner, we are going to take it all," he told Piccolo on the phone upon arriving in Arizona. "Come on over and let's discuss our strategy."

Piccolo and his wife went to the Banks's hotel room and as Joy Piccolo and Eloyce Banks relaxed on one bed, eating potato chips and watching television, their husbands sat on the other bed and plotted how they would win the tournament for Chicago. Their plans fell through as soon as the ball was teed up, however. The pair finished far behind the leaders but at least managed a one-stroke lead on the more-glamorous team from New York of Mickey Mantle and Joe Namath. Ernie noticed that Brian was tiring as they walked the 18 holes, and for the final day, he committed a slight breach in tournament rules by showing up with a golf cart—he explained to everyone that his knee was acting up—to help his stricken teammate navigate the course.[2]

As spring training broke, Ernie was as bright and optimistic as ever. "The Cubs will glow in seven-oh," he pronounced. The Cubs were still a strong team with little change to the everyday lineup from 1969. The only essential difference for the season would be at first base. Ernie Banks began to break down for good. The fountain of youth the media reveled in throughout the summer the previous year appeared to have finally dried up. This time there would be no recovery, only a slow, agonizing decline.

Ernie had finished the 1969 season with 497 home runs. At the time, 500 was a magical number—topped only by eight true greats: Babe Ruth, Mickey Mantle, Ted Williams, Mel Ott, Eddie Mathews, Jimmie Foxx, Hank Aaron, and Willie Mays. It was as sure a ticket-puncher for the Hall of Fame as was known at the time.

The buildup to 500 had increased feverishly throughout the 1969 season and continued to be a big topic during the winter. Three weeks into the 1970 season, Ernie hit his first home run. Number 499 came 14 days later, a towering blast onto Waveland Avenue off Reds rookie Don Gullett, who, at 19 years old, was not quite half Ernie's age. The watch for 500 intensified, with media hounding Ernie every day, watching every at-bat. Kids from throughout Chicago snuck transistor radios into their classes, lest they might miss the historic shot during a weekday game.

On May 12, 1970, Ernie achieved the milestone. Number 500, a low line drive into the Wrigley Field left-field bleachers, came off an inside fastball from the Braves' Pat Jarvis in the second inning in front of only 5,264 Tuesday afternoon fans. Jack Brickhouse told Cubs fans, "That's a fly ball, deep to left, back, back, that's it, that's it. Hey, hey, he did it. Ernie Banks got number 500." Banks jogged quickly around the bases with his head down and tipped his hat to the crowd while touching home plate.

After the game there were on-camera interviews for four TV stations, then several radio interviews, and finally a news conference. An hour after the game, Ernie was still cavorting in the outfield, singing, jumping, and clicking his heels: "I feel like I'm 12 years old," he said, adding, "Now we want to go on and win the National League pennant and the World Series."[3] When he finally made it to the nearly deserted clubhouse, Santo and Beckert were there to congratulate him, and there was a hand-lettered sign in his locker: "Congratulations to the greatest."

There were a few other highlights, for example, June 17, when Ernie and Willie Mays both homered at Wrigley Field, marking the first time in baseball history two members of the 500 Home Run Club did so in the same game, and June 29, when Ernie hit two home runs against St. Louis. On a good day, he could still get the bat around quickly, but his knees were getting worse and good days became rare. He visibly limped in the clubhouse and on the field. He missed most of August while on the disabled list for the first time in his career.

The Cubs stayed close to the top throughout the year. The cruel month of September 1969 had stolen some of the magic and enthusiasm, but this was still a formidable team—certainly strong enough to have a shot at the pennant. They occupied first place for two months, then a 12-game losing streak in late June dropped them back. They recovered to pull to within a half game of first place on September 3, and as late as September 15, the Cubs trailed the Pirates by only one game. After returning from the disabled list, Ernie hit .326 in 14 games in September to help with the chase, but the team went 14–14 in the final month, while the Pirates pulled out and won by five games. Ernie finished the season with 12 home runs and 44 RBI while playing less than half the season (72 games).

Ernie released his autobiography, titled *Mr. Cub*, in 1971. As the life story of one of baseball's least controversial players, the production of the book was accompanied by surprising intrigue and acrimony. No less than three publishers were involved in the project in a two-year period, two different agents lined up deals, and at least three different writers were engaged.

Jerry Holtzman of the *Chicago Sun-Times*, one of the most respected writers in the business, originally approached Ernie about a book in the spring of 1969, and got what he thought was an approval. He took the idea to a Chicago publishing house and was given a contract and a cash advance for $12,000, which was to be split between the writer and the player. Everything went well until Ernie began to shy away from the deal. Holtzman had a clubhouse shouting match with Durocher in mid-season, and it was suspected that Ernie, always sensitive to relations with his manager, began to have second thoughts about Holtzman at this point. Holtzman's blowup with Leo may or may not have been the reason, but Ernie failed to show up to a scheduled meeting to sign with the publisher and began to look for a different writer.

Banks's agent, Jack Childers, settled on Brent Musburger, a young sports director at WBBM radio in Chicago, as a replacement. Meanwhile, Ernie, unknown to Childers, decided to go with his personal friend, Jim Enright.

When Holtzman learned of the other deals, he forced a meeting with himself, Banks, and Enright in an Atlanta hotel following a game. Holtzman and Enright argued, and when the meeting broke up Holtzman was officially out.

Upon returning to Chicago, Enright learned of Musburger's potential involvement and confronted him. Musburger apologized for the confusion and backed off. Childers pulled out of the deal as well, and Enright's friend, Frank Scott, became the agent for the project. A new publisher, Viking Press of New York, was chosen.

Unfortunately for those involved, Enright had more enthusiasm than actual writing ability. Viking received Enright's first manuscript in January 1970 and rejected it. They also rejected the rewrite. The following January, Scott found another publisher, and after one more overhaul, the manuscript was accepted and published (Durocher later claimed George Vass of the *Chicago Daily News* had performed the last rewrite).[4]

The result of the maneuverings was a pedestrian, cliché-filled book that failed to do justice to its subject. Since Ernie was still in the game and perhaps felt pressure to preserve the image he had cultivated, there was absolutely nothing negative. Unfortunately, neither was there much actual substance. This was entirely in keeping with Ernie's personality. He gave ample thanks to everyone and threw no one under the bus. All anecdotes had a happy ending. Durocher, never one to sugarcoat his feelings, later wrote of the book,

> All the writers in the country rushed to write what a great book it was, and all of them said in private, "If he wanted to write a book, with all the goodwill he has going for him, why didn't he get himself a writer?" I don't know why it is, but where Ernie is concerned everybody is always ready to fall over and play dead.[5]

Buoyed by the strong last month of the 1970 season, Ernie dismissed every question about retirement during the winter, reminding one and all that he had a two-year contract he intended to fulfill. "They tell me I have the knees of a 60-year-old, but I feel fine and hope I'll be able to play 120 or more games this year," he said. "I want to keep on playing. I still love this game. It's the greatest life in the world."[6] But Ernie's batting average in September 1970 had been fool's gold. The 60-year-old knees failed to respond to treatments and workouts in the spring, and Ernie started the season on the 21-day disabled list—failing to appear in the Opening Day lineup for the first time since 1953.

He returned, but the season became one of agony and embarrassment—for both Ernie and his watching fans. He had clearly waited a year too long to stop playing baseball. At times, the left knee blew up like a balloon; they were draining it twice a week. He could hardly walk. Ernie rarely played an entire game, and most of his appearances came as a pinch-hitter. He managed just three home runs; the final, number 512, came on August 2, off the Reds' Jim McGlothlin. Indicative of just how immobile he had become was the fact that he scored a mere four runs—only once all year did his legs carry him across home plate on anything other than his own home run trot.

There was still drama with the manager. Leo later complained that Ernie set him up for embarrassment throughout the year. Before games, writers would ask Ernie how he felt, and he would tell them, "Great." Then Ernie would tell the trainer he couldn't play and Leo would write him out of the lineup. After the game, writers would ask Ernie why he didn't play, and he would shrug, "The man says I play, I play." Durocher caught heat from the writers, then the fans, who thought he was benching Banks for no reason. He was infuriated that Ernie never defended him or told the writers the truth.[7]

On May 4, 1971, against the Mets, Ernie suffered the indignity all aging sluggers face: He was removed for a pinch-hitter in a clutch situation. Teammates felt Leo purposely compounded the humiliation by allowing him to bat three times against Nolan Ryan, only to pinch-hit for him with right-handed batter Jim Hickman later when soft-throwing lefty Ray Sadecki was on the mound in the eighth inning with men on first and third, and the Cubs trailing, 2–1. Ernie was in the on-deck circle when he unexpectedly saw the shadow of Jim Hickman. Hickman sheepishly told him, "I gotta hit for you."

Banks nodded without emotion, walked back, put his bat in the rack slowly, and sat down on the bench—right next to Leo—and never said a word.

"Hickman told me later it was one of the toughest things he ever had to do," wrote Brickhouse.[8]

Ernie wasn't the only one having problems with Durocher. The good feelings generated by the successful 1969 and 1970 seasons were completely gone by mid-1971. It was a dissension-filled clubhouse. Ken Holtzman, tired of being called a "gutless Kike," despised Leo. So did newcomers Milt Pappas and Joe Pepitone. Even Ron Santo, once a Durocher favorite, grew weary of the incessant acrimony.

The clubhouse tension finally exploded. During a team meeting, Leo, Pepitone, Pappas, and Santo all ended up red-faced and screaming. At one point, Santo had to be restrained from punching the 66-year-old manager. Leo stormed out of the room, telling everyone to hell with it, he was quitting. After the clubhouse fight, Ernie and coach Joey Amalfitano tried to talk Leo into staying. According to Durocher, Ernie pleaded, "Please Leo, don't quit. We want you here. We need you. Don't go doing something you might regret."[9] Leo cooled down, and the crisis was averted temporarily, but it was clear he had irretrievably lost the clubhouse.

On September 3, in wake of the fight, P. K. Wrigley ran an infamous full-page ad in the *Chicago Today* backing Durocher. He concluded with, "P.S. If only we could find more team players like Ernie Banks." While not saying anything openly against Ernie, most players resented the very public implication that they were not team players, only he was.

As the team staggered to the end, the Cubs played the Phillies in a meaningless series, the final homestand of the season. The Cubs were barely over .500 and headed for a third-place finish. It was a miserable, rainy day, with a brisk wind blowing in from Lake Michigan. The outfield ivy had turned brown. It was so cold the teams rarely bothered to throw the ball around the horn after an out—merely returning it to the pitcher so they could all get the hell out of there sooner. Perhaps the weather was appropriate for the conclusion of Ernie's playing career.

Although newspapers had loudly proclaimed it would be Ernie's final game, the team had made absolutely no announcement, and Ernie had said little. As such, only 18,000 fans came out. A pack of frozen reporters followed Ernie's every move before the game. "You must remember those who have to work for a living," he said with a smile. "You must put it in the proper perspective. . . . Isn't it a beautiful day? The Cubs of Chicago versus the Phillies of Philadelphia in beautiful, historic Wrigley Field. It's Sunday in America, let's go." With that, he climbed into the batting cage for the final time as a player.

Durocher had announced previously that Banks would start all three of the final home games (he had only played seven complete games all year). Ernie went 0-for-4 in the first game, then 2-for-4 with a double on a brutally cold Saturday afternoon. In the final game, he got one hit in three at-bats. The hit was questionable—a seeing-eye infield poke that the fielder mishandled. No one complained when the official scorer gave Ernie the benefit of the doubt with an "H"—sort of a thanks-for-the-memories decision. The Cubs then left for the last three games of the season in Montreal, but Ernie stayed home. He was done.

Although Ernie's playing career was over, he was still listed on the roster as a coach. The once-promising Cubs ship had begun to leak oil late in 1970. Now it was dead in the water and listed grievously. Everyone other than the most naïve, die-hard fans realized that the window of opportunity had closed for this group of players and their manager. Amid increasing cries from the public and media to fire Durocher, Wrigley resolutely stuck with him but fired the entire coaching staff other than Pete Reiser and Ernie Banks before the 1972 season. Wrigley had long stated there would always be a place for Ernie with the Cubs as long as he was living and he kept his word.

John Holland announced Ernie would serve as first-base coach and also stay in shape for the possibility of being activated as a pinch-hitter should the Cubs make the postseason; it was a nice sentiment, but everyone realized that was not going to happen. Leo was not overly thrilled with having the owner choose one of his coaches, particularly one who carried the team name, but by this time he knew better than to argue the point. Suffice it to say, the manager rarely spoke to the first-base coach, and he trusted him with no baseball decisions.

The Cubs continued their rapid descent, and Durocher finally stepped down on July 24, 1972. Whitey Lockman was chosen as the new manager, and Ernie remained on the coaching staff. Some civil rights leaders were upset Ernie was not considered for the top job. Beginning in the late 1960s, Ernie's name was usually mentioned, along with Maury Wills and Frank Robinson, whenever discussions took place regarding possibilities for the first black manager in Major League Baseball. When questioned directly, Ernie did his usual dodge; he remarked that he was honored to be included in the conversation but neither confirmed nor denied any level of interest.

Interested or not, Ernie got his shot at managing, albeit only briefly and by unforeseen circumstances. On May 8, 1973, Lockman was ejected early in a game in San Diego. Assistant coach Reiser was out with an injury, and pitching coach Larry Jansen was also absent, caring for his wife after surgery. That left Ernie Banks to assume the mantle. The Cubs trailed, 2–0, when Ernie took over but rallied to tie it up in the top of the eighth. In the 12th inning, with a man on second and the pitcher coming up, Ernie went against convention and had left-hander Joe Pepitone pinch-hit against a left-handed pitcher. Pepitone responded with a double for the go-ahead run. When the Padres went down in order in the bottom of the inning, Ernie had a perfect managing record of 1–0. Writers erroneously assumed Ernie was the first African American to ever manage in a major-league game. The story was picked up and repeated many times by major media outlets and appeared to become common knowledge throughout the years. Ernie himself believed the claim and several times admitted he was proud of the fact. But, in reality, Ernie was the second. None other than his old double play partner, Gene Baker, had achieved the honor, to little fanfare, in similar circumstances with the Pirates all the way back in 1963.[10] Since Baker's team lost that game to the Dodgers, Ernie did achieve the distinction of being the first African American manager to win a game.

After the 1973 season, Lockman got rid of most of the coaching holdovers, and Ernie was reassigned to roving minor-league instructor. In 1974, with the Cubs continuing to plummet after the jettison of Ernie's former teammates, Lockman resigned in mid-season. Jesse Jackson, who had become a prominent voice in the Civil Rights Movement after starting his Chicago-based Operation PUSH (People United to Save Humanity) in 1971, had been demanding a black manager in baseball. Jackson jumped on the opportunity and loudly pushed for the Cubs to hire Ernie Banks. When Wrigley promoted third-base coach Jim Marshall to be manager, Jackson accused the owner of racism for overlooking Banks. Wrigley countered by stating that Ernie was "too nice" for the job and that he had no indication he even wanted it.

This was basically the same response Wrigley had made to inquiries regarding Banks in the past. "I'm too fond of Ernie to make him a manager of anything," he had said. He went on to state that Ernie was headed to the Hall of Fame and didn't deserve to be saddled with so dirty a job as managing.[11] Others in the organization intimated off the record that Banks wasn't organized enough. Also, most felt he was too nice to manage a clubhouse of men, and the thought of Ernie Banks kicking dirt on an umpire's feet was just too impossible to imagine.

Marshall, who had played for the Cubs in 1958 and 1959, inherited Ernie on the coaching staff and was glad of it. "When I got there as manager, Ernie was on the staff," he says. Marshall continued,

> Everybody understood he was an automatic; no one questioned it. Ernie hadn't changed on the surface from when I played with him. He still said the same things. He made you feel comfortable. He had kind of a rhythm to his speech. A lot of repetition. You almost knew what he was going to say before he said it. A lot of constantly encouraging his teammates. Always saying something good to keep everybody up. Always positive. He made you feel good to be at the ballpark. He was a special guy in that regard. I always had a lot of respect for Ernie.[12]

Ernie appeared relaxed and enjoyed his coaching duties. He often spent his time in the first-base coaching box chatting with the opposing first baseman or the umpire. Occasionally, he wandered over to the rail to entertain fans. Signs, sometimes, were of secondary importance. "One day I was on first base and I missed the sign from the third-base coach," said Jose Cardenal. "So I turned around and looked at Ernie and said, 'Ernie, I missed the sign. What am I supposed to do?' So Ernie told me, 'Well, I missed the sign, too, so you're on your own.'"[13]

For his part, whatever level of interest he had in the managing job, Ernie said the right things in public—he claimed to be happy with any job in baseball and expressed no disappointment in not getting the spot. In 2006, Ernie admitted Wrigley called him and counseled him against becoming a manager, telling him, "It's a tough, dirty business."[14]

If Ernie did actually entertain ideas of managing, he had not made an effort to prepare himself for the job. There was an offer in the late 1960s to manage in the Puerto Rican Winter League, as Frank Robinson did, to learn the managing game. But he turned it down, citing the need to spend the winter in Chicago with his family and to look after his business interests.

In a 1976 article in *Jet* magazine, in what was termed an exclusive, Ernie was quoted as saying that he really did want to manage the Cubs. At the time, he was once more working as a minor-league instructor, a job many considered to be beneath a Hall of Fame player but that Ernie enthusiastically said he loved. He said he took the job to gain experience working with young players and better learn the internal structure of the game. The writer for *Jet* stated that Banks should at least have gotten first refusal rights when the Cubs managerial job opened. He quoted Ernie as saying, "I sure would love to manage the Cubs."[15]

Ernie's sentiments were publicly ignored by the team brass. The Cubs managing job changed hands seven times in the first decade after Ernie's retirement from playing, going from Durocher to Lockman to Marshall to Franks to Amalfitano to Gomez to Amalfitano and again to Elia (Jim Marshall once remarked that the Cubs considered having a managers' reunion, but they had to cancel due to the expense—there were too many of them), but Ernie was never given serious consideration. Other than the *Jet* article, he never expressed public remorse but eventually must have realized it was never going to happen, and within a few years, the subject was closed.

In 1977, as expected, Ernie was elected to the National Baseball Hall of Fame on the first ballot. At the time, first-ballot winners were still a rarity—Ernie became only the eighth man to win the honor. He received 312 votes in 383 ballots (288 was needed for election). Eddie Mathews was second, with 239 votes, and Gil Hodges third, with 224. It was noted that Ernie's total of 512 career home runs was only 42 less than the combined total hit by the 10 shortstops previously enshrined. Almost half of Ernie's home runs came while playing other positions, but the 277 he hit were still the record for shortstops until later broken by Cal Ripken's 345 (Ripken had 86 other home runs as a designated hitter or third baseman).

When news of the impending Cooperstown induction broke, papers were filled with cheery quotes about Ernie's sunny disposition and philosophy of life. Milt Richman of United Press International wrote, "Ernie Banks doesn't discriminate. To him everybody and everything is the same. Beautiful."[16]

"It [Ernie's smile] is perhaps the most famous smile in sports," Ira Berkow wrote in the *New York Times*.[17]

"Playing baseball was like waking up every day to a pile of toys underneath a Christmas tree," wrote Will Grimsley of the Associated Press.[18]

"He's the kind of guy who'd tell you that the nice part about a nuclear war is that it would kill all the mosquitoes," wrote Chicago's Bob Verdi.[19]

On induction day, it was gray and overcast, but as Ernie prepared to speak, the heavens appropriately cleared and the sun came out. After being introduced by commissioner Bowie Kuhn, Ernie began, "We've got the setting. Sunshine. Fresh air. We've got the team behind us. So, let's play two." In his brief speech of just less than four minutes, Ernie thanked his parents and family, had his wife and children stand in the crowd to polite applause, and thanked the fans and those who had helped him. Then he added a special recognition to his former owner, who had died just that April. He declared,

There is one man who is not here today to whom I owe a great debt of gratitude. One man who I've respected and admired since we first met in 1953. And that man is Phillip K. Wrigley, one of the finest gentlemen that I ever met in my life. My career and this honor certainly belong to Mr. Wrigley. I only wish he was here today to be with me.[20]

When the Cubs retired Ernie's number 14 in a ceremony on August 22, 1982, making him the first member of the team to receive the honor, the baseball career of Ernie Banks was officially deified. Although he was certifiably immortal, he was still only 51 years old. There were many more years to live.

LIVING AS MR. CUB

Ernie Banks was certified baseball royalty, but that distinction did not guarantee long-term riches like it would a few decades later after the memorabilia market exploded. In the 1970s, anyone suggesting that a baseball Hall of Famer could make $60,000 for a weekend of scribbling his name would have been asked what he'd been smoking. Back then, former players, no matter how immortal, still needed employment to put food on the table.

After P. K. Wrigley died in 1977, his son took over the team and continued the family tradition with regard to keeping Mr. Cub somewhere on the payroll. But others in the organization continued to step over Ernie's head on their way up the ladder. In 1974, Hank Aaron, while strongly criticizing the powers of the game for not allowing African Americans to hold executive or managing positions, had stated he was disappointed Ernie had not been afforded the opportunity of a more meaningful baseball position instead of being relegated to the token spot of first-base coach, which he called the "lowest coaching job in baseball."[1]

Perhaps a mutual understanding was reached that coaching was not Ernie's forte, or perhaps Ernie himself realized he could not progress any higher in the profession—he later said that while coaching, he didn't feel "really productive or valuable."[2] He soon gave up his uniform for a suit and settled exclusively into public relations work for the team. There was no question that this was a perfect fit for Ernie Banks—getting paid to carry out the same role he had been performing for two decades. He shook hands with company executives while trying to sell them half a grandstand for a day, attended business conferences to push season tickets, encouraged Elks and Rotary clubs to set up ballpark picnics, and made appearances and speeches all over town, always in a happy, joking manner—smiling, signing, and telling old war stories. Buy a ticket, meet Ernie Banks—at one point a person could actually walk up to the Wrigley Field ticket office, ask to talk to Ernie about season tickets and be shown to his office, as simple as that. It was a great deal during those long, losing Cubs seasons when there were few other reasons to go to the ballpark aside from beer and sunshine. Ernie was great with the public, and he clearly enjoyed his work.

"Once in the late '70s when I was in college, me and some buddies were at Wrigley Field," says journalist Ed Sherman, who later wrote for the *Tribune* sports department for several decades. Sherman continued,

> We got there early and sat in the grandstand watching batting practice. We heard someone calling out to us and turn around, and here's Ernie Banks, walking down the aisle. "Hey guys, how're you doing? It's a great day. Gonna be a great game." We were blown away. And, you know, he didn't have to do that. He could have just walked on by; we wouldn't have even seen him probably. But he made the effort.[3]

By 1981, the Cubs were hemorrhaging money, and William Wrigley III, buried under the combined weight of inheritance taxes and a recent divorce, finally pulled the plug and sold the franchise to the Tribune Company. With the team no longer under the dominion of the House of Wrigley, Ernie's patronage situation was suddenly in jeopardy. He was initially downgraded to part-time. Then, in a move said to be due to budget cutting, his $25,000-a-year position was eliminated altogether in 1983, something many felt was an inevitable part of General Manager Dallas Green's purge of former Cubs.

While Ernie refused to say anything publicly about the coldhearted release after 30 years with the team, his representatives let it be known he was hurt. Sportswriters throughout the country reacted to the Cubs decision with equal parts rage, indignation, rhyme, and alliteration. One headline read, "Cubs Snub Mr. Cub," another "Cubs' Cowardly Cur Crass in Cutting up Legendary Banks." Simon Legree and Ebenezer Scrooge looked like Mother Teresa next to the Cubs after newsmen finished with them. What was next on their agenda: shoot Bambi's mother, attack baby seals with bats, or maybe go to the senior citizens home and take the rubber tips off the crutches?

The team's official response was as follows: "There are always two sides to every story. The Ernie Banks story also has two sides, and he apparently has chosen to let the newspapers do his talking for him."[4] There was little argument that Ernie had performed his ambassador's job very well, but unnamed team officials leaked that he had been unreliable and missed an unacceptable number of planned appearances, even after being assigned a personal secretary to help with scheduling.

Everyone close to the team had long known that had been part of Ernie's baggage, the accepted price for his popular personality. "Ernie could never say no," says Chuck Shriver, Cubs public relations man from 1967 to 1975. Shriver added,

> He was just so agreeable; he didn't want to turn anybody down. That had always caused some headaches for me as a PR guy. Back then fans had a lot more access to players than they do now. During batting practice Ernie would wander over to the rail and just talk to anybody who was there. Somebody might say, "Hey Ernie, we've got a kids banquet in January, can you come speak?" And it would always be, "OK." Then later he might forget about it. Sometimes I'd find out that he was promised to three places at the same time.[5]

Ernie admitted he had missed some appearances but added that the no-shows had been few and due to scheduling mix-ups. "Two or three in a hundred, and when I did, I'd send a note of apology afterward, and maybe a Cub cap and a ball. I didn't want them to think I ignored them intentionally."

An again-unnamed member of the Cubs staff, only identified as a "high-ranking spokesman," told the *Chicago Sun-Times*, "I hate to say it, but in a few years, people are going to forget Ernie Banks."[6]

Ernie concluded the debate by saying, "I feel I'll always be a Cub. And I feel if there's anything I can do for them, I'll be happy to do it."[7] He would speak of the situation no more.

Ernie had been right. He would always be a Cub; the bond was too strong to ever be broken. He was soon back. As the Cubs charged to the division title in 1984, the club reached out, Ernie was made a honorary member of the team, and the disagreeable episode—a mere stumble on the basepath for both the team and its greatest symbol—was forgotten.

With special permission from the Padres and MLB's commissioner's office, Ernie was allowed to sit on the bench—in uniform—for the National League Championship Series. He wore a big smile as he strolled around the batting cage before the game, bat in hand, joking with members of both teams. Then he threw out the first pitch in the first postseason game at Wrigley Field in 39 years, bowing deeply to everyone in the ballpark before firing the ball toward home plate behind his back.

Thereafter, Ernie would remain part of the Cubs organization for the rest of his life; never full-time employment, but part-time in public relations. Although he was on the team payroll, he would never have a job with any responsibility other than to be Ernie Banks.

In addition to his baseball jobs, Ernie stayed busy with civic duties. He served on the boards of a number of organizations, including the Jackson Park Hospital, LaRabida Children's Hospital, Glenwood Home for Boys, the Metropolitan YMCA, the Joint Negro Appeal, Woodlawn Boys Club, the Chicago Rehabilitation Institute, and Big Brothers. But he also needed regular employment to fill his checking account. While Ernie appeared to be in better financial position than most recently retired baseball players—he had never lived extravagantly and had been laying the groundwork in various businesses for more than a decade before he stopped playing—his future plans were still relatively unsettled. He had taken college classes several times but had never been able to make anything of it; his near-nightly duties of celebrity had always prevented anything more than dabbling in education.

During the winter of 1966, Ernie had opened a gas station at 115th and Racine on the far South Side. Area kids enjoyed running to the station for autographs and pictures, and business appeared to go well. Experience in that venture prepared Ernie for a major move. In August 1967, Ernie and a partner started the Nelson–Banks Ford agency on the South Side. This was no ordinary opening of a car lot. Ernie and his partner, Robert Nelson Jr., were the first black men in the nation to acquire a Ford new-car dealership. At the time, it was only the second black-owned new-car dealership in the United States among 29,000 dealers (the other one was a Chrysler franchise in Detroit). This was big news and made national headlines.

Ford had been carefully looking for a replacement for a dealership that had closed in the area. P. K. Wrigley was valuable in assisting Ernie's startup in the business. "I called Mr. Wrigley and said, 'Mr. Wrigley, I'm going into this business and I don't know a lot about it, I need your help,'" Ernie said in 2000. "He said, 'okay,' and he called up Mr. Ford [Henry Ford II], and they set me up."[8] P. K. Wrigley then bought the first car, reportedly a station wagon.

The 46-year-old Nelson, who had eight years' experience in the auto business, was president and owned 51 percent. He had been a pioneer himself. A member of the Tuskegee Airmen, he had been the first nonwhite commissioned officer in the U.S. Army Air Force and flew 130 missions in Italy during World War II and 66 more in Korea. While Nelson performed most of the business duties, Ernie, who owned 49 percent, provided name recognition and functioned as a handshaking public relations man.

Ernie quickly sold cars to teammates Kessinger, Santo, and Jenkins, as well as such opponents as Juan Marichal and Art Shamsky. By February 1970, it was reported that the dealership was valued at $300,000 and employed 65 people, with a planning volume for the year of 1,800 new cars and 100 trucks. Ernie announced he was scheduled to start in a training program with Ford for more expansion.

In an article in *Ebony*, Ernie discussed his operation, sounding like a business school professor.

> You've got to be aware of the people you're going into business with. You have to know the person, know something about his background, know something about his interest in the particular business you're going into. You have to be very much aware of customer relations. You have to be seen at that business. You have to be involved in the relationship between the business and the people. You have to spend a lot of time with figures and percentages, and how to make profits, and work at it. . . . You have to make plans and how to motivate people. . . . You have to feel that you're making a contribution back to the community.[9]

One of the contributions to the community they made was to sponsor a local Little League team, one of whose members was future ESPN journalist Michael Wilbon. Born in 1958, and raised on the South Side, Wilbon had long viewed Ernie as his hero.[10] And now he was as accessible as looking down at the name on the jersey.

Everything appeared to be going well for Nelson–Banks. Then, a recession swept the country, causing a general declining market, which combined with increasing costs, caused Ford to close the dealership even though local sales had remained steady. Ernie was out of the car-selling game.

He then moved to banking. He had earlier held a part-time job and received executive training at Seaway National Bank on 87th. In 1979, he was hired by the Bank of Ravenswood. He was put through an entire program, starting with teller, and eventually was given a vice president's title. Ernie spoke enthusiastically to reporters about how much he enjoyed working with people and proudly noted he was only one year away from a degree in finance at Northwestern. He said he was busy forming ties with Chicago's most influential power brokers and his goal was to one day become president of his own bank and "do something for the working man."

Ernie said to do that, however, he needed to establish an identity away from the game that had made him famous. "Baseball is really the past now," he explained, adding,

> I don't like to talk about baseball. It's the '80s now, not the '50s. The downtrodden need access. They have to influence the decision-makers. . . . It's hard to

show the world that a ballplayer can be something else. Well, I want to be seen as something else, too, a thinking, highly competent banker. . . . Being a pathfinder, that's what I want . . . I want to help people. Not just here, but around the world.[11]

Despite Ernie's ambition, altruism, and desire to become known as Ernie Banks, international financier and not Ernie Banks, ex-baseball star, his actual duties at the bank didn't seem to amount to much more than playing on the company softball team and sitting in the lobby behind the nameplate that announced to everyone who he was. "I went to interview Ernie when I had just started," says longtime Chicago sports journalist and Cub historian George Castle. He continued,

> He was working at the Bank of Ravenswood. It was a neighborhood bank about two miles from Wrigley. He was sitting at a desk with bank business going on all around him. But he had a clean desk and plenty of time to talk to me. He appeared to have nothing to do, like he was just there for show, just to be Ernie Banks.[12]

Ernie left banking in 1983, and jumped into the insurance business, latching on with the Equitable Life Insurance Company on Michigan Avenue. He talked of enlisting in courses and taking the exam to get his insurance license. But the insurance job only lasted two years. Insurance people were no more willing to forget about Mr. Cub's baseball heroics than bankers had been. "They always thought of me as Ernie Banks the ballplayer," he explained. "It was hard to make a new identity."[13] There would be many other similar positions during the next three decades, always some type of executive position, almost never full-time, rarely lasting more than five or 10 years, and then on to the next phase.

Ernie also tried broadcasting. He had hosted a radio show in the late 1950s, as well as functioned in other radio and TV spots throughout his playing career. For several years in the late 1960s, he did the Sunday night sports on local TV, not uncommonly cheering the Cubs as game highlights rolled: "It was three to three in the ninth, and then I came up . . ." While he was on the disabled list in 1970, he filled in as Jack Brickhouse's color man on Cubs broadcasts. Brickhouse, who worshipped Ernie, worked hard to help him with his enunciation, to break the habits of Southern speak that made it difficult for Northern audiences to understand him. Unfortunately, the efforts resulted in Brickhouse picking up bad habits as often as Ernie forming good ones. Moreover, Ernie could not bring himself to criticize former teammates; he continuously made alibis for them, no matter the circumstances. Brickhouse enjoyed a private game of trying to make Ernie say something critical but always failed. While Ernie looked natural on television and his personality was a good fit, he was obviously not play-by-play material, and nothing came of broadcasting that would make a long-term career.

Then there was the Chicago Transit Authority gig. In 1969, Ernie had been appointed by Republican governor Richard B. Ogilvie to serve on the CTA board. The appointment was for a seven-year term and came with a salary of $15,000 a year. Ernie was still playing at the time and was assured duties would not interfere with his baseball activities. Again, this was big news, and Ernie was a pioneer: He became the first African American to serve on the board.

On the surface, this was a major opportunity for Ernie to make a real difference, particularly for his people, and an overdue, positive step for the city. But there were some negative comments from activists in the black community who saw the appointment as nothing more than a publicity move—appointing an agreeable, conservative African American who didn't know anything about the problems of minority CTA riders. They had a point. With Chicago ghettos growing worse due to crime and dreadful schools, the CTA always seemed to build or extend L routes that ended in white neighborhoods; the level of service in black neighborhoods, where the greatest need for reliable public transportation existed, was spotty at best. Someone was needed in the position who could stand up and fight—loudly and defiantly, if necessary—for improvements.

But that wasn't Ernie's style, and everyone knew it. Despite prominent enthusiasm at the beginning, he was unable to help make significant progress in the areas of need. He seemed to function more in public relations than policy-making. Upon accepting the appointment, Ernie told a reporter, "For one thing, I want to make sure that the elevated always stops at Wrigley Field."[14] There were pictures in the paper of Ernie, or Ernie and his sons, standing in front of trains, accompanied by pithy slogans, but no noticeable improvements for African American neighborhoods. And by 1973, there were complaints in print about Ernie's lack of reliability with the board. The required attendance was one regularly scheduled meeting a month. It was reported that Ernie's attendance record was only .277—less than his batting average during his heyday. There was even some suggestion that the Illinois governor could remove him due to the lack of attendance, most likely a politically motivated move since the governor, by that time, was a Democrat. Rather than be removed, however, Ernie was reappointed when his term expired in 1976, and he served one more term. He never commented publicly on his CTA service, but it was generally felt to be a disappointment.

The different careers kept coming. And going. Ernie later admitted that during the transition period from baseball to business, he experienced panic attacks.

There were times . . . that I felt I had to leave, run away from everything and be a fugitive from myself. I felt trapped. No one looked at me as a human being. There was no reality, just image, image, image. I couldn't get on with my life. I had to be this famous ballplayer, or what people wanted me to be. I couldn't be my own man. . . . I just wanted to be alone so I could find some answers.[15]

Ernie had created the magnificent Mr. Cub character, and that's what everyone wanted. No one seemed interested in the real Ernie Banks, if there was a real Ernie Banks outside of Mr. Cub anymore. The feelings were conflicting. Baseball had been his savior, his refuge; armed with a bat and glove, he had been a true knight of an elite realm. Now, he was just a guy who used to play ball.

"When I got out of baseball, I was like brain dead. I said, 'Gosh, I don't know anything, and I don't know anybody outside of baseball, and I don't have any skills.'"[16]

He saw a psychologist. "She helped me adjust, to get the right perspective on things. It's fabulous being a baseball star. But too many people direct your life. . . . Functioning later on is so difficult."[17]

In 1983, perhaps in a bid to establish a personal identity away from his baseball hometown, Ernie moved to Los Angeles. But his new sources of employment seemed to evolve from his baseball character, as before. He took a job working for Associated Film Promotions, a company that got products placed in movies. The owner, Bob Kovoloff, had worked as a vendor at Wrigley Field when Ernie played and jumped at the opportunity to have Mr. Cub work for him.

At about the same time, Ernie took a position in Los Angeles as executive vice president of New World Van Lines, a moving company based in Chicago. The company was only two years old, and when the owner, Edward Marx, and his wife Shirley spotted Ernie eating at a club, they immediately thought of a great idea: What better way to increase the exposure of a new Chicago company than by having Mr. Cub as a public relations man? They introduced themselves, invited him to their room, and a few hours later Ernie left with a job. Again, Mr. Cub opened business doors.

By the early 1990s, Ernie seemed to have reconciled the struggle between his personal identity and public image, and was splitting his time between Chicago and Los Angeles. His kids had settled in California, and Ernie enjoyed the time with them, frequently playing golf with his sons. Joey had played baseball in college and eventually had a long career in Hollywood working as a stunt man and movie consultant. His specialty was baseball. In addition to providing technical assistance on numerous baseball movies, he had acting roles in *Brewster's Mil-*

lions and *Soul of the Game*, and played a Vulcan baseball player on *Star Trek: Deep Space Nine*. Jerry was a stockbroker, and Jan was a local chef.

Ernie, meanwhile, ran Ernie Banks International Enterprises, a sporting goods marketing firm. He had an office in Pasadena and later Compton. He was also vice president of Compensation Resource Group, which developed executive benefits packages for corporations, and continued to work for New World Van Lines.

But Chicago would always be home, and baseball would always hold Ernie's heart. He made appearances at card shows and banquets, and continued to be a popular participant in old-timer's games throughout the country. Former Cubs players were the first to enjoy a phenomenon that would eventually become a staple for every team: the fantasy camp. The Cubs fantasy camp was started by Randy Hundley in 1982. For years, Ernie and former Cubs, especially the members of the 1969 team, traveled to Arizona each January and entertained rich, middle-aged would-be major leaguers, while playing and having fun themselves. It was a chance to squeeze into a uniform, take the field, and exchange insults with the guys again.

"Randy Hundley's fantasy camps were great," says Don Kessinger. He elaborated,

> We all went to those from the early years because we were still young enough to move and play a little. It was always great to see all the guys every year—Beckert, Santo, Williams, Ernie—great people. And it was just like a big reunion, a lot of laughs and memories, just like we had never left.[18]

At one of the early camps, a contrite Leo Durocher, only months removed from open heart surgery,[19] participated and, at the farewell banquet, stood up and tearfully made amends with team members, particularly Ernie Banks, for how he had treated them.

Ernie enjoyed interacting with former teammates at Hundley's camp and in chance meetings in other places. "Ernie never changed over the years," said Jerry Kindall. He continued,

> After I got out of baseball, I coached at the University of Arizona. Once I took my boys, I think they were 10 and 12, to see the Cubs play the Dodgers. Ernie was a coach with the Cubs then. We were in the crowded clubhouse before the game, and I introduced the boys to Ernie. He lit up and said, "Oh, I am so glad to meet Doug and Bruce. Boy, I'm so glad to meet you. Your daddy was an outstanding player, he could really hit." That was a bit of an exaggeration [the slick-fielding

Kindall hit .213 in his nine-year major-league career], but it was very kind. It elevated me in my boys' eyes. He went out of his way and made me feel like such a valued former teammate. But that's the way he was.[20]

Ernie treated every former teammate the same, even the ones who only played with him briefly, a remarkable feat since the Cubs roster turned over regularly in his early years. "I saw Ernie about 10 years ago at a BAT [Baseball Assistance Team] function," says Doug Clemens, an outfielder who played with the Cubs in 1964 and 1965 (coming to the team as part of the infamous Lou Brock deal). "There was a long line for autographs, but Ernie spotted me in the crowd and jumped up with a huge smile on his face and gave me a big hug. We'd only played together briefly 40 years earlier, yet it was like we were buddies. He was just such a good guy."[21]

Ernie was a regular at Hall of Fame events, hamming it up during the parade and on the podium. In Cooperstown, he was like a kid in a toy factory. He returned every year for the induction weekend festivities and renewed his lasting friendships with other Hall of Famers the likes of Harmon Killebrew and Stan Musial. He frequently joked (with arguably a little truth) with Hank Aaron, Willie Mays, and Musial that his 10 best years were better than theirs.

Despite the misgivings early after he retired as he tried to establish his own identity, Ernie grew to hold immense pride in his status as Mr. Cub. His public personality rarely changed. He talked nonstop to reporters, pouring out the spiel. He told them his goal was to make at least one new friend each day. It was not uncommon for him to break into a song in public appearances or interviews. He would call out to couples, "Are you married?" and to passing women, "Where's your smile? Don't you know it will increase your face value?"[22] He became an ordained minister and performed weddings at Wrigley Field. He could be counted on to provide vintage Mr. Cub enthusiasm at a parade, in an interview, or with unknowns, thrown together by circumstance, for instance, the time he led calisthenics on an airplane that was delayed on the tarmac.

"For 35 years all I did was deal with people I didn't know," Ernie said in a mix of honest introspection and Mr. Cub shtick in 1989. He further commented,

> But the façade was also me. I view people as if they have a sign on their chest which says, "Make me happy," and I got happy by making them happy. . . . I try to focus attention off myself and onto them to make them feel important. . . . The other side of me, though, is that I like to be alone. I never had that opportunity.[23]

Although in his later years Ernie did intimate on occasion the regret of not having enough time alone, he seemed to thoroughly enjoy the fact that he was recognized almost every time he went out. Otherwise, how to explain the fact that he usually spent the first 15 minutes in a public place calling to strangers and making sure everyone knew Ernie Banks was in the house? Ernie never slunk into a back room and had a quiet dinner incognito.

Ernie's public personality could either delight or frustrate journalists. Always with a smile, he put on the same act, regardless of their agenda. "Ernie was different," says Ed Sherman, adding,

He was a complicated guy. I grew up here [Chicago] and followed Ernie's career growing up. He was my idol. I first met Ernie during the strike of '94 at a golf outing. During the strike we [*Chicago Tribune*] were writing accounts of past games to fill the void, and we had just run a story about Ernie Banks Day and had a picture of him and his kids. I asked him if he had seen the article. He said, "No, but I'd love to get ahold of that picture." So I said, "There must be a thousand pictures of you in the file, why don't you come down some day and we'll go through it."

Two days later, I'm at my desk and the front desk calls up: "Mr. Sherman, Ernie Banks is here to see you." He hadn't called or anything, just showed up. But can you imagine? I'm 35 at the time; suddenly I turned into a 10-year-old. It was staggering—I grew up worshipping him; he was larger than life. And here is the front desk saying, "Ernie Banks is here to see you." So I bring him up and we're sitting in the library, pulling out files. And he stayed perfectly in character. He was calling out to people passing by, smiling and shouting out to everyone. He's having a great time, looking at all the pictures and telling stories.

Then it was time for me to go to a meeting for planning the next day's paper. I said I had to go but that he could stay in the files as long as he liked. He asked where I had to go and I told him, and he said, "I'd love to see that." So I bring Ernie to the meeting. And here's Ernie Banks walking into the newsroom meeting, smiling and talking to everyone, just having a ball. And he sat through the whole meeting. Every story presented, he goes, "That sounds like it's gonna be a great story."

I ran into Ernie quite a bit after that, especially when I was covering golf. He was a real golf fan. He loved playing golf, and he loved watching Tiger Woods. He followed Tiger from the first Masters. He later said he stalked Tiger in as many tournaments as he could, just walking along with the gallery, following him. He appreciated that Tiger was a pioneer. He said he always wanted to play with Tiger, but I don't think he ever got to. If not, that's Tiger's loss.

But I saw Ernie a lot, and he was always the same. Sure, there was some shtick involved, but I think Ernie really had a generally positive outlook on life. I don't see how he could have put on an act like that so much and never let down if it wasn't real.

Author Rich Cohen (*The Chicago Cubs: Story of a Curse*) met Ernie several times throughout the years, beginning in his living room when he was young, courtesy of his famous lawyer father. He met him again on the field of the Cracker Jack Classic in 1982, when he was 14, and, in 2014, conducted what was probably Ernie's last major interview. "When I was a kid, he was great," says Cohen. Continued Cohen,

> He talked to me like I was important and joked with me. At the Cracker Jack Classic, he handed me a glove and gave me pointers on fielding ground balls. He was remarkably consistent each time I met him. If his act or persona was a line of bull, it was so practiced and so deep a part of his personality that it became who he was. Ernie never cracked, he never slipped. I never heard of one single incident where he was rude or inappropriate or got mad. At some point along the way, he decided he wanted to be a positive person, and he willed himself to be that way. And he was truly great with kids. He took his time and had fun. He didn't have to be nice to me when I was a kid. No one would have ever known the difference. But he did.[24]

"I grew up in Gary, Indiana, watching Ernie Banks," says Fred Mitchell, who wrote sports for the *Chicago Tribune* for four decades starting in 1974.

> He was magnificent and charismatic, and him being the first African American on the Cubs was significant as well. He was a crossover star who was loved by everyone. At an event with Ernie about 10 years ago, I made the comment that 1959 was a big year for both of us. He was the National League MVP, and I was the West Gary Little League MVP. He got a big kick out of that.
>
> We developed a professional relationship when I joined the *Tribune* as a writer, and later I got to know him better and we became friends. A lot of times he would make random phone calls just to see how I was doing. Initially he asked me to help him write a script for a video he did on the history of great black ballplayers. He had a good sense of history. He came to the realization that I was the first African American with the *Tribune*. He commented on my pioneer status.
>
> As a reporter, when you asked Ernie about things, he gave a lot of stock answers. Into the '80s and '90s he would not touch a controversial topic. I know that frustrated a lot of guys. You just could not get Ernie to make a statement on certain things or get deep into his past. He had a default response when they would get too close. He would turn the conversation around, ask the reporter a question, and deflect the conversation to keep from having to answer an uncomfortable question.
>
> Once later, after we had been friends, I asked him something about race, and he said, "You're the first person who ever asked me that." And he gave me a very

eloquent answer. As the years went by Ernie would talk more about race and certain things; you could get hints about the kinds of things he had to endure silently. There were just so many instances where African Americans were treated differently no matter how they did on the field. Occasionally Ernie talked to me about going through the segregated background in Dallas, and then barely segregated in the army, then the Monarchs, then coming here to Chicago and what a big adjustment he had to make with the white teammates, traveling together. It made me appreciate what he went through.[25]

Ernie "managed to show not a sliver of his inner self in two decades of being in the spotlight" wrote Paul Hemphill in *Sport* in 1971.[26] And he continued that for the rest of his life. He freely gave interviews—almost never turned one down—but while he appeared happy and cooperative, he artfully dodged any true insight. Assiduously refusing to give up the slightest personal detail, he doled out only a few well-worn tidbits from his early years and never elaborated. Unfailingly polite with the media, he would hold forth at length spouting his well-worn phrases and meaningless optimistic proclamations, and at the end of a half hour, the interrogator would have absolutely nothing. Sometimes after listening to Ernie, writers would walk away asking, "What did he say?"

Teammates had been amused. "It seemed like Ernie would never give a straight answer to a reporter's direct question," wrote Ron Santo. "After a while, Billy and I would chuckle to ourselves when reporters would try over and over again to get some controversial quote from Ernie."[27] Most likely, Ernie knew exactly what he was doing. For whatever reason, he had decided he would not discuss subjects painful to himself or others. His image was a hard-candy protective coating. No one was ever able to crack it open to find out what was inside. Some athletes react rudely when prodded with annoying questions; answers range from a terse "No comment" while walking away to suggestions of what the reporter can go do with himself. Ernie's polished dance with writers was his way of saying the same thing but doing it while still looking like a nice guy. Writers who accepted this at face value and were content with the status quo were allowed to remain pleasant acquaintances, even friends. Those who didn't were doomed to frustration.

"One of the things that was infuriating about Ernie was trying to interview him and get any real information," says George Castle. He further commented,

He was not the type to sit down and talk. It was hard to pin him down. I saw a dark side of Ernie also. In 2003, Vinnie Lloyd, the longtime Cubs announcer, died. Vinnie was one of the nicest guys in the world. Everybody loved him. And he was one of the four people who were with Ernie his entire career; Wrigley,

Brickhouse, and clubhouse man Yosh Kawano were the others. I was trying to put together a tribute to Lloyd, and I wanted to get Ernie to say something about him. I met Ernie at Wrigley, but he kept putting me off. We danced for seven innings with me trying to get some sort of comment. Finally, Ernie said, "Just because somebody's with you a long time doesn't mean he's your friend." That amazed me. I mean everybody liked Vinnie. I'm not sure what the deal was.

But Ernie was like that. I grew up in Chicago and was a big fan, but it was disappointing to meet him and find out how he was with the media. He could be very evasive and off-putting when you wanted a serious interview. He was lighter on his feet after his career than he ever was at shortstop. Ernie was great, everybody in Chicago loved him, but he was human like everybody else.

Jim Brosnan, an inquisitive sort, knew Ernie both as a player and a member of the media. Perhaps because he was a writer longer than a player, Brosnan experienced his own exasperation and disappointment at trying to get to the real person behind the image. "I didn't know that Ernie Banks had any opinions except, 'Let's play at beautiful Wrigley Field,'" Brosnan said. "Within those safe confines, he had all kinds of clichés he'd mutter, never venturing an opinion if he had one. He had an act, and he was very good at it."[28]

"Ernie was the ultimate politician," Brosnan said on another occasion, adding,

> He was like that right from the start. It was almost impossible to get to know Ernie Banks. He would say exactly what he was supposed to say. . . . I don't recall having more than a couple minutes conversation with him. . . . You never knew what Ernie was feeling. . . . Jerry Holtzman once told me he and Ernie once were together in a bar late at night after a game. Holtzman said to him, "Ernie, cut the bullshit and tell me what you really think." And Holtzman says he thinks he did, but he's not sure. That's the way Jerry put it. There is another side to Ernie Banks, and I would like to know it. . . . I never heard him take an opposite viewpoint, resenting the discrimination, wishing something else was done. But you couldn't get to him, especially if you were press, 'cause he's got a reputation and doesn't want to foul it in any way.[29]

Similar to his baseball career, Ernie's marriage history was prolific but never reached the postseason. In fact, he was 0-for-4 in terms of long-term matrimonial bliss. The fourth wedding for Ernie came in 1997. The bride, the former Elizabeth Ellzey of Chicago, was 41 years old; he was 66. They told reporters they had met on a blind date. The wedding took place in Barbados with singer Charlie Pride a groomsman and Hank Aaron the best man.

Ernie's three previous marriages had ended in divorce. The first, to Mollye, lasted from 1953 to 1959. They had married young and found themselves thrust into a complicated, rapidly expanding universe—carried in opposite directions by a world they could neither have foreseen nor comprehended when they married before Ernie's final year with the Monarchs. The second and longest marriage, to Eloyce, lasted from 1959 to 1982, and produced three children.

Ernie and Eloyce made a fashionable couple and were often photographed stylishly dressed at charity events throughout the city. By the time they married, Ernie was a universally recognized celebrity, a city-owned property, and they knew what they were in for. There were plenty of good times. Each spring, they would take the kids to Arizona, where Ernie reported a week early for camp. During the 1966 offseason, Ernie and Eloyce took a three-week vacation in Europe, visiting London, Vienna, Paris, Budapest, Rome, and Florence, and stopping off at the Vatican to meet Pope Paul. Ernie told reporters, "Imagine, a poor boy from Dallas, visiting the Pope, eating in sidewalk cafes, dining in the best restaurants with gypsy music in the background. Unbelievable."[30]

But Eloyce eventually grew irritated by the obstacle all of Ernie's wives faced: the need to share their husband's time, to come to grips with the fact that, despite Ernie's intentions, sometimes they felt like they were firmly in second place in the race for his affection—and there was a 3 million–way tie for first. With 81 games a year on the road and a seemingly always full schedule of appearances, both during the season and in the offseason, there was precious little time left for matrimonial solitude. His star was too bright, the demands of the public too great, and the life Ernie chose for himself did not include his father's idea of coming home every night and playing dominoes on the porch.

In 1969, Eloyce told a reporter that she spent most of her time at home with the children to compensate for his schedule of almost nightly testimonial dinners and autograph events. She belonged to no social clubs, and they went to only a few movies a year and rarely entertained. "It would be kind of silly for me to invite people over when my husband will be out making public appearances," she said. Asked about longing for a more normal life, she replied, "You bet I do. And I wonder if it will ever happen. Not as long as Ernie is in a position where he'll never say no." She added he was much different at home compared to the ballpark or out in public—introspective and even moody—and that sometimes she felt compelled to tell him "Ernie, life is not just all ballpark."[31]

"I remember Eloyce got frustrated with Ernie sometimes," says Chuck Shriver. He further related,

She could be very possessive. She seemed to be afraid he was ducking out all the time. I never saw it; I don't think he did. If he did, he hid it very, very well. It's interesting thinking about ballplayers from back then. The guys who were straight arrows seemed to have the most suspicious wives. The ones who ran around a lot seemed to have the wives who never suspected a thing.

But sometimes that caused problems for Ernie. I remember one time he was booked as the main speaker at a big thing up in Wisconsin, the Red Smith Sports Banquet. He called me that day and said, "I can't go, Eloyce is mad at me." I told him it was too late to back out because he was the main event, and he said, "Well, she's going to have to come along." And, oh yeah, "Can you drive?" So I picked them up and drove up there, about a two-and-a-half-hour drive. And the whole time she was arguing with him, just working the poor guy over.

While few breakups are ever pleasant, Ernie's were particularly trying, especially the divorce from Eloyce. It came during his difficult transition period from baseball to the world of business. Perhaps due to the absence of P. K. Wrigley's lawyers, who helped him through his first divorce, Ernie fared about as well as a Cubs pitcher with a strong wind blowing toward Waveland Avenue. While he didn't exactly lose his shirt, it can be accurately stated that he lost his shower clogs. Eloyce retained possession of much of Ernie's personal items and memorabilia in the settlement and soon sold the lot to a collector. Ernie, along with his fans and nationwide media, could only watch with embarrassment as the stuff was auctioned off. Newspapers printed the loot and its haul: A four-foot-tall National League 500–home run trophy netted $14,000, the baseball hit for his 500th home run went for $13,000, a Sterling Silver Bat Award brought $13,500, and a 12-inch brass trophy cup inscribed "Red Smith Nice Guy Sports Award, 1969" went for $425. The auctioneer also sold off a pair of Ernie's wooden shower clogs ($80) and a brass buckle ($50). In all, 85 trophies and mementos from his career were sold for $82,000. While the auction spawned indignant rage among sportswriters, Ernie had no public comment. And he refused to try to buy any of the stuff back.

The third marriage, to Marjorie, lasted from 1984 to 1997. She had been director of human resources for the CTA, and they had been friends for years. Marjorie played a pivotal role in the Marge Schott scandal, serving as part of a group that met with MLB executives and helped with Schott's exit after the Reds owner had made numerous racist comments in public.

The final wife, Elizabeth, became actively involved in the Ernie Banks business. She helped run his foundation and also was founder and president of the 500 Home Run Club, LLC, which provided a website with facts about the men who had hit 500 major-league home runs and attempted to license and market them. She enlisted Ernie's friend Fred Mitchell to write articles for the site.

In 2000, the couple bought a three-story, open-air, lavishly furnished home in a private community overlooking the harbor in Marina del Rey, California.[32] It was a nice neighborhood; Kareem Abdul-Jabbar lived just down the street.

Ernie's trend, if one looks for those sorts of things, was that he married progressively younger women each time, and when the marriages ended he quickly jumped into a new one. Although he was divorced three times, from the time he was 22 years old, there was never a period of more than half a year in which he was unmarried. Someone looking for personality traits might say he didn't want to be alone. But a longtime friend intimates, "Ernie didn't make good decisions when it came to wives sometimes."

Perhaps with his marriages in mind, sometime after 2000, Ernie began changing his answer when asked by journalists why he was always so happy at the ballpark. He once commented,

> Wrigley Field and the baseball diamond was my whole life, a place I could make decisions, when to swing, when to run, when to talk, when not to talk. But when I was at home, none of that existed, I had a wife. . . . I couldn't wait to get to the park. That's where I could control my life, be at ease and friendly and socialize with people.[33]

As Ernie entered his 70s, he remained active. He had thrown himself into his post-baseball passion of golf with the same enthusiasm he had baseball. He spent much time at golf courses throughout Southern California and the Chicago area, rarely missing a charity tournament. He was full of advice and encouragement for anyone on the course or in the clubhouse, not infrequently announcing, "Let's play 36." He was a regular at Cog Hill, Chicago's finest public course, and was on a first-name basis with the pros and workers at numerous courses and driving ranges. His golf game slowed until he finally had the ancient knees replaced in 2004 (afterward, he felt so good he joked about making a comeback in baseball).

And he never stopped thinking large. "I have a lot of goals," he told Fred Mitchell in 2004, continuing,

> First of all, I want to achieve my masters in finance from Northwestern. I want to build an image as a businessperson. . . . I want to write two books. One would be called, *Live Above and Beyond*. Because that is what I think of my life. I want to be around people who live above and beyond, and write a book about them. It doesn't have to be something done in sports. It could be a woman who raises five kids by herself.

My last, but not least, goal is to become the first former professional athlete to win the Nobel Peace Prize. I used to dream about this 30 years ago. . . . I called up a friend of mine—actor Sidney Poitier. I said, "Sydney, I want to win the Nobel Peace Prize. How do I get there?" He said, "Well, Ernie, you have no chance." And we laughed. He said, "You have to be known in America and some other country for doing something worthwhile. And you haven't done that yet." I said, "Well, I still have a little time."[34]

It was not a spurious thought. For the last decade of his life, Ernie talked wistfully to reporters of wanting to win the award. "When he talked about the Nobel Peace Prize people laughed," says Mitchell. "But he was serious. I think that represented his personality. He always fashioned himself as a peacemaker, bringing people together, being a bridge-builder. That is certainly the story of his life here in Chicago."

Ernie never lost his zeal for benevolent causes. He wrote letters to sick patients and frequented hospitals and old folks' homes, visiting, talking, and spreading cheer. He was a regular volunteer for Little Brothers–Friends of the Elderly in Chicago, an organization dedicated to alleviating isolation and loneliness among the elderly. He was honorary president of the Chicago-based Fatherhood Education Institute, which provides resources and education for fathers in impoverished neighborhoods. He set up and ran the California-based Ernie Banks Live Above and Beyond Foundation, which supported under-served communities, senior citizens, and children through various events and programs. It also educated family members and caregivers about palliative care for senior citizens, a project close to Ernie's heart and dedicated to his mother, Essie, who died in 2009, at the age of 97.

Ernie was honored with a statue at Wrigley Field in 2008. The team had never before bestowed such an honor on a player, but there had been talk of an Ernie Banks statue for decades. Most Chicagoans felt it was long overdue. Jesse Jackson helped finally get the project started—first publicly suggesting the idea on Mike North's WSCR-AM morning radio show in 2007, and later meeting with the president of the Cubs to discuss details. The seven-foot, 300-pound bronze statue depicted Ernie in his batting stance wearing his trademark smile. A plaque at the base read, "Ernie Banks: Mr. Cub." The other side of the base had, "Let's Play Two." There was some initial conster-nation when it was discovered that the sculptor had left off the apostrophe in "let's," but it was quickly corrected.

The cold weather and rain did nothing to dampen the spirits of the crowd at the dedication ceremony on March 31, 2008, which included remarks from

Hank Aaron, Ron Santo, Billy Williams, and Jesse Jackson. "I just wish it was 10 or 15 years earlier," Aaron told the gathered crowd.

"He is more than just a baseball player," said Jackson. "This is a great day for Chicago."

"There's nobody who deserves this statue more than Ernie Banks," added Santo.

Amid cries of "We love you, Ernie," and "You're the best, Ernie," the man of the hour stepped up to the microphone. "Seeing this statue makes me think of my dad, who only made it through third grade, and my mother, who only made it to the sixth grade," Ernie told the crowd. He added,

> They might not have been educated, but they were wise. They taught me one of the greatest lessons of my life, and that was to be satisfied. A professional athlete who played his entire career in one city, Chicago, one mayor, Richard J. Daley, one owner, P. K. Wrigley, one park, Wrigley. And I played all my home games under one light, and that's God's light. I was satisfied. It's a miracle I made it from there to here.

Pointing to the statue, he added, "Long after I'm not here, I'll still be here."[35]

No matter who owned the Cubs, it was understood Ernie Banks came with the purchase price, along with the ivy on the outfield wall and the fixtures in the restrooms at Wrigley Field. Ernie became more visible after the Ricketts family acquired the team in 2009, representing the team in a variety of capacities. His salary with the team eventually reached a reported six figures.

Some people may have been surprised to see Ernie riding the Cubs float in Chicago's Gay Pride Parade in 2010. Laura Ricketts, who owns the Cubs, along with her three brothers, was the first openly gay owner of a sports franchise and undoubtedly influenced Ernie's decision to appear, but Ernie had his own personal connection to the cause. He had revealed in an interview in 2004 that one of his sisters had lived with a lady for years, and the family later discovered they were a couple.

Ernie's benevolence and forgiveness showed when he tried to reach out to Steve Bartman and with his approach to steroid-tainted sluggers. While many former greats lashed out indignantly at suspected steroid cheats who eclipsed their records, Ernie took the calm, nonaccusatory approach. In 2010, he publicly urged Sammy Sosa to come forward and answer questions truthfully about steroids. Ernie had maintained a relationship with Sosa since the latter had arrived at Wrigley as a skinny 23-year-old in 1992. Ernie had graciously cheered when Sosa broke his team record for home runs, even as skeptics pointed to Sosa's overbulked physique and rumors of use of performance-enhancing drugs. In the years after his exit from the Cubs, Sosa had become a pariah in Chicago.

Ernie publicly said he wanted to see Sosa and the new Cubs ownership embrace one another, and for Sammy to once again become a fan favorite in Chicago. He told the *Chicago Tribune* he planned to meet with him and convince him how it was possible: "Come clean with it. Explain it to them. . . . Just say, 'This is what happened.' Just admit it and live with it and understand it. I am sure a lot of people will forgive him."[36] Skeptics were moved to ask, was Ernie optimistic or naïve? Either way, it never happened. Ernie traveled to the Dominican Republic to talk to Sosa, but nothing changed.

"That's another example of Ernie being a bridge-builder," says Mitchell. Mitchell further related,

> Sosa had become persona non grata with the Cubs due to his personality, the cork, and the steroid allegations. He wasn't even invited to the big Cubs celebration for the 100th anniversary. Ernie was the only one who came out publicly and wanted to see Sammy and the Cubs reconcile. Ernie didn't have to say anything. He could have just silently gone along with everyone else. But he thought that was horrible and spoke out. He had a very forgiving nature.
>
> He did the same thing with A Rod. When A Rod broke Ernie's record for most home runs by a shortstop, I brought up that he had used steroids. Ernie said, "No, Alex is a great player. I've spent time with him golfing and getting to know his family. He deserves the honor."

Although Ernie never won the Nobel Prize for his efforts, there were plenty of other significant humanitarian honors. He received the Living Legend Award from the Library of Congress, given in honor of contributions to American life, in 2009. He was given the Major League Baseball Beacon of Life Award, which honors civil rights pioneers, in 2011.

His biggest honor came in 2013, when he was invited to the White House to receive the Presidential Medal of Freedom. Established by John F. Kennedy in 1963, the Medal of Freedom is the highest civilian honor bestowed by the United States, given to those who have made "an especially meritorious contribution to the security or national interests of the U.S., world peace, cultural, or other significant public or private endeavors." Appearing on the podium with fellow recipients Bill Clinton and Oprah Winfrey, Ernie became the ninth baseball player awarded, after Hank Aaron, Roberto Clemente, Joe DiMaggio, Stan Musial, Buck O'Neil, Jackie Robinson, Ted Williams, and Frank Robinson. He listened as the official announcement stated, "With an unmatched enthusiasm for America's pastime, Ernie Banks slugged, sprinted, and smiled his way into the record books."

Former teammates Billy Williams, Fergie Jenkins, and their wives, along with friends Shirley Marx of New World Van Lines and Chicago financier John Rogers, accompanied Ernie to the White House for the ceremony.

Ernie had once been a wealthy man, but there were reports he was having cash-flow problems in his old age. He admitted in an interview in 2000 that he had "lost a lot of money" throughout the years.[37] Multiple divorces tend to do that to a guy. During his playing days, Ernie had allowed P. K. Wrigley to withhold half of his salary to invest; he was reportedly one of the only players to take Wrigley up on the offer. He later said that when he turned 55, the investment had grown to $4.5 million. But it appeared to have dissolved throughout time.

Ernie's financial situation puzzled many. "I don't understand why Ernie never could cash in on the goodwill he had in Chicago," says George Castle, continuing,

> He was never able to find stable employment. It's a mystery. He was a conservative African American—the first major African American athletic superstar in the city—who was nonthreatening to whites; he was accepted everywhere in Chicago. In the late '60s, he worked for both WGN and the *Tribune*, the two biggest media outlets, and that gave him a platform in the city. He broke through barriers, and Wrigley was his patron. He could have done anything. His name was golden. He had built up so much goodwill, he could have owned the city. But he seemed to just flit from job to job. He frittered away lifetime security. It was kind of sad that he was so unstable.

Ernie participated in the sports memorabilia boom and attended paid signing events, but that merely gave him walking-around money. He had a website with things for sale but refrained from completely selling his soul to memorabilia dealers. And he gave away as many autographs as he sold. He never signed with a professional, no marketing-savvy lawyer or agency to fully mine the money-making potential of his name. He seemed content to allow his wife or friends to perform the chores. He obviously left a pile of cash on the memorabilia table. Maybe he didn't care; maybe he made a conscious choice not to prostitute his image in an effort to squeeze out every buck; maybe he felt other things were more important than money. It's anyone's guess.

"Ernie worked for us as a public relations man for about 30 years," says the now-retired Shirley Marx, who took over as CEO of the New World Van Lines company after her husband died in 1995. Marx elaborated,

We were very good friends. He was just such a great guy. I'll never say a bad word about him; he didn't have any bad habits. But Ernie didn't have any idea how to manage money. The hardest thing for him to learn was that, for 20 years, in the military and then baseball, from when he was a kid, only 20, somebody told him when to get up, when to go to bed, where to be, when to show up. Then all of the sudden, he's out of baseball. He had never had to do any of those things. It was a very hard transition. And he had no idea what to do with money because he had never had any growing up.

Also, a lot of times, family members and other so-called friends would ask him for money. Ernie never could say no to anybody. Once he was kind of sad and he said to me, "You think all these people who are always asking for something are really friends, but later you find out they're not." Then Liz made him stop working for us. She came and said we weren't paying him enough. I said that was what the contract called for. And she said, "I've decided he's not going to work for you anymore."[38]

Although Ernie had battled high blood pressure for more than two decades, he had otherwise remained in remarkable shape—active and energetic. As he neared 80, however, friends noticed his health was declining. He seemed to visibly shrink, and the once-brisk, athletic gait slowed. He developed a slight stoop and occasionally shuffled his feet.

Those close to Ernie knew there were problems developing in his latest go-round with marriage. While Elizabeth and Ernie were pictured prominently in formal attire at a charity event on the website of the Ernie Banks Foundation, they were rarely spotted together anymore. With great fanfare, media celebrated the adoption by Ernie, then 77, and Elizabeth of an infant daughter in 2008. In reality, the couple had been estranged for more than a year, and the adoption was made solely by Elizabeth, who lived in the house in Marina del Rey, while Ernie spent more and more time in Chicago, living alone in a condominium.

In 2010, Ernie began to be seen in public with Regina Rice, a 51-year-old Chicago talent management agent and lounge singer whose specialty was a Diana Ross tribute show. In 2015, Rice described herself to reporters as a "friend and confidante [of Ernie Banks] for over 12 years."[39] Rice accompanied Ernie to autograph events and personal appearances, and posted YouTube videos of trips to Wrigley Field, Harry Caray's restaurant, and other places. She traveled with him to Cooperstown for Hall of Fame weekends. It was Rice who was photographed at Ernie's side—not his wife Elizabeth—when he received the Medal of Freedom at the White House in 2013. While Elizabeth Banks continued to run the 500 Club, Rice became the registered agent for "Ernie Banks, LLC." As Ernie's health continued to decline, she became his caretaker.

Journalist Ron Rappaport, who had become a friend throughout the years, spent time with Ernie working on a never-completed autobiography and sensed rumination, sadness, and regret. Rappaport later wrote that he was told Ernie was afraid to be alone but at the same time noticed he began to withdraw from friends and family. He still had great fun with guys like Billy Williams and Fergie Jenkins when they got together at Cubs conventions and sports shows, but away from those organized events, contact grew much less frequent. He spent more time alone, hanging around Cog Hill and eating at Harry Caray's restaurant, still smiling and calling out to strangers, but often with seemingly nowhere else to go.

Rappaport questioned whether Ernie had ever really come to terms with his fame, writing that while other baseball stars had an image away from the game, "Ernie escapes all context. He is nothing but sunshine and smiles. Just as he was defined by his image, so was he imprisoned by it."[40]

If Ernie was battling depression, he hid it well in public. He still kept up a busy schedule and looked good at most appearances, but there were reports he was making mistakes when telling stories—the same stories he had been telling for 60 years—sometimes confusing a Hank Thompson for a Bill Blair, or a Dizzy Dismukes for a "Cool Papa" Bell. They were small mistakes but telling and important ones he wouldn't have normally made. But it was little cause for concern, as there had been reports posted online of Ernie repeating stories or missing some obvious facts when talking to fans as early as 2007.[41]

"I thought he was very sharp when I interviewed him," says Rich Cohen, who conducted a lengthy interview with Ernie for *Sports Illustrated* in 2014. Added Cohen,

> I had talked to Roger Angell, who had talked to him at the Hall of Fame the year before, and he said Ernie seemed a little confused at that time. But with me he had great recall and was very interesting. I didn't see any signs of problems. He took my phone number and called me back two weeks later.

Journalist and baseball collector Zach Sanzone watched Ernie at the Hall of Fame weekend in Cooperstown in late July 2014. "Ernie had the biggest smile on his face the entire time," he says. Sanzone continued,

> He was completely engaged with all those he was talking to. When he got out of the van and people called to him, he stopped, turned, and made sure he acknowledged them. Most Hall of Famers just kind of waved and gave a small smile and kept moving, but Ernie stopped completely and waved at everyone. There was a long line of people who had bought tickets to get his autograph, but it took

him about an hour to get through the first 10 or so because he wanted to talk to everyone. Finally, the people running the show asked him to speed it up because the line was out the door.[42]

Ernie could look back on an incredible life. He had swapped handshakes and greetings with nine presidents ("Sons of poor black folks from Dallas don't get the opportunity to meet the president of the United States very often"[43]), played golf with Bill Gates and Warren Buffett at Augusta National ("I golfed with half of the U.S. economy, is this a great country or what?"[44]), chatted up Nelson Mandela, and had a private audience with the pope. More importantly, he had lived through events and seen changes that would have seemed like hopeless fantasy to him as a child. He had seen the day that, given enough money, his family could buy a house anywhere, in any neighborhood, and attend any school they desired, that when two rookies were granted starting assignments in the middle of the infield, the only news was that they were rookies and nothing else, that when two black men opened a new-car dealership, there was essentially no news at all, and that when he visited the White House for the last time, it was a black man who welcomed him into his home.

In 1969, when asked about his life without baseball, Ernie had said to a reporter, "What would I have been? A bread salesman, probably. Or working for a soft drink company, loading trucks in Dallas. I can't think of anything that would have got me out of Dallas and being poor. Timing is everything in life. I was fortunate with the timing."[45] Ernie never let anyone doubt that baseball had been his savior and that he considered himself to be fortunate. To judge the incredible arc of Ernie's life—and the unlikelihood of it—one only has to look at his siblings, raised in the same household, by the same parents, with the same opportunities. Ernie was one of only three who graduated high school. Six of the 11 passed away before the age of 60; two died violently. One hauled laundry, one drove a bus, one drove a truck locally, and several worked in custodial jobs. Few ever left Dallas. Ernie described them all as "brilliant" but noted, "Some people got stuck in time and places, and just couldn't move."[46] Only Ernie made it out.

Ernie never forgot his past and never completely mended ways with the city of Dallas; there were too many complicated feelings. In 1971, he had become the first African American athlete to be elected to the Texas Sports Hall of Fame. In 1977, he had become the first Dallas native to be enshrined in Cooperstown. Yet, old friends felt he had never been given his due by the city, perhaps because city leaders also held complicated feelings and preferred to forget the past rather than deal with unpleasant memories. Ernie rarely returned to Dallas except to visit his mother or for funerals. Few people in Dallas even knew the city was the hometown of Ernie Banks. Several of his friends pitched the idea for a statue or some sort of permanent marker for Ernie in North Dallas as he passed his 80th birthday. After a few years of trying, they got the city to agree to honor Ernie at the reopening of a park in his old neighborhood.

"I had talked to some people at City Hall," says Robert Prince, adding,

> And we had finally gotten approval. There was a Negro Park—the only one in our part of the city. They were going to dedicate it and have a ceremony for Ernie. I talked to Ernie. He was going to come to Dallas for it. He said, "I'll come if you'll invite Charlie Pride.[47] He pitched against me one time, and he's been spreading for years that he struck me out, which he never did. Tell him I'm bringing my bat, and we'll settle this once and for all."[48]

Pride agreed to come and bring his glove, but Ernie never made it back to settle the score.

Ernie fell while alone in his Chicago condominium on October 8, 2014, and was taken to Northwestern Memorial Hospital. He was discharged on October 11, with a recommendation for 24-hour assistance and outpatient physical therapy. His condition continued to decline.

"He missed the last Cubs convention [January 2015]," says Fred Mitchell. "It's a huge event, and Ernie never missed it. He always had a good time. That surprised me that he wasn't there. He used to call me quite a bit but hadn't in a while so I called him and didn't get any response." Within a week, Ernie died of a reported heart attack, on January 23, 2015. He was 83 years old.

Amid the mourning, fond memories, and celebrations of Ernie's life and legacy, an unfortunate postscript was soon added. The man famous for cooperation and peace was the subject of a nasty public battle after his death. Initially, the legal conflict concerned the disposition of his remains. Elizabeth Banks filed a petition to prevent Regina Rice from having him cremated. Rice claimed Ernie had expressed a desire to be cremated and have his ashes spread on Wrigley Field. Although Ernie had once made a similar comment to Jerome Holtzman, preferably with the wind blowing out to left, his will did not contain any such written instructions. While the public learned Ernie had filed for divorce from Elizabeth as early as 2012, citing cruelty, according to Illinois law, disposition determination of the deceased in the absence of written instructions goes to the surviving spouse, regardless of divorce proceedings. The issue was resolved shortly, and Ernie was laid to rest among many of Chicago's past prominent citizens in beautiful Graceland Cemetery, not far from Wrigley Field. This was only the start, however.

Soon, Ernie's wills—there were two of them in question—became hotly debated topics. Elizabeth, along with Ernie's children, contended Rice had exerted undue influence in coercing him into signing a will that gave her control of his estate. They announced they would contest it. Ernie had been driven to an attorney by Rice and signed a will dated October 17, 2014 (nine days prior to his fall and three months prior to his death), giving 100 percent of his estate to the Ernest Banks Declaration of Trust—everything went to the trust to be disposed of under the terms of the trust, of which Regina Rice was the sole trustee. His will also contained wording that he was "making no provisions" for his wife and children, "not for a lack of love and affection for them and for reasons best known by them."[49] A previous will, dated 2008 (drafted by a different attorney), also named Rice as executor and left the estate to a separate trust.

Elizabeth Banks filed the will contest on July 24, challenging Ernie's state of mind at the time of the last will. The children did not join in or file their own contest. Elizabeth charged Ernie had been recently diagnosed with "moderate to severe dementia" and "severe global cognitive impairment," based on an October 14 neuropsychological evaluation performed shortly after his fall.

The public soon learned the extent of Ernie's cash flow problems. At a probate court hearing on February 24, Rice told the judge the initial estimate of Ernie's known assets (held solely in his name) was a mere $16,000. This number was later revealed to be an underestimation of his total worth, as it did not include assets held jointly with his wife and did not include the value of his personal memorabilia, which was significant. The rights to Ernie's name and likeness had been transferred by Banks to his trust in 2014 (to be administered by Rice), and most felt the true value of the estate was in future sales of his name and publicity rights. At the present time, however, there was not even enough in the estate to pay for the burial. On March 6, it was reported that Donnellan Family Funeral Services filed a claim for $35,000 in unpaid funeral expenses. The Cubs quickly agreed to cover the full amount, and the claim was dropped.

During the next two months, a number of other claims were made on the Ernie Banks estate: The Dussias Law Group filed a claim for expenses incurred by Ernie in his pending divorce; Grund & Leavitt, PC, filed a claim for $27,000 in unpaid attorney fees incurred by Ernie; the Law Offices of Jeffrey M. Leving, Ernie's initial attorney when he filed for divorce in 2012, submitted a claim for unpaid attorney fees of $27,000; Barry H. Greenberg filed for $11,000 for fees incurred by Elizabeth; and an accounting firm, Kipnis, Rosen and Bloom, Ltd., filed for $5,100 for representation at an audit. At discovery, it was revealed that Ernie had entered into an installment agreement with the IRS for payment of taxes in 2009 and 2011, in excess of $75,000. In August 2015, Shirley Marx, longtime friend and employer, filed a claim for in excess of $80,000 in unpaid loans. She said Ernie had experienced liquidity problems in the past few years and that she had made personal loans to help him out. Once she found out the state of his affairs, she voluntarily withdrew her claim.

The will was given "proof of will" at a hearing on March 31. The court certified that the signatures were genuine and confirmed the circumstances surrounding the execution ceremony. Two paralegals from the attorney's office testified Ernie arrived with Rice for the 15-minute meeting, that he did not appear to be under duress, and that he appeared to be of sound mind and no illness.[50] No determination was made by the court on the validity of the claims made by Elizabeth Banks. Rice and Elizabeth Banks failed to reach an agreement in several negotiation meetings, and the case remains pending.

Amid these reports, the public mourned the loss of Ernie Banks. There were memorials in both Chicago and Dallas. The Cubs announced they would honor him throughout the 2015 season. The city of Chicago made the unprecedented move of transporting his Wrigley Field statue—it had been in storage while the field was being renovated—to the city's civic center at Daley Plaza for viewing by fans. Perhaps it was only fitting. In 1967, the city of Chicago had erected a 50-foot, 160-ton metal abstract sculpture, an enlargement of a commissioned work by Pablo Picasso, in the plaza. The bewildering statue was met with scorn. Alderman Joe Hoellen introduced a formal resolution in the City Council declaring that instead of Picasso's fiasco, a "rusting heap of iron," they should replace it with a five-story image of Ernie Banks, a "living symbol of a vibrant city."[51] Although the council rejected Hoellen's suggestion at the time, more than four decades later, Ernie finally got his day in Daley Plaza.

EPILOGUE

The happiness he gives, is quite as great as if it cost a fortune.

—Ebenezer Scrooge in *A Christmas Carol*,
by Charles Dickens

Much has been written about Ernie Banks throughout the years. Unfortunately, his image, so pleasant and inimitable in sports, became malleable, used to fit whatever the holder intended. He was turned into a monolithic caricature of good and optimism, and little else. But such a characterization is condescending and misguided, and it obscures the real person behind the image. And there was a real person behind Mr. Cub.

Ernie Banks was a paradox: at once absurdly simple and impossibly complex. Few baseball players have been as recognizable and misunderstood, successful individually while playing on unsuccessful teams, accommodating off the field while remaining cautiously secretive. The questions remain: Was Ernie trapped in the image he had created? Or was he content hiding in it? How did he really feel about the things he had witnessed in his life, the racism, the bad teams, and his personal struggles? It's anyone's guess because he never really said. Perhaps it is wise to stick to the facts and resist the trap of attempting to explain that which cannot be explained accurately.

His on-field performance speaks for itself: Through 1980, he was universally acknowledged with Honus Wagner as one of the two best shortstops the game has ever known. No argument. It's unfortunate that many modern fans do not understand exactly how good and how revolutionary Ernie Banks was at his first position. Many consider the 6-foot-4 Cal Ripken to be the prototype of the big, slugging modern shortstop, but Ripken only topped 30 home runs in a season once and never hit more than 34. Ernie was almost a half-century ahead of his time—it was not until the confluence of advanced weight training and chemical enhancement in the 1990s that Ernie's home run totals were approached by other shortstops.

Ernie's legacy as a pioneer is undeniable. The first African American to play for the Chicago Cubs, he was the only man to ever go directly from the Negro Leagues to Major League Baseball to the Hall of Fame without at least a brief stop in the minors. There were numerous other firsts, for example, the first African American to hold a seat on the Chicago Transit Authority and the first African American to own a Ford new-car dealership. Like his baseball career, he performed these duties with grace and optimism, if not ultimate triumph.

Despite the great accomplishments, it was his personality and actions in dealing with the public that made a place for Ernie in the hearts of fans everywhere, particularly in his adopted city of Chicago. His was one of the most unique personalities in baseball history. He was possibly the most accessible superstar in recent time. Accessible? Approachable? He often *initiated* the conversation with strangers; he made sure everyone in a restaurant knew who he was. After signing events, instead of bolting, he often spent hours wandering the premises, talking to people, on his own time.

Throughout the years, seemingly everyone in the Chicago area had a personal story of meeting Ernie, often in unexpected places, as he seemed to be everywhere. For Chicago residents, it was like finding Superman waiting for a bus in Metropolis—unusual the first time, but after a while he just came with the landscape. But these kinds of things don't happen nowadays. Celebrities are sequestered and cautious; they've learned that everyone wants something from them. Heroes don't mix with regular people anymore. Oh, they might come down from Olympus occasionally for well-crafted, well-protected events, to bestow a signature and maybe a picture or a handshake (don't push it)—for a price of course—and then disappear in a cadre of handlers as soon as the time limit is up. But not Ernie. He was different to the end. He had an extraordinary ability, and seemingly a desire, to connect with strangers.

The stories are impossible to ignore and remarkably similar. Eyes sparkling, grinning widely, Ernie was always cheerful. Sit next to Ernie on an airplane or get on an elevator with him and by the end of the ride, you would exit feeling like he was an old friend.

Ernie could converse at length on any subject, with anyone. He seemed fascinated by other people's lives—their families, their employment, their hobbies. Time didn't seem to matter to Ernie. He could talk to a new acquaintance in a restaurant for more than an hour, happily handing out advice and words of wisdom about patience, forgiveness, avoiding hate, and the joys of children, but, most often, he listened and asked questions—question after question—encouraging his new friend to talk. For kids, his entire face exploded with bright-eyed smiles as he joked and laughed. While most celebrities abhor cameras, Ernie often insisted on a picture. Ernie thought selfies were the greatest invention since the basket in front of the Wrigley left-field bleachers.

On subsequent meetings with regulars at golf courses or restaurants, he amazed people with his ability to remember names and details (the result of an old trick he learned in a memory class: Repeat someone's name several times upon introductions and memorize things about them). He invariably started off with, "How's the wife and kids?" If the answer was, "Ernie, I still don't have either," he would respond, "Well, what are you waiting for?"

The stories of Ernie Banks meetings number in the thousands, but three are presented here to illustrate his initiative in caring about other people and the impact he was able to have on their lives.

"Ernie Banks was my hero," says 70-year-old Darrel Chaney, who had an 11-year major-league career with the Reds and Braves. Chaney grew up near Chicago, in Hammond, Indiana, and never forgot his first meeting with Ernie. Or his second. He continued,

> I would come home from school every day and turn on the TV to catch the last part of the Cubs game and see Ernie hit once or twice. He was a great role model. I admired his commitment to the military—during the national anthem he took his hat off, put his hand over his heart, and sang his heart out. At my 12-year-old Little League banquet [1960] Ernie was the guest speaker. I got a special award for being the Most Valuable Player, and when they called me up, Ernie shook my hand and gave me an autograph. He signed it, "I'll see you in the big leagues."
>
> Well, nine years later, I'm a rookie playing for the Reds, and we go into Chicago in June for our first series there. That was special for me because a lot of family and friends came over from Hammond. Early in the game I got a double and didn't stop at first, but later I beat out an infield hit for a single. I'm standing there on first and all of a sudden, there's an arm around my shoulders and Ernie Banks is standing there with a big smile. "Darrel Chaney! Welcome to the big leagues. I told you I'd meet you some day in the majors." I think there had been an article in the local paper or something and Ernie had seen the story and was waiting for me, but it was just such a huge thrill; standing there in Wrigley Field with Ernie hugging me and my parents in the stands.

Chaney went on to play on three pennant-winners and one world championship team, but he remembers that moment as his number-one major-league thrill.

"It is just so great when you meet your idol and he turns out to be such a good guy. He was an incredible role model. I still have the picture and autograph in a collage on my wall. It meant a lot to me because he took his time to do it."[1]

"I was a combat medic assigned to the 9th Infantry Unit in Vietnam in 1968," says Jerry Schuebel, adding,

> We basically lived on a boat in the Mekong Delta. We would go out on the boat for six or seven days and try to make contact, then get maybe one day back and then go out again. Not a real good time for a 20-year-old kid. One day, a helicopter lands and a guy gets out wearing fatigues and a Cubs hat, and it's Ernie Banks. He was visiting Vietnam as part of a tour with some other guys and had flown into base camp at Dong Tam and heard there were troops out on a boat and flew out to see us. I wasn't really a baseball fan, but I thought it was great that he came out there. Nobody else came out there. Most guys were afraid to. But it was great for us because we got out of no-man's land for a day and the old man put out a steak fry and beer.
>
> When Ernie got off the helicopter he pretty quickly took his shirt off because it was sweltering there in the jungle. He hollered, "Anybody here from Illinois?" Then he called out for Iowa and the bordering states. I was from a small town in Wisconsin, so when he got to Wisconsin I held up my hand, and he came over and we talked. He was real friendly, very personable. He made sure he shook everybody's hand. Somebody had a little camera, and we snapped a shot.
>
> When I got home I started collecting Ernie Banks baseball cards because he had made such an impression. Twenty-five years later, my brother-in-law mentioned that he knew him through the bank he worked at, and so I gave him the book of cards and sent a copy of the picture of us from Vietnam and a little note telling him who I was. Ernie signed every one of those cards and sent a nice note back thanking me for my service in Vietnam. I just thought the whole thing was so nice of him. He didn't have to do any of that but I'll never forget it.[2]

"In 1963, my father had been stricken with a disease that would later be diagnosed as ALS," says Chicago resident Kathy Hounihan. She continued,

> He was a huge Ernie Banks fan. Ernie made an appearance at an opening of a gas station near our neighborhood, and my cousin's husband went down and got an autograph and mentioned to Ernie that my father was a big fan but couldn't make it because he was incapacitated. Ernie acted real interested and talked about him, and I guess got our address.
>
> Well, one Saturday, I was resting in the living room and the doorbell rang. I looked up and there was my dad in his wheelchair talking to Ernie Banks and his wife! They were all dressed up. Ernie said they were on their way to dinner with friends but had some time. He shook hands with everybody and said he

was happy to meet us. Ernie seemed a little reserved and formal at first, but Dad recalled a bunch of highlights from Ernie's career and Ernie's face lit up and soon he was joking and talking about the games. My mom asked them to sit down and got them a drink, and they stayed an hour and just chatted. Ernie was very polite and gentlemanly. He had a big smile. His wife was very gracious.

When they were ready to leave, Ernie pulled out an 8 by 10 picture and signed it. My parents kept the picture on the mantelpiece until the day Dad died. My sister still has it put away. I was 16 at the time and just mesmerized. It was such a big surprise. He acted so interested. I can't tell you how much that meant to my father that Ernie came that far out of his way and took time out of his day on a Saturday afternoon just to meet him. It was so thoughtful of him. He didn't have to do it. There were no cameras around. Nobody in the media would ever know.[3]

Despite occasional suggestions that he was too good to be true or hiding something or putting on an act, there is little evidence that Ernie Banks was anything other than exactly what he appeared to be: a basically good person who tried to do the right thing, who genuinely cared about other people. He was also was one of the best baseball players on the planet but didn't feel that entitled him to anything more than what he had already received from the game.

The basic personality traits Ernie exhibited as a child persisted throughout his life, regardless of the circumstances. Of course, he wasn't perfect. He was as human as everyone else. But that, possibly, makes his public personality even more impressive. Confronted with the choice each morning of how he would conduct himself, he chose to be happy, whether circumstances, win–loss records, social unrest, or family or money problems dictated differently. He chose to be happy and give that happiness to others.

APPENDIX: ERNIE BANKS CAREER STATISTICS

Year	Batting Avg.	Games	At-Bats	Runs	Hits	Doubles	Triples	Home Runs	RBI
1953	.314	10	35	3	11	1	1	2	6
1954	.257	154	593	70	163	19	7	19	79
1955	.295	154	596	98	176	29	9	44	117
1956	.297	139	538	82	160	25	8	28	85
1957	.285	156	594	113	169	34	6	43	102
1958	.313	154	617	119	193	23	11	47	129
1959	.304	155	589	97	179	25	6	45	143
1960	.271	156	597	94	162	32	7	41	117
1961	.278	138	511	75	142	22	4	29	80
1962	.269	154	610	87	164	20	6	37	104
1963	.227	130	432	41	98	20	1	18	64
1964	.264	157	591	67	156	29	6	23	95
1965	.265	163	612	79	162	25	3	28	106
1966	.272	141	511	52	139	23	7	15	75
1967	.276	151	573	68	158	26	4	23	95
1968	.246	150	552	71	136	27	0	32	83
1969	.253	155	565	60	143	19	2	23	106
1970	.252	72	222	25	56	6	2	12	44
1971	.193	39	83	4	16	2	0	3	6
Total	.274	2,528	9,421	1,305	2,583	407	90	512	1,636

NOTES

CHAPTER 1. DALLAS

1. Comments in this chapter by Robert Prince are from a personal interview.

2. Comments in this chapter by Joe Kirven are from a personal interview.

3. Comments in this chapter by Robert Stinnett are from a personal interview.

4. W. Marvin Dulaney, "African Americans," *Texas State Historical Association*, www.tshaonline.org/handbook/online/articles/pkaan (12 December 2016).

5. Dulaney, "African Americans."

6. Edward Everett Davis, *The White Scourge* (San Antonio, TX: Naylor Company, 1940).

7. Harvey J. Graff, *The Dallas Myth: The Making and Unmaking of an American City* (Minneapolis: University of Minnesota Press, 2008).

8. Bill Minutaglio, *In Search of the Blues: A Journey to the Soul of Black Texas* (Austin: University of Texas Press, 2010).

9. "Call to Action," Role of Dallas, *Sixth Floor Museum*, https://www.jfk.org/event/call-to-action-dallas-at-the-crossroads/ (19 December 2016).

10. Tom Siler, "Good Field, Terrific Hit," *Saturday Evening Post*, 21 April 1956.

11. "Ernie Banks," NVLP Oral History Archive, *National Visionary Leadership Project*, 2004, http://www.visionaryproject.org/banksernie/ (3 January 2017).

12. Phillip T. Drotning and Wesley South, *Up from the Ghetto* (New York: Cowles Book Company, 1970).

13. "Negro Workers in YMCA Drive Top $50,000 Aim, Get $65,949," *Dallas Morning News*, 26 November 1947.

14. Siler, "Good Field, Terrific Hit."

15. Randy Galloway, "From Dallas to Cooperstown," *Dallas Morning News*, 20 January 1977.

16. Joe Booker, "Signing Jackie Robinson Killed Negro Leagues, Said Blair," *Black Athlete Sports Network*, 18 June 2005, http://blackathlete.net/2005/06/signing-jackie-robinson-killed-negro-leagues-said-blair/ (14 September 2015).

17. John Hoffman, "Ernie Banks Played His First Game at 17," *Sporting News*, 20 July 1955.

18. Cathy Harasta, "100 Years of Texas High School Football," *Dallas Morning News*, 23 June 2016, https://sportsday.dallasnews.com/high-school/high-schools/2018/05/23/flashback-donnas-1961-football-championship-rio-grande-valleys-one-texas-true-cinderella-story (27 November 2016).

19. William Blair, *A Life Lived: The Story of William "Bill" Blair from the Negro Baseball League to Newspaper Publisher* (Bloomington, IN: AuthorHouse, 2013).

20. Galloway, "From Dallas to Cooperstown."

21. Drotning and South, *Up from the Ghetto*.

22. Dave Condon, "The Cubs' $500,000 Shortstop," *Sport*, July 1956.

23. Harasta, "100 Years of Texas High School Football."

24. Drotning and South, *Up from the Ghetto*.

25. Drotning and South, *Up from the Ghetto*; "Ernie Banks," interview by Julienna Richardson, *History Makers*, 18 July 2014, http://abc7chicago.com/society/historymakers-seeks-to-chronicle-african-american-experience-/145262/ (15 September 2015).

26. Timothy Gilfoyle, "From Wrigley Field to Outer Space: Interviews with Ernie Banks and Mae Jemison," *Chicago History* 27, no. 3 (Winter 1998–1999).

CHAPTER 2. BASEBALL

1. Edward Prell, "The Ernie Banks Story," *Chicago Tribune*, 8 July 1955.

2. Sam Lacy, "From Dime Store Mitt to National League's Best—Ernie Banks," *Afro-American*, 6 August 1955.

3. "Chicago Treasures: Ernie Banks and Minnie Minoso," Chicago History Museum, *WBEZ News*, 12 October 2006, https://www.wbez.org/shows/wbez-news/chicago-treasures-ernie-banks-minnie-minoso/acb77170-8a05-4bf0-aa30-0d28f0b6dd8a (3 January 2017).

4. James Enright, "Banks, Even as a Kid, Was Real Blaster," *Sporting News*, 17 February 1960.

5. Enright, "Banks, Even as a Kid, Was Real Blaster."

6. Tom Siler, "Good Field, Terrific Hit," *Saturday Evening Post*, 21 April 1956.

7. Randy Galloway, "From Dallas to Cooperstown," *Dallas Morning News*, 20 January 1977.

8. Sixty years later he could still tell an interested party every move he made when he scored the series' first touchdown for Washington against Lincoln in 1939.

9. Barry Horn, "Mr. Cub Still Surprises Residents in His Hometown," *Dallas Morning News*, 19 September 1977.

10. Galloway, "From Dallas to Cooperstown."

11. Dave Condon, "The Cubs' $500,000 Shortstop," *Sport*, July 1956.

12. John Hoffman, "Ernie Banks Played His First Game at 17," *Sporting News*, 20 July 1955.

13. Galloway, "From Dallas to Cooperstown."

14. Horn, "Mr. Cub Still Surprises Residents in His Hometown."

15. Jimmy Jordan, "Cubs First Negro Player in Game Here Yesterday," *Pittsburgh Gazette*, 14 September 1953.

16. Galloway, "From Dallas to Cooperstown."

17. Horn, "Mr. Cub Still Surprises Residents in His Hometown."

18. Horn, "Mr. Cub Still Surprises Residents in His Hometown."

19. William Blair, *A Life Lived: The Story of William "Bill" Blair from the Negro Baseball League to Newspaper Publisher* (Bloomington, IN: AuthorHouse, 2013).

20. Kevin Sherrington, "Ernie Banks's Greatness Started with Bill Blair," *Dallas Morning News*, 9 June 2012.

CHAPTER 3. KANSAS CITY MONARCHS

1. Steve Wulf, "The Guiding Light," *Sports Illustrated*, 19 September 1994.

2. Arlene Howard and Ralph Wimbish, *Elston and Me: The Story of the First Black Yankee* (Columbia: University of Missouri Press, 2001).

3. Brent P. Kelley, *I Will Never Forget: Interviews with 39 Former Negro League Players* (Jefferson, NC: McFarland, 2003).

4. Comments in this chapter by Sam Taylor are from a personal interview.

5. Comments in this chapter by Bill Bell are from a personal interview.

6. Comments in this chapter by Ernest Johnson are from a personal interview.

7. "First Negro Coach in Majors," *Ebony*, August 1962.

8. "Buck O'Neil: 1911–2006," *Chicago Tribune*, 8 October 2006.

9. Howard and Wimbish, *Elston and Me.*

10. Howard and Wimbish, *Elston and Me.*

11. Howard and Wimbish, *Elston and Me.*

12. William Blair, *A Life Lived: The Story of William "Bill" Blair from the Negro Baseball League to Newspaper Publisher* (Bloomington, IN: AuthorHouse, 2013).

13. Gregory Simms, "Ernie Banks Recalls His Days in Old Negro Leagues," *Jet*, 10 February 1977.

14. Joe Posnanski, *The Soul of Baseball: A Road Trip through Buck O'Neil's America* (New York: William Morrow, 2007).

15. Maury Allen, "Elston Howard: Portrait of a Key Yankee," *Sport*, May 1965.

16. Posnanski, *The Soul of Baseball.*

17. Fay Vincent, *The Only Game in Town: Baseball Stars of the 1930s and 1940s Talk about the Game They Loved* (New York: Simon and Schuster, 2006).

18. Timothy Gilfoyle, "From Wrigley Field to Outer Space: Interviews with Ernie Banks and Mae Jemison," *Chicago History* 27, no. 3 (Winter 1998–1999).

19. Lee Greene, "Where Does Banks Get All That Power?" *Sport*, December 1958.

20. Greene, "Where Does Banks Get All That Power?"

21. John Hoffman, "Ernie Banks Played His First Game at 17," *Sporting News*, 20 July 1955.

22. Dave Condon, "The Cubs' $500,000 Shortstop," *Sport*, July 1956.

23. Personal interview with Robert Prince.

24. Russ Cowans, "Bolstered Rivals to Challenge Flag Reign of Clowns," *Sporting News*, 6 May 1953.

25. Posnanski, *The Soul of Baseball*.

26. "Ernie Banks Plugs Hole for Kaycees," *Chicago Defender*, 2 May 1953.

27. Larry Lester, *Black Baseball's National Showcase: The East–West All-Star Game, 1933–1953* (Lincoln: University of Nebraska Press, 2001).

28. Buck O'Neil and David Conrads, *I Was Right on Time* (New York: Simon and Schuster, 1997).

29. O'Neil and Conrads, *I Was Right on Time*.

30. Robert Cromie, "West Defeats East 5–1," *Chicago Tribune*, 17 August 1953.

31. Wendell Smith, "All-Star Tilt Fails to Impress Scouts from Big Leagues," *Pittsburgh Courier*, 22 August 1953.

32. Jerry Holtzman, "Banks Given Best Chance to Tie Bambino," *Sporting News*, 3 September 1958.

33. Hoffman, "Ernie Banks Played His First Game at 17."

34. Condon, "The Cubs' $500,000 Shortstop."

35. Brad Wilson, "Dom Caniglia: The Scout Who Knew Ernie Banks Would Be a Star," *Daytona Beach News-Journal*, 7 August 1977.

36. Hoffman, "Ernie Banks Played His First Game at 17."

37. Tom Siler, "Good Field, Terrific Hit," *Saturday Evening Post*, 21 April 1956.

38. Phillip T. Drotning and Wesley South, *Up from the Ghetto* (New York: Cowles Book Company, 1970).

39. Dave Condon, *Chicago Tribune*, 28 August 1975.

40. Greene, "Where Does Banks Get All That Power?"

41. Condon, "The Cubs' $500,000 Shortstop."

42. Siler, "Good Field, Terrific Hit."

43. R. G. Lynch, "Top Negroes Gone Before Gates Opened," *Sporting News*, 15 June 1955.

44. "Dallas Negro Set to Become First in Cubs' Lineup," *Dallas Morning News*, 15 September 1953.

45. Jimmy Jordan, "Cubs First Negro Player in Game Here Yesterday," *Pittsburgh Post-Gazette*, 14 September 1953.

CHAPTER 4. CHICAGO

1. "NAACP in Attack on Segregation," *Chicago Defender*, 28 June 1952.
2. Mike Royko, *Boss: Richard J. Daley of Chicago* (New York: Signet, 1971).
3. Royko, *Boss*.
4. Phil Rogers, *Ernie Banks: Mr. Cub and the Summer of '69* (Chicago: Triumph, 2011).
5. Tom Siler, "Good Field, Terrific Hit," *Saturday Evening Post*, 21 April 1956.
6. Carrie Muskat, "Banks Grew from Early Baker Influence," *MLB.com*, 13 April 2012, https://www.mlb.com/news/c-38614862 (3 January 2017).
7. James Enright, *Chicago American*, 25 August 1953.
8. "Cubs to Bring Gene Baker Up," *Chicago Defender*, 3 September 1953.
9. Revealed in a quote by former player Hank Wyse in Peter Golenbock, *Wrigleyville: A Magical History Tour of the Chicago Cubs* (New York: St. Martin's, 1996).
10. Comments in this chapter by Ransom Jackson are from a personal interview.
11. Personal interview with Jim Willis.
12. Rogers, *Ernie Banks*.
13. Paul Sullivan, "Banks, Baker Cubs' Dynamic Duo," *Chicago Tribune*, 31 March 1997.
14. Comments in this chapter by Bob Talbot are from a personal interview.
15. Rich Cohen, *The Chicago Cubs: Story of a Curse* (New York: Farrar, Straus and Giroux, 2017).
16. "Ernie Banks," NVLP Oral History Archive, *National Visionary Leadership Project*, 2004, http://www.visionaryproject.org/bankssernie/ (3 January 2017).

CHAPTER 5. BINGO BANGO

1. Neil Gazel, "For Cubs He's Money in the Banks," *Baseball Digest*, June 1955.
2. Edgar Munzel, "Bang-Up Batting Labels Banks as Cub Rookie Star," *Sporting News*, 24 March 1954.
3. Peter Golenbock, *Wrigleyville: A Magical History Tour of the Chicago Cubs* (New York: St. Martin's, 1996).
4. Dave Condon, "The Cubs' $500,000 Shortstop," *Sport*, July 1956.
5. Edgar Munzel, "Cubs Traded Smalley Just to Help Him, Says Wrigley," *Sporting News*, 31 March 1954.
6. Hugh Trader, "Banks Won't Stick beyond June, Dykes Wagers Scribe," *Sporting News*, 31 March 1954.
7. "Two Negro Rookies May Solve Cavarretta's Problem," Associated Press, in *Milwaukee Journal*, 3 March 1954.

8. "Cubs' Boss Thinks Pair of Colored Rookies Will Be Hot," *Lewiston Evening Journal*, 3 March 1954.

9. *Sporting News*, 7 April 1954.

10. Danny Peary, *We Played the Game: 65 Players Remember Baseball's Greatest Era, 1947–64* (New York: Hyperion, 1994).

11. Edgar Munzel, "White, Negroes in Game First Time in Hattiesburg," *Sporting News*, 14 April 1954.

12. Lui Virgil Overbea, "Large Crop of Negroes in Majors," *Chicago Defender*, 16 January 1954.

13. Comments in this chapter by Ransom Jackson are from a personal interview.

14. Paul Sullivan, "Banks, Baker Cubs' Dynamic Duo," *Chicago Tribune*, 31 March 1997.

15. George Castle, *The Million-to-One Team: Why the Cubs Haven't Won a Pennant since 1945* (South Bend, IN: Diamond Communications, 2000).

16. Comments in this chapter by Jim Willis are from a personal interview.

17. Timothy Gilfoyle, "From Wrigley Field to Outer Space: Interviews with Ernie Banks and Mae Jemison," *Chicago History* 27, no. 3 (Winter 1998–1999).

18. Comments in this chapter from Bob Talbot are from a personal interview.

19. Sullivan, "Banks, Baker Cubs' Dynamic Duo."

20. Peary, *We Played the Game*.

21. Peary, *We Played the Game*.

22. "Chicago Treasures: Ernie Banks and Minnie Minoso," Chicago History Museum, *WBEZ News*, 12 October 2006, https://www.wbez.org/shows/wbez-news/chicago-treasures-ernie-banks-minnie-minoso/acb77170-8a05-4bf0-aa30-0d28f0b6dd8a (3 January 2017).

23. Sullivan, "Banks, Baker Cubs' Dynamic Duo."

24. "Ernie Banks," NVLP Oral History Archive, *National Visionary Leadership Project*, 2004, http://www.visionaryproject.org/banksernie/ (3 January 2017).

25. "Chicago Treasures."

26. Sullivan, "Banks, Baker Cubs' Dynamic Duo."

27. Sullivan, "Banks, Baker Cubs' Dynamic Duo."

28. "Bruins Label Baker–Banks Combination 'Bingo Bango,'" *Sporting News*, 26 May 1954.

29. Carrie Muskat, "Banks Grew from Early Baker Influence," *MLB.com*, 13 April 2012, https://www.mlb.com/news/c-38614862 (3 January 2017).

30. "Keystones Kept Cubs Out of Alcoholics Anonymous," *Sporting News*, 1 December 1954.

31. Phil Rogers, *Ernie Banks: Mr. Cub and the Summer of '69* (Chicago: Triumph, 2011).

32. Edward Prell, "They Star for the Cubs," *Chicago Tribune*, 3 July 1955.

33. Peary, *We Played the Game*.

34. "Hit in Face by Pitch, Shows That He Knows about Noses," *Sporting News*, 20 July 1955.

35. Peary, *We Played the Game.*

36. Personal interview with Hobie Landrith.

37. Edgar Munzel, "Banks Bolsters MVP Bid on Shortstop Homer Mark," *Sporting News*, 14 September 1955.

38. Personal interview with Lindy McDaniel.

39. "Ernie Banks Refuses 'Day,'" *Sporting News*, 21 September 1955.

40. "Ernie Banks Refuses 'Day.'"

41. Gazel, "For Cubs He's Money in the Banks."

42. Tom Siler, "Good Field, Terrific Hit," *Saturday Evening Post*, 21 April 1956.

43. Bill Surface, "Ernie Banks Has It Made," *Sport*, March 1960.

44. "Banks Receives New Car, Scroll on 'Day' in Dallas," *Sporting News*, 19 October 1955.

45. Siler, "Good Field, Terrific Hit."

46. Sam Lacy, "Cubs Reassign Ernie Banks' Brother after Dixie League Is Hit by Bias," *Afro-American*, 7 April 1956.

47. "Chicago Cubs," *Sports Illustrated*, 9 April 1956.

48. "Cubs Turned Down Cardinal Offer of $500,000 for Banks," *Sporting News*, 19 December 1956.

49. Personal interview with Jerry Kindall.

50. Personal interview with Don Kaiser.

51. Personal interview with George Incledon.

52. James Enright, "Injured Kid's Wish Spurs Banks's Drive for HR Title," *Sporting News*, 25 September 1957.

CHAPTER 6. MOST VALUABLE PLAYER

1. Dave Condon, "Condonsations," *Sporting News*, 18 June 1958.

2. Jerry Holtzman, "Banks Labeled Top Bet to Break Babe Ruth's Record," *Sporting News*, 27 August 1958.

3. Jerry Holtzman, "Banks Given Best Chance to Tie Bambino," *Sporting News*, 3 September 1958.

4. Comments in this chapter from Dick Ellsworth are from a personal interview.

5. Comments in this chapter from Jerry Kindall are from a personal interview.

6. Personal interview with Hobie Landrith.

7. Comments in this chapter from Jim Marshall are from a personal interview.

8. Personal interview with Lindy McDaniel.

9. Personal interview with Pete Richert.

10. Jerry Holtzman, "Ernie Thanks All for MVP Award—Orchid to Wife," *Sporting News*, 31 December 1958.

11. Jim Murray, "Ernie Banks: Baseball's Pollyanna," Associated Press, in *Spokesman-Review*, 6 June 1965.

12. Tom Siler, "Good Field, Terrific Hit," *Saturday Evening Post*, 21 April 1956.

13. Ted Williams and John Underwood, *The Science of Hitting* (New York: Simon and Schuster, 1970).

14. Holtzman, "Banks Given Best Chance to Tie Bambino."

15. Rick Talley, *The Cubs of '69: Recollections of the Team That Should Have Been* (Chicago: Contemporary Books, 1989).

16. Holtzman, "Banks Labeled Top Bet to Break Babe Ruth's Record."

17. Jerry Holtzman, "Homer Goal? 'Not for Me,' Says Banks," *Sporting News*, 21 January 1959.

18. Oscar Kahan, "Players Pick Glove Whizzes of Senior Loop," *Sporting News*, 23 November 1960.

19. Dave Condon, "Condonsations," *Sporting News*, 14 May 1958.

20. "Indestructible Ernie Banks Is Now Baffling Everyone," Associated Press, in *Ocala Star-Banner*, 17 August 1959.

21. Ernie Banks and James Enright, *Mr. Cub* (Chicago: Follett, 1971).

22. James Enright, "Banks, Even as a Kid, Was Real Blaster," *Sporting News*, 17 February 1960.

23. *Jet*, 15 January 1959.

24. *Jet*, 23 April 1959.

25. *Jet*, 16 July 1959.

26. Siler, "Good Field, Terrific Hit."

27. *Jet*, 22 October 1959.

CHAPTER 7. BECOMING MR. CUB

1. Edgar Munzel, "Bruins Nixing All Offers for Biffer Banks," *Sporting News*, 22 November 1961.

2. Carl Sandburg, "Chicago Poems," *Poetry*, March 1914.

3. "Shortstop Ernie Banks Brightens Cubs' Hopes," United Press International, in *Milwaukee Journal*, 1 September 1954.

4. "Bert Wilson Interviews Ernie Banks in 1955," *Bert Wilson and the Chicago Cubs*, http://www.bertwilsonchicagocubs.com/index.html (26 October 2017).

5. Wendell Smith, "Robbie Was Rip-Roarer—Banks Big Breeze," *Sporting News*, 20 May 1959.

6. "Chicago Treasures: Ernie Banks and Minnie Minoso," Chicago History Museum, *WBEZ News*, 12 October 2006, https://www.wbez.org/shows/wbez-news/chicago-treasures-ernie-banks-minnie-minoso/acb77170-8a05-4bf0-aa30-0d28f0b6dd8a (26 October 2017).

7. Monte Irvin, "This Is Where the Negro Ballplayer Stands Today," *Sport*, April, 1957.

8. Personal interview with Larry Davidson.

9. Personal interview with Mike Filipiak.

10. Personal interview with Dennis Freres.

11. Hal Lagerstam, "That Warm Feeling Is Mr. Ernie Banks," *Telegraph-Herald*, 14 October 1964.

12. Personal interview with Jerry Kindall.

13. Lee Greene, "Where Does Banks Get All That Power?" *Sport*, December 1958.

14. "Banks, Mays, Friend Praised by Alston," Associated Press, in *Lodi News-Sentinel*, 12 July 1960.

15. Jerry Holtzman, "Banks Given Best Chance to Tie Bambino," *Sporting News*, 3 September 1958.

16. Greene, "Where Does Banks Get All That Power?"

17. Personal interview with Dick Ellsworth.

18. Personal interview with George Altman.

19. Michael Wilbon, "Banks Was First among Chicago Idols," *ESPN.com*, 24 January 2015, http://carnageandculture.blogspot.com/2015/01/banks-was-first-among -chicago-idols.html (13 January 2018).

20. Jack Koffman, "Banks Is 'Little' Man but Only Off the Field," *Ottawa Citizen*, 5 February 1960.

21. "Ralph Bertam Puckett, Radio Name Bert Wilson," *Bert Wilson and the Chicago Cubs*, http://www.bertwilsonchicagocubs.com/index.html (26 October 2017).

22. Jim Enright, "Cubs SRO Gate 'Three-Way Perfect Day' to Wrigley," *Sporting News*, 10 August 1968.

23. Personal interview with Don Kaiser.

24. Personal interview with Hobie Landrith.

25. Joe Posnanski, "No. 55: Ernie Banks," *JoePosnanski.com*, 30 January 2014, http://joeposnanski.com/no-55-ernie-banks/ (4 March 2016).

26. Personal communication with George Altman.

27. James Enright, "Cub Boss Sets Precedent by Honoring First Player," *Sporting News*, 22 August 1964.

28. Jerome Holtzman, "Banks, Honored by 20,000, Thankful He's an American," *Sporting News*, 29 August 1964.

CHAPTER 8. THE OLD COLLEGE EFFORT

1. James Enright, "P. K. Defies Critics of 'Coaching College,'" *Sporting News*, 25 January 1961.

2. Walter Bingham, "The Cubs and All Their Coaches," *Sports Illustrated*, 10 April 1961.

3. Bingham, "The Cubs and All Their Coaches."

4. Peter Golenbock, *Wrigleyville: A Magical History Tour of the Chicago Cubs* (New York: St. Martin's, 1996).

5. Edgar Munzel, "Bruins' Teddy Bear Road Act Traced to Slipshod Discipline," *Sporting News*, 6 September 1961.

6. Danny Peary, *We Played the Game: 65 Players Remember Baseball's Greatest Era, 1947–64* (New York: Hyperion, 1994).

7. Tom Siler, "Good Field, Terrific Hit," *Saturday Evening Post*, 21 April 1956.

8. Edgar Munzel, "Al Tabbed Leader for Cubs' Infield," *Sporting News*, 28 May 1958.

9. Peary, *We Played the Game*.

10. "Ernie Banks to Try Extra Batting Practice," Associated Press, in *Pittsburgh Post-Gazette*, 26 April 1961.

11. Golenbock, *Wrigleyville*.

12. Personal interview with Don Kessinger.

13. Lou Brock and Franz Schulze, *Stealing Is My Game* (Englewood Cliffs, NJ: Prentice Hall, 1976).

14. "Edgar Munzel, "Banks Lands Kayo Rap on Injuries Hex," *Sporting News*, 8 November 1961.

15. "Ernie Banks Back in Lineup and He Smacks Three Homers," Associated Press, in *Lawrence Journal-World*, 30 May 1962.

CHAPTER 9. WINDMILLS

1. "Ernie Banks Plans Career in Politics," *Pittsburgh Press*, 21 December 1962.

2. Jerome Holtzman, "Old-Pro Politicians Try to Whiff Banks in Alderman's Race," *Sporting News*, 2 February 1963.

3. "Cubs' Banks to Run for Alderman's Seat," *Chicago Tribune*, 21 December 1962.

4. Ray Gillespie, "Diamond Facts and Facets," *Sporting News*, 19 January 1963.

5. "Cubs' Banks to Run for Alderman's Seat."

6. "Cubs' Banks to Run for Alderman's Seat."

7. John Kuenster, "Slugger Banks Swings for HR in Ballot Box," *Sporting News*, 16 February 1963.

8. Mike Royko, *Boss: Richard J. Daley of Chicago* (New York: E. P. Dutton, 1971).

9. Kuenster, "Slugger Banks Swings for HR in Ballot Box."

10. "Cubs' Banks to Run for Alderman's Seat."

11. "Political Curves 'Much Easier' Says Ernie Banks," Associated Press, in *Herald-Journal*, 23 February 1963.

12. "Ernie Banks Strikes Out in First At-Bat in Politics," Associated Press, in *Eugene Register Guard*, 27 February 1963.

13. Red Smith, "Banks Ran Better Race Than Cubs," syndicated in *Miami News*, 5 April 1963.

14. Jerome Holtzman, "Banks, Political Whiff Victim, Ready to Take Cut Again in '67," *Sporting News*, 16 March 1963.

15. Lester Biedermann, "Ernie Banks Expects to Take Another Whirl at Politics," *Pittsburgh Press*, 8 May 1963.

16. Smith, "Banks Ran Better Race Than Cubs."

17. Timothy Gilfoyle, "From Wrigley Field to Outer Space: Interviews with Ernie Banks and Mae Jemison," *Chicago History* 27, no. 3 (Winter 1998–1999).

18. "Metro Wonders If Bruins Will Take or Play 'Marbles,'" *Sporting News*, 20 April 1963.

19. Personal interview with Lindy McDaniel.

20. Edgar Munzel, "Banks's Spirit High—Weary Feeling Gone," *Sporting News*, 25 January 1964.

CHAPTER 10. LEO FEROCIOUS

1. Leo Durocher, with Ed Linn, *Nice Guys Finish Last* (Richmond Hill, Ontario: Pocketbooks, 1976).

2. Leonard Shecter, "Leo Durocher Is 60 Years Old," *Sport*, November 1966.

3. Edgar Munzel, "P. K. Asks Lippy to Lead Cubs to Light," *Sporting News*, 6 November 1965.

4. Arthur Daley, "Leo Earns a Reprieve," *New York Times*, 25 November 1971.

5. Billy Williams, with Fred Mitchell, *My Sweet-Swinging Lifetime with the Cubs* (Chicago: Triumph, 2008).

6. Edgar Munzel, "Cubs' Biggest Sin? Those Mental Miscues, Says Lip," *Sporting News*, 22 January 1966.

7. Edgar Munzel, "Lip Gets Head Start Pumping Confidence into Mauled Bruins," *Sporting News*, 29 January 1966.

8. "Banks Finally Tells of Durocher's Many Insults," *Jet*, 2 June 1977. For the record, Ernie Banks stole four bases in seven attempts in the six seasons he played for Leo. It was never recorded whether Leo actually ponied up the $700.

9. Fergie Jenkins and Lew Freedman, *Fergie: My Life from the Cubs to Cooperstown* (Chicago: Triumph, 2008).

10. Durocher, with Linn, *Nice Guys Finish Last*.

11. Jack Brickhouse, *Thanks for Listening* (South Bend, IN: Diamond Communications, 1986).

12. David Llorens, "Ernie Banks: New Life for an Old Man," *Ebony*, October 1967.

13. James Enright, *Baseball's Great Teams: Chicago Cubs* (New York: Routledge, 1975).

14. Durocher, with Linn, *Nice Guys Finish Last*.

15. Edgar Munzel, "Cubs Cash Quick Dividend in Trade for Lee Thomas," *Sporting News*, 11 June 1966.

16. Edgar Munzel, "End of the Line for Vet Banks? Ernie Loses Post to Boccabella," *Sporting News*, 16 July 1966.

17. Personal interview with Lee Thomas.

18. Comments in this chapter by Don Kessinger are from a personal interview.

19. Rich Cohen, "Catching Up with Cubs Legend Ernie Banks," *Sports Illustrated*, 7 July 2014.

CHAPTER 11. RESPECT

1. Jerome Holtzman, "A Dual Role for Banks—Professor-Performer," *Sporting News*, 18 March 1967.

2. "Ernie Banks Cubs Coach," United Press International, in *Baltimore Afro-American*, 4 March 1967.

3. Jerome Holtzman, "Cubs Stagger at Halfway Point as Swatters Fall into Swoon," *Sporting News*, 22 July 1967.

4. Holtzman, "Cubs Stagger at Halfway Point as Swatters Fall into Swoon."

5. Comments in this chapter from Rich Nye are from a personal interview.

6. Banks vigorously defended Rose and stated it was his own fault for not pulling his foot off the bag in time.

7. Edgar Munzel, "In a Year of Bruin Surprises, Banks Was the Biggest," *Sporting News*, 28 October 1967.

8. Munzel, "In a Year of Bruin Surprises, Banks Was the Biggest."

9. Edgar Munzel, "Leo Won't Make Same Error—He'll Find Spot for Vet Banks," *Sporting News*, 30 December 1967.

10. Ira Berkow, "Banks, Cubs' Elder Statesman, Plays and Sings with Earnest," NEA, in *Times-News*, 5 May 1969.

11. Peter Golenbock, *Wrigleyville: A Magical History Tour of the Chicago Cubs* (New York: St. Martin's, 1996).

12. Rick Talley, *The Cubs of '69: Recollections of the Team That Should Have Been* (Chicago: Contemporary Books, 1989).

13. Leo Durocher, with Ed Linn, *Nice Guys Finish Last* (Richmond Hill, Ontario: Pocketbooks, 1976).

14. Ernie Banks and James Enright, *Mr. Cub* (Chicago: Follett, 1971).

15. See what he did there?

16. Bob Verdi, "Ernie Makes Cubs' Day a Little Brighter," *Chicago Tribune*, 4 March 1975.

17. "Banks Finally Tells of Durocher's Many Insults," *Jet*, 2 June 1977.

18. Bob Verdi, "Banks Goes to Bat for Cubs, Even on First Tee," *Chicago Tribune*, 10 January 1985.

19. Talley, *The Cubs of '69*.

20. Rich Cohen, *The Chicago Cubs: Story of a Curse* (New York: Farrar, Straus and Giroux, 2017).

21. Jim Murray, "Ernie Banks Is Bright Gem in Chicago," *Los Angeles Times*, 19 September 1962.

22. Comments in this chapter from Don Kessinger are from a personal interview.

23. Monte Irvin, "Monte Irvin, This Is Where the Negro Ballplayer Stands Today," *Sport*, April 1957.

24. Branch Rickey, "Branch Rickey Discusses the Negro in Baseball Today" (condensed from *Ebony*), *Baseball Digest*, July 1957.

25. Sam Lacy, "Can These 10 Years Match Decade Just Ended," *Baltimore Afro-Amercan*, 5 January 1960.

26. Dan Daniel, "Bias Beef on Negroes in Mag Story Untrue, Scott Says," *Sporting News*, 6 April 1960.

27. Wendell Smith, "Negro Ball Players Want Rights in South," *Chicago American*, 23 January 1961.

28. "The Negro in Baseball: Year of the Big Money," *Ebony*, June 1962.

29. Bill White, with Gordon Dillow, *Uppity: My Untold Story about the Games People Play* (New York: Grand Central Publishing, 2011).

30. Billy Williams, with Fred Mitchell, *Billy Williams: My Sweet-Swinging Lifetime with the Cubs* (Chicago: Triumph, 2008).

31. Personal interview with Dick Ellsworth.

32. White, with Dillow, *Uppity*.

33. Buck O'Neil and David Conrads, *I Was Right on Time* (New York: Simon and Schuster, 1997).

34. Edgar Munzel, "Cubs Sign O'Neil as Coach, First Negro in Majors," *Sporting News*, 9 June 1962.

35. Carrie Muskat, "O'Neil's Hire Progressive, but Not Far Enough," *MLB.com*, 3 February 2012, http://wap.mlb.com/chc/news/article/2012012826502180/?locale =es_CO (3 January 2017).

36. O'Neil and Conrads, *I Was Right on Time*.

37. *Pittsburgh Courier*, 14 March 1964.

38. Williams, with Mitchell, *Billy Williams*.

39. "Ernie Banks," NVLP Oral History Archive, *National Visionary Leadership Project*, 2004, http://www.visionaryproject.org/banksernie/ (3 January 2017).

40. Personal interview with Chuck Shriver.

41. Bill Surface, "Ernie Banks Has It Made," *Sport*, March 1960.

42. Steve Gelman, "Bill White: A Man Must Say What He Thinks Is Right," *Sport*, July 1964.

43. Jackie Robinson and Bill Russell, "Sound Off! Where the Negro Goes from Here in Sports," *Sport*, September 1966.

44. Bob Sudyk, "Baseball Leads in Reducing Bias, Negro Players Agree," *Sporting News*, 20 April 1968.

45. Sudyk, "Baseball Leads in Reducing Bias, Negro Players Agree."

46. Sudyk, "Baseball Leads in Reducing Bias, Negro Players Agree."

47. Sam Lacy, "What Has Baseball Done Lately," *Baltimore Afro-American*, 17 February 1970.

48. Personal interview with Nate Oliver.

49. White, with Dillow, *Uppity*.

50. Timothy Gilfoyle, "From Wrigley Field to Outer Space: Interviews with Ernie Banks and Mae Jemison," *Chicago History* 27, no. 3 (Winter 1998–1999).

51. Talley, *The Cubs of '69*.

52. "Banks to Head Chicago NAACP Drive," *Baltimore Afro-American*, 3 September 1957.

53. Banks and Enright, *Mr. Cub*.

54. Gilfoyle, "From Wrigley Field to Outer Space."

55. Personal interview with Lindy McDaniel.

56. Banks and Enright, *Mr. Cub*.

57. "Ernie's Only Race Problem: To Beat Throw to First Base," *Sporting News*, 22 August 1964.

58. Banks and Enright, *Mr. Cub*.

59. A slur used to indicate black on the outside but white on the inside.

60. Mark Kram, "A Tale of Two Men and One City," *Sports Illustrated*, 29 September 1969.

61. Bill Libby, "Why They Call Ernie Banks Baseball's Beautiful Man," *Sport*, June 1969.

62. Craigh Barboza, "Ernie Banks: A Beacon for Baseball," *AARP Bulletin*, 10 May 2011.

63. Comments in this chapter by Pete Richert are from a personal interview.

64. Stan Isle, "Vietnam Soldiers Cheer Banks, No. 1 Morale Booster," *Sporting News*, 14 December 1968.

65. Isle, "Vietnam Soldiers Cheer Banks, No. 1 Morale Booster."

66. "Voice of the Fan," *Sporting News*, 14 December 1968.

67. Jerome Holtzman, "Mr. Cub Doffs Lid to GIs in Vietnam," *Sporting News*, 7 December 1968.

CHAPTER 12. THAT SUMMER OF '69

1. Jim Enright, "Birthday Cake for Banks after Signing," *Sporting News*, 18 February 1967.

2. "Year of the Holdouts," *Ebony*, June 1966.

3. Milton Richman, "Everything Is Beautiful to Banks," United Press International, in *Pittsburgh Press*, 20 January 1977.

4. Personal conversation with Fred Mitchell, Billy Williams's biographer.

5. Jerome Holtzman, "Elated Cubs Hail Abby as Flag Factor," *Sporting News*, 25 January 1969.

6. "Ernie Issues Annual Phrase," Associated Press, in *Altus Times-Democrat*, 24 February 1969.

7. Bill Libby, "Why They Call Ernie Banks Baseball's Beautiful Man," *Sport*, June 1969.

8. Comments in this chapter by Don Kessinger are from a personal interview.

9. Comments in this chapter by Nate Oliver are from a personal interview.

10. Jim Murray, "Ernie Banks: Baseball's Pollyanna," *Los Angeles Times*, 6 June 1965.

11. Jim Murray, "Ernie Banks: The Eternal Optimist," *Los Angeles Times*, 17 May 1967.

12. Edgar Munzel, "Scribes Honor Banks; Record 1,180 at Feed," *Sporting News*, 23 January 1965.

13. Murray, "Ernie Banks: Baseball's Pollyanna."

14. Ira Berkow, "Banks, Cubs' Elder Stateman, Plays and Sings with Earnest," NEA, in *Times-News*, 5 May 1969.

15. Mark Kram, "A Tale of Two Men and One City," *Sports Illustrated*, 29 September 1969.

16. Libby, "Why They Call Ernie Banks Baseball's Beautiful Man."

17. Libby, "Why They Call Ernie Banks Baseball's Beautiful Man."

18. David Llorens, "Ernie Banks: New Life for an 'Old Man,'" *Ebony*, October 1967.

19. "Ageless Ernie: Keeper of a Dream," *Ebony*, June 1969.

20. Libby, "Why They Call Ernie Banks Baseball's Beautiful Man."

21. Billy Williams, with Fred Mitchell, *Billy Williams: My Sweet-Swinging Lifetime with the Cubs* (Chicago: Triumph, 2008).

22. Paul Sullivan, "Cubs Legend Ernie Banks Remembered as a Man Who Loved Life, People," *Chicago Tribune*, 1 February 2015.

23. Carrie Muskat, "Williams Saddened by Loss of Former Teammate, Friend Banks," *MLB.com*, 24 January 2015, https://www.mlb.com/cubs/news/billy-williams-saddened-by-loss-of-ernie-banks/c-107330268 (3 January 2017).

24. Jerome Holtzman, "Do-It-All Banks Powering Cubs along Victory Route," *Sporting News*, 21 June 1969.

25. Comments in this chapter by Rich Nye are from a personal interview.

26. "Ernie Banks on 'Pass' to 1969 All-Star Tilt," United Press International, in *Rome News-Tribune*, 22 July 1969.

27. Peter Golenbock, *Wrigleyville: A Magical History Tour of the Chicago Cubs* (New York: St. Martin's, 1996).

28. Holtzman, "Do-It-All Banks Powering Cubs along Victory Route."

29. Golenbock, *Wrigleyville*.

30. Golenbock, *Wrigleyville*.

31. Golenbock, *Wrigleyville*.

32. Personal interview with Chuck Shriver.

33. Sullivan, "Cubs Legend Ernie Banks Remembered as a Man Who Loved Life, People."

34. Jerome Holtzman, "Cubs' Billy Fires Home Run Barrage—Leaps into Race for RBI Title," *Sporting News*, 28 September 1968.

35. Comments in this chapter by Jerry Kindall are from a personal interview.

36. Jerome Holtzman, *The Jerome Holtzman Baseball Reader* (Chicago: Triumph, 2003).

37. The game mentioned actually took place in 1961.

38. Holtzman, "Do-It-All Banks Powering Cubs along Victory Route."

39. Dave Anderson, "Ernie Banks: He's Almost Too Good to Be True," *New York Times*, 21 January 1977.

40. Personal communication with George Altman.

41. Ron Santo, with Randy Minkoff, *Ron Santo: For Love of Ivy* (Chicago: Bonus Books, 1993).

42. Bill Surface, "Ernie Banks Has It Made," *Sport*, March 1960.

43. Paul Sullivan, "Ken Holtzman Shares Fond Memories of Ernie Banks," *Chicago Tribune*, 27 January 2015.

44. Paul Hemphill, "The Last Days of Ernie Banks," *Sport*, December 1971.

45. Robert Boyle, "Leo's Bums Rap for the Cubs," *Sports Illustrated*, 30 June 1969.

46. *The Tim McCarver Show*, 28 January 2006.

47. Llorens, "Ernie Banks."

48. John Roseboro, with Bill Libby, *Glory Days with the Dodgers and Other Days with Others* (New York: Atheneum, 1978).

49. Rick Talley, *The Cubs of '69: Recollections of the Team That Should Have Been* (Chicago: Contemporary Books, 1989).

50. Talley, *The Cubs of '69*.

51. Talley, *The Cubs of '69*.

52. Rich Cohen, *The Chicago Cubs: Story of a Curse* (New York: Farrar, Straus and Giroux, 2017).

53. Talley, *The Cubs of '69*.

CHAPTER 13. IMMORTAL

1. Edgar Munzel, "Leo Plans to Curb Cubs' Outside Interests," *Sporting News*, 18 October 1969.

2. Jeannie Morris, *Brian Piccolo: A Short Season* (Chicago: Rand McNally, 1971).

3. "Pressure Almost Got to 'Mr. Cub,'" United Press International, in *Palm Beach Post*, 13 May 1970.

4. Kent Hannon, "Ernie Banks's Autobiography, 'Mr. Cub,' Is a Book Whose Time Almost Never Came," *Sports Illustrated*, 19 July 1971.

5. Leo Durocher, with Ed Linn, *Nice Guys Finish Last* (Richmond Hill, Ontario: Pocketbooks, 1976).

6. "Banks Ready When Needed," Associated Press, in *Times-Daily*, 31 January 1971.

7. Durocher, with Linn, *Nice Guys Finish Last*.

8. Jack Brickhouse, *Thanks for Listening* (South Bend, IN: Diamond Communications, 1986).

9. Durocher, with Linn, *Nice Guys Finish Last*.

10. "Baker First Negro at Major 'Helm,'" *Sporting News*, 5 October 1963.

11. Arthur Daley, "Leo Earns a Reprieve," *New York Times*, 25 November 1971.

12. Personal interview with Jim Marshall.

13. Fred Mitchell, "Fans, Former Teammates, Friends Pay Respects at Ernie Banks Visitation," *Chicago Tribune*, 30 January 2015.

14. "Chicago Treasures: Ernie Banks and Minnie Minoso," Chicago History Museum, *WBEZ News*, 12 October 2006, https://www.wbez.org/shows/wbez-news/chicago-treasures-ernie-banks-minnie-minoso/acb77170-8a05-4bf0-aa30-0d28f0b6dd8a (3 January 2017).

15. "'I Want to Manage the Chicago Cubs'—Ernie Banks," *Jet*, 29 January 1976.

16. Milton Richman, "Everything Beautiful to Banks," United Press International, in *Pittsburgh Press*, 20 January 1977.

17. Ira Berkow, "Ernie Bank's Story Has Two Sides," *New York Times*, 13 June 1983.

18. Will Grimsley, "Baseball Delight for Ernie Banks," Associated Press, in *Spokane Daily Chronicle*, 20 January 1977.

19. Bob Verdi, "Banks Goes to Bat for Cubs, Even on First Tee," *Chicago Tribune*, 10 January 1985.

20. "Ernie Banks's Enshrinement Greeted by Sunshine," Associated Press, in *Daytona Beach Morning Journal*, 9 August 1977.

CHAPTER 14. LIVING AS MR. CUB

1. "Aaron Lower Boom on Baseball," *Washington Afro-American*, 15–19 January 1974.

2. Edward Kiersh, *Where Have You Gone, Vince DiMaggio?* (New York: Bantam, 1983).

3. Comments in this chapter by Ed Sherman are from a personal interview.

4. Ira Berkow, "Ernie Banks's Story Has Two Sides," *New York Times*, 13 June 1983.

5. Comments in this chapter by Chuck Shriver are from a personal interview.

6. John Schulian, "Cubs' Cowardly Cur Crass in Cutting Up Legendary Banks," *Chicago Sun-Times*, 15 June 1983.

7. Berkow, "Ernie Bank's Story Has Two Sides."

8. Michael Craig, "Ernie Banks Talks Baseball and Business," *Salon.com*, 25 September 2000, http://dir.*salon.com*/business/green/2000/ 09/25/banks/index.html?pn=2 (13 January 2018).

9. A. S. (Doc) Young, "The Athlete in Business," *Ebony*, December 1970.

10. Michael Wilbon, "Banks Was First among Chicago Idols," *ESPN.com*, 24 January 2015, http://carnageandculture.blogspot.com/2015/01/banks-was-first-among -chicago-idols.html (13 January 2018).

11. Kiersh, *Where Have You Gone, Vince DiMaggio?*

12. Comments in this chapter by George Castle are from a personal interview.

13. Berkow, "Ernie Banks's Story Has Two Sides."

14. Thomas Buck, "Ernie Banks Put on CTA Board with $15,000 Salary," *Chicago Tribune*, 9 August 1969.

15. Kiersh, *Where Have You Gone, Vince DiMaggio?*

16. Dave Cunningham, "Not-So-Funny Ernie Banks the Effervescent Mr. Cub Is Battling Hypertension at 68 and Is Well Aware of Its Health Repercussions, but the Hall of Fame Infielder Still Has Kind Words for Everyone He Encounters," *Orlando Sentinel*, 12 March 1999.

17. Kiersh, *Where Have You Gone, Vince DiMaggio?*

18. Personal interview with Don Kessinger.

19. Contrary to the belief of some former players and virtually all media members, the surgeon *did* find a heart during the procedure.

20. Personal interview with Jerry Kindall.

21. Personal interview with Doug Clemens.

22. Cunningham, "Not-So-Funny Ernie Banks the Effervescent Mr. Cub Is Battling Hypertension at 68."

23. Rick Talley, *The Cubs of '69: Recollections of the Team That Should Have Been* (Chicago: Contemporary Books, 1989).

24. Comments in this chapter by Rich Cohen are from a personal interview.

25. Comments in this chapter by Fred Mitchell are from a personal interview.

26. Paul Hemphill, "The Last Days of Ernie Banks," *Sport*, December 1971.

27. Ron Santo, with Randy Minkoff, *Ron Santo: For Love of Ivy* (Chicago: Bonus Books, 1993).

28. Danny Peary, *We Played the Game: 65 Players Remember Baseball's Greatest Era, 1947–64* (New York: Hyperion, 1994).

29. Peter Golenbock, *Wrigleyville: A Magical History Tour of the Chicago Cubs* (New York: St. Martin's, 1996).

30. Lester Biederman, "Banks Feels Like Winner Despite Team," *Pittsburgh Press*, 10 August 1967.

31. Lois Wille, "Few Love the Game as Much as Cubs' Ernie Banks," *Toledo Blade*, 13 July 1969.

32. The house would be listed for $2.75 million in 2017.

33. *The Tim McCarver Show*, 28 January 2006.

34. Fred Mitchell, *Chicago Cubs, Where Have You Gone? Ernie Banks, Andy Pafko, Ferguson Jenkins . . .* (New York: Sports Publishing, 2004).

35. "Cubs Unveil Ernie Banks Statue at Wrigley Field," YouTube video, *Daily Herald.com*, 5 April 2008, https://www.youtube.com/watch?v=wjd5px5cUyM (21 December 2017).

36. Matt Snyder, "Ernie Banks Urges Sammy Sosa to Come Forward, Answer Questions," *AOL News*, 25 January 2010, www.aolnews.com/ernie-banks-urges-sammy -sosa-to-come-forward-answer-questions/ (14 July 2016).

37. "Ernie Banks," interview by Julienna Richardson, *History Makers*, 18 July 2014, http://abc7chicago.com/society/historymakers-seeks-to-chronicle-african-american -experience-/145262/ (15 September 2015).

38. Personal interview with Shirley Marx.

39. Cheryl Burton, "ABC Exclusive," 12 February 2015.

40. Ron Rappaport, "The Last Years of Ernie Banks," *Chicago Magazine*, October 2015.

41. "Ernie Banks: His Life, Career, and Memory," *SB Nation*, 18 February 2007, https://www.bleedcubbieblue.com/2015/1/26/7918927/ernie-banks-life-career-mem ory (4 November 2017).

42. Personal interview with Zach Sanzone.

43. Ernie Banks and James Enright, *Mr. Cub* (Chicago: Follett, 1971).

44. David Haugh, "Mr. Cub Takes on the World," *Chicago Tribune*, 24 July 2005.

45. Lois Wille, "Few Love the Game as Much as Cubs' Ernie Banks," *Toledo Blade*, 13 July 1969.

46. "Ernie Banks," interview by Julieanna Richardson.

47. Country singer Charley Pride, who later made his home in Dallas, pitched for the Memphis Red Sox and Birmingham Black Barons in the mid-1950s. In 1956, he pitched in an exhibition against major-league stars, including Willie Mays, Hank Aaron, Gene Baker, and Ernie Banks, losing, 2–1, but he did manage to strike out 12 in the game.

48. Personal interview with Robert Prince.

49. Annie Sweeney, "Ernie Banks's Will Confirmed; Witnesses Say Mr. Cub Was of 'Sound Mind,'" *Chicago Tribune*, 31 March 2015.

50. Sweeney, "Ernie Banks's Will Confirmed."

51. "Let Paris Have Picasso, Chicagoan Wants Ernie," Associated Press, in *Milwaukee Journal*, 8 July 1967.

EPILOGUE

1. Personal interview with Darrel Chaney.

2. Personal interview with Jerry Schuebel.

3. Personal interview with Kathy Hounihan.

BIBLIOGRAPHY

Altman, George, with Lew Freedman. *George Altman: My Journey from the Negro Leagues to the Majors and Beyond.* Jefferson, NC: McFarland, 2013.

Banks, Ernie, and James Enright. *Mr. Cub.* Chicago: Follett, 1971.

Blair, William. *A Life Lived: The Story of William "Bill" Blair from the Negro Baseball League to Newspaper Publisher.* Bloomington, IN: AuthorHouse, 2013.

Brickhouse, Jack. *Thanks for Listening.* South Bend, IN: Diamond Communications, 1986.

Brock, Lou, and Franz Schulze. *Stealing Is My Game.* Englewood Cliffs, NJ: Prentice Hall, 1976.

Castle, George. *The Million-to-One Team: Why the Chicago Cubs Haven't Won a Pennant since 1945.* South Bend, IN: Diamond Communications, 2000.

———. *Where Have All Our Cubs Gone?* Dallas, TX: Taylor Trade, 2005.

Claerbaut, David. *Durocher's Cubs: The Greatest Team That Didn't Win.* Dallas, TX: Taylor, 2000.

Cohen, Rich. *The Chicago Cubs: Story of a Curse.* New York: Farrar, Straus and Giroux, 2017.

Dedmon, Emmett. *Fabulous Chicago.* New York: Atheneum, 1981.

Dickson, Paul. *Leo Durocher: Baseball's Prodigal Son.* New York: Bloomsbury, 2017.

Drotning, Phillip T., and Wesley South. *Up from the Ghetto.* New York: Cowles Book Company 1970.

Durocher, Leo, with Ed Linn. *Nice Guys Finish Last.* Richmond Hill, Ontario: Pocketbooks, 1976.

Enright, James. *Baseball's Great Teams: Chicago Cubs.* New York: Routledge, 1975.

Freedman, Lew. *African American Pioneers of Baseball.* Westport, CT: Greenwood Press, 2007.

Fussman, Cal. *After Jackie: Pride, Prejudice, and Baseball's Forgotten Heroes.* New York: ESPN Books, 2007.

Golenbock, Peter. *Wrigleyville: A Magical History Tour of the Chicago Cubs.* New York: St. Martin's, 1996.

Graff, Harvey J. *The Dallas Myth: The Making and Unmaking of an American City.* Minneapolis: University of Minnesota Press, 2008.

Heylar, John: *The Lords of the Realm: The Real History of Baseball.* New York: Random House, 2011.

Holtzman, Jerome. *The Jerome Holtzman Baseball Reader.* Chicago: Triumph, 2003.

———, and George Vass. *The Chicago Cubs Encyclopedia.* Philadelphia, PA: Temple University Press, 1997.

Howard, Arlene, and Ralph Wimbish. *Elston and Me: The Story of the First Black Yankee.* Columbia: University of Missouri Press, 2001.

Jackson, Ransom, Jr., with Gaylon H. White. *Handsome Ransom Jackson: Accidental Big-Leaguer.* Lanham, MD: Rowman & Littlefield, 2016.

Jenkins, Fergie, and Lew Freedman. *Fergie: My Life from the Cubs to Cooperstown.* Chicago: Triumph, 2009.

Kahn, Roger. *The Boys of Summer.* New York: Harper and Row, 1971.

Kelly, Brent P. *I Will Never Forget: Interviews with 39 Former Negro League Players.* Jefferson, NC: McFarland, 2003.

Kiersh, Edward. *Where Have You Gone, Vince DiMaggio?* New York: Bantam, 1983.

Lester, Larry. *Black Baseball's National Showcase: The East–West All-Star Game, 1933–1953.* Lincoln: University of Nebraska Press, 2001.

Madden, Bill. *1954: The Year Willie Mays and the First Generation of Black Superstars Changed Major League Baseball Forever.* Boston, MA: Da Capo Press, 2014.

Minutaglio, Bill. *In Search of the Blues: A Journey to the Soul of Black Texas.* Austin: University of Texas Press, 2010.

Mitchell, Fred. *Chicago Cubs, Where Have You Gone? Ernie Banks, Andy Pafko, Ferguson Jenkins . . .* New York: Sports Publishing, 2004.

Morris, Jeannie. *Brian Piccolo: A Short Season.* Chicago: Rand McNally, 1971.

O'Neil, Buck, and David Conrads. *I Was Right on Time.* New York: Simon and Schuster, 1997.

Peary, Danny. *We Played the Game: 65 Players Remember Baseball's Greatest Era, 1947–64.* New York: Hyperion, 1994.

Posnanski, Joe. *The Soul of Baseball: A Road Trip through Buck O'Neil's America.* New York: William Morrow, 2007.

Rogers, Phil. *Ernie Banks: Mr. Cub and the Summer of '69.* Chicago: Triumph, 2011.

Roseboro, John, with Bill Libby. *Glory Days with the Dodgers and Other Days with Others.* New York: Atheneum, 1978.

Royko, Mike. *Boss: Richard J. Daley of Chicago.* New York: E. P. Dutton, 1971.

Santo, Ron, with Randy Minkoff. *Ron Santo: For Love of Ivy.* Chicago: Bonus Books, 1993.

Stout, Glenn. *The Cubs: The Complete Story of Chicago Cubs Baseball*. New York: Houghton Mifflin, 2007.

Talley, Rick. *The Cubs of '69: Recollections of the Team That Should Have Been*. Chicago: Contemporary Books, 1989.

Vincent, Fay. *The Only Game in Town: Baseball Stars of the 1930s and 1940s Talk about the Game They Loved*. New York: Simon and Schuster, 2006.

———. *We Would Have Played for Nothing: Baseball Stars of the 1950s and 1960s Talk about the Game They Loved*. New York: Simon and Schuster, 2008.

Vorwald, Bob. *Cubs Forever: Memories from the Men Who Lived Them*. Chicago: Triumph, 2008.

White, Bill, with Gordon Dillow. *Uppity: My Untold Story about the Games People Play*. New York: Grand Central Publishing, 2011.

White, C. C. *No Quittin' Sense: Growing Up Black in East Texas*. Austin: University of Texas Press, 1969.

Will, George. *A Nice Little Place on the North Side: Wrigley Field at One Hundred*. New York: Crown Archetype, 2014.

Williams, Billy, with Fred Mitchell. *Billy Williams: My Sweet-Swinging Lifetime with the Cubs*. Chicago: Triumph, 2008.

Wood, Gerald, and Andrew Zucha, eds. *Northsiders: Essays on the History and Culture of the Chicago Cubs*. Jefferson, NC: McFarland, 2008.

INDEX

ABOUT THE AUTHOR

Doug Wilson is a former college baseball player and a member of the Society for American Baseball Research. He is author of *Fred Hutchinson and the 1964 Cincinnati Reds* (2010), *The Bird: The Life and Legacy of Mark Fidrych* (2013), *Brooks: The Biography of Brooks Robinson* (2014), and *Pudge: The Biography of Carlton Fisk* (2015). Wilson's books have been selected as finalists for the Casey Award and SABR's Seymour Medal as the best baseball books of the year. He and his wife live in Columbus, Indiana. Visit him at dougwilsonbaseball.blogspot.com. *Photo courtesy Kentucky Wesleyan College and Charles Mahlinger.*